THE LETTERS OF
ARNOLD STEPHENSON
ROWNTREE
TO MARY KATHERINE
ROWNTREE,
1910–1918

THE LETTERS OF ARNOLD STEPHENSON ROWNTREE TO MARY KATHERINE ROWNTREE, 1910–1918

edited by
IAN PACKER

CAMDEN FIFTH SERIES
Volume 20

CAMBRIDGE
UNIVERSITY PRESS

FOR THE ROYAL HISTORICAL SOCIETY
University College London, Queen Street, London WC1 6BT
2002

Published by the Press Syndicate of the University of Cambridge
The Edinburgh Building, Cambridge CB2 2RU, United Kingdom
40 West 20th Street, New York, NY 10011-4211, USA
477 Williamstown Road, Port Melbourne, VIC 3207, Australia

First published 2002

A catalogue record for this book is available from the British Library

Library of Congress Cataloging-in-Publication Data applied for

ISBN 0 521 80000 5 hardback

SUBSCRIPTIONS. The serial publications of the Royal Historical Society, *Royal Historical Society Transactions* (ISSN 0080-4401) and Camden Fifth Series (ISSN 0960-1163), volumes may be purchased together on annual subscription. The 2002 subscription price (which includes postage but not VAT is £63 (US$102 in the USA, Canada and Mexico) and includes Camden Fifth Series, volumes 19, 20 and 21 (published in July and December) and Transactions Sixth Series, volume 12 (published in December). Japanese prices are available from Kinokuniya Company Ltd, P.O. Box 55, Chitose, Tokyo 156, Japan. EU subscribers (outside the UK) who are not registered for VAT should add VAT at their country's rate. VAT registered subscribers should provide their VAT registration number. Prices include delivery by air.

Subscription orders, which must be accompanied by payment, may be sent to a bookseller, subscription agent or direct to the publisher: Cambridge University Press, The Edinburgh Building, Shaftesbury Road, Cambridge CB2 2RU, UK; or in the USA, Canada and Mexico; Cambridge University Press, Journals Fulfillment Department, 110 Midland Avenue, Port Chester, NY 10573-4930, USA.

SINGLE VOLUMES AND BACK VOLUMES. A list of Royal Historical Society volumes available from Cambridge University Press may be obtained from the Humanities Marketing Department at the address above.

Cover illustration: Arnold Rowntree. Reproduced by kind permission of Michael Rowntree.

Printed and bound in the United Kingdom by Butler & Tanner Ltd, Frome and London

CONTENTS

ACKNOWLEDGEMENTS

My greatest debt is to the late Mrs Tessa Cadbury, Arnold Rowntree's eldest daughter, without whom this project would not have been possible. Not only did she collect her father's letters, prepare a typescript of them, and deposit them in Friend's House in London, but when I wrote to her suggesting an edition of the letters, she responded with enormous enthusiasm and made many helpful suggestions. It is a great sadness that she did not live to see the publication of this edition. I would also like to thank Mr Michael Rowntree for his generous help.

I have accumulated many other debts of gratitude in the course of the research for this book. Professor David Eastwood, as Literary Director of the Royal Historical Society, not only commissioned the project but provided invaluable guidance. The staff at Friends House Library and Mrs Elizabeth Jackson, Librarian of the Joseph Rowntree Foundation, were endlessly patient when assisting me through the intricacies of Quaker and Rowntree family history. Dr Michael Hart and Professor Cameron Hazlehurst helped me track down some elusive sources and references. Dr Martin Lynn and Professor Peter Jupp were a constant source of sound advice on Quakerism and the process of editing, respectively. As ever, Tony Sheehan solved all technical difficulties. My parents were, as always, supportive and hospitable.

Once again, Lynda made it all worthwhile.

Abbreviations

Amb.	Ambassador
A.S.R.	Arnold Stephenson Rowntree
Asst	Assistant
b.	born
Bd	Board
bro.	brother
Bt	Baronet
cand.	candidate
Chanc.	Chancellor
Chmn	Chairman
CO	Conscientious Objector
Co.	Company
Con.	Conservative
cr.	created
CSIR	Council for the Study of International Relations
Cttee	Committee
d.	died
DBE	Dame of the Order of the British Empire
Dep.	Deputy
Dept	Department
Dir.	Director
DN	*Daily News*
Ed.	Editor
FAU	Friends' Ambulance Unit
FOR	Fellowship of Reconciliation
FSC	Friends' Service Committee
Fin.	Financial
GBE	Knight Grand Cross of the Order of the British Empire
GCB	Knight Grand Cross of the Order of the Bath
GCSI	Knight Grand Commander of the Order of the Star of India
Gen.	General
Gov.	Governor
Govt	Government
HofC	House of Commons
HofL	House of Lords
Ind.	Independent
ILP	Independent Labour Party
JRSST	Joseph Rowntree Social Service Trust
KBE	Knight of the Order of the British Empire

KCB	Knight Commander of the Order of the Bath
KCSI	Knight Commander of the Order of the Star of India
KG	Knight of the Garter
kt.	knighted
Lab.	Labour
LCC	London County Council
Ld	Lord
Lib.	Liberal
LU	Liberal Unionist
m.	married
Min.	Minister
M.K.R.	Mary Katherine Rowntree
ML	*Morning Leader*
MP	Member of Parliament
NASU	National Adult School Union
Nat.	National
NER	North Eastern Railway Company
NLC	National Liberal Club
OM	Order of Merit
Parl.	Parliamentary
Parlt	Parliament
PM	Prime Minister
PPS	Parliamentary Private Secretary
Pres.	President
Prof.	Professor
Prog.	Progressive
PS	Parliamentary Secretary
PUS	Parliamentary Under-Secretary
QM	Quarterly Meeting
retd	retired
s.	son
Sec.	Secretary
succ.	succeeded
UDC	Union of Democratic Control
Univ.	university
US	Under-Secretary
Vt	Viscount
YM	Yearly Meeting

INTRODUCTION

Most investigations of early twentieth-century Liberalism have centred on the politics of Campbell-Bannerman and Asquith's cabinets, the thought of Liberal intellectuals, and the struggles of local parties.[1] But the world of the backbencher remains relatively obscure. When he has been studied, it has usually been in the mass as historians have sought to chart changes in the social background of Liberal MPs or tabulate their opinions, as expressed in parliamentary divisions, on topics like social reform or the relative merits of Asquith and Lloyd George.[2] Much less is known about the lives of backbench MPs.

This is largely because few of these men left any detailed records. The only published diary of a backbench Liberal MP for this period is that of R.D. Holt, MP for Hexham 1907–1918, and this can be supplemented by a handful of similar sources in archives around the country.[3] The letters which Arnold Rowntree wrote to his wife, Mary, while he was MP for York in 1910–1918 provide an important addition to the existing material. They are particularly significant for three reasons. Firstly, Rowntree was, in many ways, a fairly typical Liberal backbencher. He was a middle-aged nonconformist businessman, sitting for a constituency that was his home and the location of his business. But he provides an important corrective to the idea that all men from this background were, like R.D. Holt, necessarily enemies of the New Liberalism.

Secondly, Rowntree's letters are not just concerned with parliamentary politics. They cover all his interests, including his family, business, and religion and his charitable work. The letters forcefully illustrate the point that politics was only a part of the lives of backbench MPs and their political activities and opinions cannot be understood without reference to this wider context. Finally, though Arnold Rowntree had no ambitions for office, he was not without political significance. As a leading member of the Rowntree family of confectionary

---

[1] P. Rowland, *The Last Liberal Governments*, 2 vols (London, 1968–1971); P. Clarke, *Liberals and Social Democrats* (Cambridge, 1978); D. Tanner, *Political Change and the Labour Party, 1900–18* (Cambridge, 1990).

[2] G. Searle, 'The Edwardian Liberal Party and business', *English Historical Review*, 98 (1983), pp. 28–60; H.V. Emy, *Liberals, Radicals and Social Politics, 1892–1914* (Cambridge, 1973); E. David, 'The Liberal Party divided, 1916–18', *Historical Journal*, 13 (1970), pp. 509–532.

[3] D. Dutton (ed.), *Odyssey of an Edwardian Liberal: the Political Diary of Richard Durning Holt* (Gloucester, 1989). Other backbench diaries include those of E.W. Davies in the National Library of Wales, Aberystwyth, A. MacCallum Scott in the University of Glasgow Library, and A. Ponsonby in private hands.

manufacturers he was closely involved with many of the projects for moral and social reform associated with the family. He was also one of seven Quaker Liberal MPs elected in December 1910. After the First World War broke out his commitment to the peace testimony of his faith made him an important spokesman in parliament for Conscientious Objectors. His letters give a valuable insight into the problems and policies of 'pacifist' MPs in 1914–1918 and the difficulties Quakers faced in reconciling their historic witness for peace with the pressures of a nation at war.

Background and religious influences

Arnold Stephenson Rowntree was born on 28 November 1872, the fifth and youngest son and eighth child of John Stephenson Rowntree, a wealthy grocer from York, and Elizabeth (nee Hotham), the daughter of a well-to-do Leeds draper.[4] Both his mother's and his father's families were Quakers. The Rowntrees were descended from a Yorkshire farmer who had been converted to Quakerism in the mid-eighteenth century, and the family had spread over the north and east of the county, mainly working in the retail trades. The York branch was founded when John Stephenson Rowntree's father, Joseph Rowntree, moved from Scarborough to open a grocer's shop in York in 1822. Joseph became an important figure in his adopted home city, serving as Honorary Secretary from 1829 to 1859 of the York Schools Committee, which administered the Quaker schools, Bootham and the Mount, and becoming a prominent local Liberal and alderman, though he declined the lord mayoralty.

Joseph also became well-known in national Quaker affairs, particularly for his part in the campaign to abolish the rule that any Quaker who married outside the denomination should automatically be expelled. John Stephenson Rowntree was Joseph's eldest son. He too became an important figure in Quakerism and went on to take over his father's role in the business and on the York Schools Committee. He was so well respected in York that he was offered and accepted the lord mayoralty in 1880–1881 without ever having served on the town council.

This ancestry ensured that Arnold Rowntree was born into both the elite of Quakerism and of York's public affairs. His early life was not untroubled, though. His mother was killed in an accident in 1875 and he was sent to live for three years with his mother's sister and her

---

[4] For A.S.R.'s background see P. Doncaster, *John Stephenson Rowntree: His Life and Work* (London, 1908); E. Vipont, *Arnold Rowntree: A Life* (London, 1955)

husband, Joel Cadbury, a Birmingham button manufacturer. Joel was a cousin of George Cadbury and the latter had worked for a time in John Stephenson Rowntree's shop before starting to build up Cadbury Bros into one of the country's leading chocolate and cocoa manufacturers. Arnold's years in Birmingham exemplified the close links that already existed between the Rowntrees and Cadburys and he was to spend much of his working life in commercial rivalry with his Cadbury relatives, while collaborating with them on many political, religious, and charitable projects.

In 1878 John Stephenson Rowntree married again to Helen (nee Doncaster) and Arnold returned home. The Doncasters were a family of steel manufacturers from Sheffield who were not only Quakers but were distantly related to the Rowntrees. Thus, Arnold acquired both a stepmother with whom relations were always cordial and a new series of links with another group of influential Quakers. In 1883 he went to Bootham School, the Quaker institution which was so closely connected to his family. He showed little interest in his studies but soon displayed an enthusiastic commitment to cricket and Liberal politics. His early Liberalism was unsurprising – all his family were Liberals, and the climate at Bootham was distinctly anti-Conservative, reflecting the fact that Quakers still tended to think of themselves as outside the Anglican and landed elite. Arnold also made two friends who remained of crucial importance throughout his public life: T.E. 'Ted' Harvey, his future brother-in-law and Liberal MP for West Leeds; and George Newman, who became the leading civil servant in the field of public health.

Arnold left Bootham in 1889 and went to work in his father's shop and then for Barrow's Stores in Birmingham, a firm owned by another cousin of George Cadbury's. But in 1892 his future was settled when he returned to York to join H.I. Rowntree & Co., a fairly small-scale but rapidly expanding firm of confectionary manufacturers. The business was owned and run by Arnold's uncle, Joseph Rowntree. Joseph was anxious to recruit younger members of his family to the firm in order to keep its growing operations entirely under Rowntree control. Arnold remained with the business all his working life and when it became a company in 1897 he was appointed to its board of directors, remaining in office until his retirement in 1941.

The firm of Rowntree & Co. provided the framework for much of Arnold's life as well as his work. In the 1890s and early 1900s his closest friend was John Wilhelm Rowntree, his cousin and the eldest son and partner of Joseph Rowntree.[5] John Wilhelm had a profound influence on his younger cousin, as he did on many Quakers of his generation.

[5] Vipont, *Arnold Rowntree*, pp. 35–48 for A.S.R.'s relationship with John Wilhem Rowntree.

Though not an original thinker, he was the key organizer and publicist of what has been dubbed the Quaker Renaissance, a new movement, similar to that in many other denominations, that urged the Society of Friends to move from the evangelical certainties of the mid-nineteenth century to a more liberal outlook.[6] John Wilhelm believed that Quakers should reject reliance on the Bible as the cornerstone of their faith and return to their early tradition of the divine 'Inner Light' in all people as the source of religious inspiration. He believed this would create a less dogmatic faith that would have a much wider appeal and would revive the significance of Quakerism in British life. But John Wilhelm also believed that Quakers should show how their faith was relevant to the world and how it could offer solutions to the world's problems. This meant reinvigorating Quakers' traditional commitment to peace, joining wider nonconformist campaigns on issues of common moral concern, especially temperance, and taking a favourable attitude to social reform. As John Wilhelm put it, the rediscovery of 'the indwelling God' in all was necessarily accompanied by 'a notable stirring of the social conscience' and the requirement to 'express in conduct and life, in social relations and ideas, the large practical consequences which that truth involved'.[7]

Arnold shared his cousin's beliefs and they were to shape his whole approach to public life. He was a regular participant in John Wilhelm's summer schools for religious study and became a close friend of many other leading figures in the Quaker Renaissance, especially the American academic Rufus Jones. After John Wilhelm's early death in 1905 Arnold was an important supporter of Woodbrooke College in Birmingham, a study centre inspired by John Wilhelm's ideas. He was also a central figure in carrying out John Wilhem's plan for a multivolume history of Quakerism, one of whose purposes was to demonstrate the links between the early Quakers and John Wilhem's ideas. But Arnold felt he was not suited to primarily religious work. As he wrote to his wife after a religious meeting, 'so often one is so conscious of one's special temptations and weaknesses and one feels a glorious old hypocrite'.[8] Instead, he chose to express his faith primarily through public work. Part of this work was in the field of politics, but this was only ever one element of Arnold Rowntree's life.

[6] E. Isichei, *Victorian Quakers* (Oxford, 1970), pp. 32–43; T. Kennedy, 'What hath Manchester wrought? change in the religious Society of Friends, 1895–1920', *Journal of the Friends' Historical Society*, 57 (1996), pp. 277–305; M. Davie, *British Quaker Theology since 1895* (Lampeter, 1997).

[7] J. Rowntree (ed.), *John Wilhelm Rowntree: Essays and Addresses*, 2nd edn (London, 1906), pp. 242–243.

[8] A.S.R. to M.K.R., 3 July 1907, transcript letters, Joseph Rowntree archive L/93/29, Joseph Rowntree Foundation, York.

Educational work

Arnold Rowntree's first forays into public life were in the field of education and this area remained a life-long interest, taking up at least as much of his time in the Edwardian era as politics. An interest in education was partly a matter of heredity. It was no surprise that in 1903–1945 he filled the post of Honorary Secretary (later Chairman) of the York Schools Committee, as the position had been held by his father and grandfather. This sort of role also fitted Arnold's naturally gregarious and outgoing temperament and his delight in the company of children, so obviously shown in his own family life. But in Arnold's youth active Quakers were also expected to take a role in teaching in the Society's adult schools and it was in this sphere that his main interests lay.

These schools, organized at a national level in the Friends' First Day Schools Association (FFDSA), had their origins in the attempt by mid-nineteenth-century Quakers to find a distinctive niche in the overcrowded field of Sunday school provision.[9] They were originally literacy schools for adults, but as the need for this sort of provision declined they gradually transformed into a combination of Bible study class, discussion group, and social venue for earnest working-class scholars. The Rowntrees were extensively involved in the adult school movement in York. Both Arnold's father and grandfather taught in adult schools and his cousins John Wilhelm, Seebohm, and Frank all ran their 'own' schools.[10] Arnold committed himself to a school in Leeman Road, a working-class district of York. He found a real joy and sense of purpose in adult school-work and he even moved into the area with his elder sister, Gertrude. But to the young men of the Quaker Renaissance, the adult school also represented a paradigm of how Quakerism could reshape Britain.[11] Just as the Society of Friends would lead the nation in a project of moral reform, so individual Quakers had the opportunity to break down the barriers between the classes and share in fellowship with working people the virtues of temperance, self-improvement and undogmatic Christianity. Possibly, the schools could act as the magnet to attract the kind of inquiring minds to which the Quaker Renaissance hoped to appeal.

In the late 1890s this seemed more likely as the adult schools received a huge input of new enthusiasm when they started amalgamating on a regional basis with non-denominational and other religious schools

---

[9] Isichei, *Victorian Quakers*, pp. 258–279.

[10] A.J. Peacock, 'Adult education in York, 1800–1947', *York History*, 5 (n.d.), pp. 266–301.

[11] J.F.C. Harrison, *Learning and Living, 1790–1960: A Study in the History of the English Adult Education Movement* (London, 1961), pp. 303–312.

providing adult learning.[12] The new National Adult School Union (NASU), formed in 1899, expanded from 45,000 members in 1901 to 113,789 in 1910. The two key figures in this process were close friends of Arnold's: W.C. Braithwaite, NASU's Chairman 1900–1922, and George Newman, the organization's Honorary Secretary 1899–1905 and editor of its newspaper, *One and All*. Both were Quakers, and although NASU was not officially linked to any religious group it was clear that its leadership remained very much in Quaker hands.

Arnold played an important role in negotiating the merger of Quaker adult schools in Yorkshire into NASU and in 1905–1919 served as the organization's Honorary Secretary. This was one of his most demanding and time-consuming roles but one that gave him most pleasure. Under his leadership, the central organization of NASU gradually expanded and started to exercise more influence on weekly adult school meetings. Arnold was anxious to strengthen the religious element in the schools and promoted the organization's own hymn book. But he also wanted it to provide more professional education, and members were soon able to take correspondence courses and receive visits from lecturers. As a further development, Arnold was closely involved in setting up educational settlements in York and Leeds in 1909, which it was hoped would develop into communities where fellowship and spiritual development could grow along with learning.

The success and expansion of NASU in the Edwardian era was a central part of the optimism of the Quaker Renaissance. But in the period of these letters the movement was visibly contracting, from 113,789 members in 1910 to 91,751 in 1914. The education it provided was far less specialized than that offered by competitors like the new Workers' Educational Association and local authority night schools, while the non-denominational religious fellowship of its meetings was also available from groups like the Brotherhood movement and the Young Mens' Christian Association. Arnold spent much of his time trying to draw NASU's rivals into schemes for co-operation, with limited success.[13] Ultimately, the movement was doomed to a long decline because its role was not sufficiently distinctive. But in the years before 1914 it was still a major force in the field of adult education and certainly a far bigger presence than groups like the Workers' Educational Association.

---

[12] W.A. Hall, *The Adult School Movement in the Twentieth Century* (Nottingham, 1985), pp. 6–22, 213.

[13] *Letters*, 26 March, 18 May, 8, 30 July 1914 for attempts to co-ordinate the work of NASU and the Brotherhood movement.

Business

Arnold had to fit NASU into his life whenever he could, just as he did with politics. Throughout his time as an MP he had a full-time job as a Director of Rowntree & Co. This combination of roles was only possible because he was able to delegate many of his day-to-day activities in the firm. But he remained its third most important figure, after Joseph Rowntree and Joseph's eldest surviving son, Seebohm. Joseph had tended to assign the younger generation of Rowntrees to specific areas of the firm, and Arnold's main area of responsibility was sales and marketing. In some ways this was an easy task. The consumer sector was growing rapidly in the late nineteenth century as real wages rose and Rowntree & Co. had already developed a dominant position in the market for pastilles and gums when Arnold joined the firm. Rowntree sales grew tenfold in 1897–1907, the factory was moved to new premises on the outskirts of York, and the workforce expanded rapidly.

However, if the firm was to continue to expand, it needed to break into the markets for cocoa and chocolate, as these offered the opportunity for really massive sales. Rowntree & Co. produced these goods when Arnold joined the firm, but only on a small scale.[14] He concentrated much of his efforts on promoting the firm's Elect cocoa as a good quality product for the mass market. Arnold engaged the leading advertising agent, S.H. Benson, to act for Rowntree & Co. and launched concerted campaigns involving everything from advertisements on buses to coupons in newspapers. However, he faced two major problems. Joseph Rowntree was intensely suspicious of advertising, which he associated with 'quackery'. He resisted increases in the advertising budget and tried to cut it when sales fell. Moreover, Arnold did not control product development. Rather than concentrating on selling a few lines, Rowntree & Co. tended to produce dozens, thus dissipating their efforts. They were also slow to respond to the development of milk chocolate and the new, less bitter, Dutch alkalized cocoa in the 1900s. This left the way open for their rivals, Cadbury Bros, to produce and market Cadburys Dairy Milk and Bournville Cocoa and establish themselves firmly as market leaders. Rowntree & Co. continued to expand but found their profits squeezed as real incomes fell in the years before 1914. In this respect the First World War was a boon to the company as it halted overseas competition and produced rising real wages once again. But the war also produced severe shortages of raw materials, most importantly sugar. Cadburys

---

[14] R. Fitzgerald, *Rowntree and the Marketing Revolution, 1862–1969* (Cambridge, 1995), pp. 75–146.

suggested the two firms merge, especially as there had always been some degree of co-operation between the two on pricing and advertising campaigns. But Joseph Rowntree refused. He and his family continued to believe their company could survive, as it did after a very shaky period in the 1920s.

Arnold's involvement with Rowntree & Co. was not separate from his wider religious and political concerns, but the significance of the firm's employment practices should be treated carefully. Though the old paternalism, when Joseph Rowntree took a personal interest in all his employees, could not survive in a company with 4,000 workers, Rowntree & Co. prided themselves on being a firm who cared for their workforce, providing relatively good wages, pensions, and sports, leisure, and welfare facilities. This has sometimes been seen as a particularly 'Quaker' approach to management, especially as much the same benefits were available from the Cadburys. But Rowntree & Co.'s provision for its workers could be matched by chocolate and cocoa manufacturers in much of the rest of Europe and North America, whatever the religion of the employers.[15] In consumer industries not susceptible to violent fluctuations of demand, it made economic sense to try and build up a pool of skilled and committed workers. But Rowntrees and Cadburys also combined good conditions with official policies to discourage drinking, gambling, and illicit sex and to 'improve' workers through education and a strong religious ethos. As Seebohm Rowntree put it, 'probably much more beneficial influence upon the character of the working classes may be exercised through the medium of their places of employment than is at present exercised through the churches'.[16] It was the combination of welfare and morality at Rowntree & Co. that was meant to be a microcosm of how Quaker leadership could create a better world, just as in the adult schools.

Moreover, Arnold did not just promote the application on a national scale of the conditions of employment at Rowntree & Co. Rather, he advocated crucial issues like minimum wages and consultation with employees in Parliament *before* they were enacted in his firm.[17] The most important influence on Arnold's thinking were his religion and his family, not his business. In fact, the activities of his firm were more often an embarrassment than an inspiration in his political career. Conservatives noted the role of the Rowntrees and the Cadburys in supporting Liberalism and targeted both firms for intense criticism.

---

[15] J. Child, 'Quaker employers and industrial relations', *Sociological Review*, 12 (1964), pp. 293–315; W.G. Clarence-Smith, *Cocoa and Chocolate, 1765–1914* (London, 2000), p. 79.

[16] Fitzgerald, *Rowntree*, pp. 237–239; B.S. Rowntree (ed.), *Betting and Gambling: A National Evil* (London, 1905), pp. 186–187.

[17] Fitzgerald, *Rowntree*, pp. 240–257; *Hansard*, 5th series, XXXVI, 290–293 (26 March 1912) on wages; *ibid*, XCIV, 86–91 (5 June 1917) on consultation with employees.

Cadbury Bros in particular were regularly charged with buying cocoa from plantations in São Tomé worked with slave labour and this led to a famous libel case in 1909.[18] Both firms were also accused of benefiting from protection, despite being ardent free-traders, as the duty on imported cocoa was lower than that on imports of manufactured chocolate. This provoked a long-running argument that was not resolved until the adjustment of duties in the 1911 budget. Arnold played an important role in brokering this agreement, but he clearly felt uncomfortable about the barrage of criticism he faced from the Tory benches.[19] Conservatives were not averse to implying his attitudes on other issues, like lowering the sugar duty, were also motivated by business concerns.[20] Criticism of Rowntree & Co. was magnified in wartime when the pacifism of the firm's owners made them deeply unpopular. The Rowntrees were accused of everything from trading with the enemy to encouraging conscientious objectors.[21] Thus, while his business career was an essential platform for Arnold's public life, it also had distinct drawbacks for him once he was in the Commons.

Newspapers

However, Arnold's business interests were not confined to Rowntree & Co. He was also a significant figure in the world of Edwardian newspapers. His uncle, Joseph Rowntree, was increasingly disgusted by the spread of what he saw as sensationalist Tory newspapers, like the *Daily Mail*, particularly because of their jingoistic coverage of the Boer War.[22] When he set up three charities in 1904 to administer much of his wealth, one of these charities, the Joseph Rowntree Social Service Trust (JRSST), was explicitly designed to support ailing but worthy Liberal papers. In this Joseph was merely following the example of George Cadbury, who had bought the *Daily News* in 1901 to secure it for the pro-Boer cause.

The first papers Joseph Rowntree bought were the Darlington-based *Northern Echo* and its weekly sister-papers in 1903. He transferred them to the ownership of the JRSST on its foundation and they were formed into the North of England Newspaper Co., with Arnold Rowntree as

[18] A.G. Gardiner, *Life of George Cadbury* (London, 1923), pp. 238–251.
[19] *Letters*, 16 May, 11 December 1911.
[20] *Hansard*, 5th series, LIII, 1665 (11 June 1913) for Sir F. Banbury's interjection to this effect during a speech by A.S.R.
[21] *Yorkshire Evening Press*, 14, 18 January, 14 August 1916.
[22] A. Vernon, *A Quaker Business Man: the Life of Joseph Rowntree, 1836–1925* (London, 1958), pp. 160–163; A.P. Duncum, *The Westminster Press Provincial Newspapers* (London, 1952), pp. 3–5.

Chairman of its Board of Directors. Perhaps his uncle considered his role in sales and marketing made Arnold particularly suitable to sell newspapers. The other leading figures in the new Company were J.B. Morrell, the only non-family Director of Rowntree & Co., and Charles Starmer, the general manager of the *Northern Echo*. The North of England Newspaper Co. soon acquired a range of titles in northern England, while Arnold and Morrell went on to buy the *Sheffield Independent* in 1909, and Morrell and Starmer purchased the *Birmingham Gazette* in 1912.

These papers were not acquired primarily as a profit-making venture. The aim was 'affording a vehicle for the promulgation of Liberal ideas', and, in particular, the ideas for social and moral reform that Arnold Rowntree and his family cared about.[23] The papers were to perform the role in print that the family carried out in their educational work and their business. To ensure this occurred, Arnold appointed like-minded editors to the papers, such as the active Unitarian and Radical Liberal, G.G. Armstrong, who took over the *Northern Echo* in 1904. But the JRSST did not have a bottomless purse and all the papers were expected to strive to reduce their losses. Armstrong was typical in attempting to mix together serious investigations into subjects like infant mortality with the best techniques of the 'new journalism' to increase sales – news appeared on the *Echo*'s front cover instead of advertisements, for instance.[24] When combined with substantial new investment, this technique was reasonably successful and most of the titles were moving towards breaking even by 1914.[25] One issue, though, posed the potential conflict between ideals and sales starkly – whether the papers should include betting news. The JRSST instructed the *Echo* to exclude such items, only to have to rescind the ban in March 1910 on the grounds that no paper could survive without it.[26]

This issue was raised in a much more acute and embarrassing way for the Rowntrees when the JRSST made its sole foray into Fleet Street.[27] In 1908 the *Morning Leader*, a national morning daily, and the *Star*, a London evening paper, two Liberal newspapers predominantly owned by the Colman family, were in serious difficulties. To save them for the Liberal cause George Cadbury and the JRSST agreed to take

[23] *Northern Echo*, 19 April 1904.

[24] G.G. Armstrong, *Memoirs of George Gilbert Armstrong: Journalist, Politician, Author, Preacher* (London, 1944), pp. 81–90.

[25] The *Sheffield Independent* went into profit in 1913 and the *Northern Echo* in 1914, the latter after initially losing £7,000–£8,000 p.a.; JRSST, minutes 22 December 1913, 12 October 1914.

[26] *Ibid.*, minutes 10 December 1907, 1 March 1910.

[27] S. Koss, *The Rise and Fall of the Political Press in Britain*, vol. 2 (London, 1984), pp. 42–43, 147–148, 172–173.

them over. Arnold played a crucial role in the negotiations that led to the acquisition of the papers and was installed as Chairman of the Board of Directors of the new joint venture.[28] However, the project was fraught with difficulties. Joseph Rowntree had been dubious of its merits from the beginning, especially as the potential financial commitment for the JRSST was huge. The Cadburys and Rowntrees soon found themselves subjected to a barrage of criticism from gleeful Tories and appalled Quakers that they continued to allow betting tips in the *Star*. The subject sparked off a pamphlet war within the Society of Friends and a committee of inquiry by its governing body, Yearly Meeting.[29] As early as 1910, Arnold Rowntree began negotiations with the Cadburys to extricate the JRSST from the imbroglio. It made more financial sense, anyway, to merge the *Morning Leader* with the Cadburys' *Daily News* and print the *Star* on the same machinery. However, it took until April 1911 to work out an agreement.

The only national venture the JRSST kept on was the weekly, the *Nation*, which it had bought in 1907.[30] Its circulation was always small and it required considerable subsidies, but it gained immense prestige under H.G. Massingham, the editor recruited by the JRSST, as the intellectual forum for the New Liberalism. The Trustees of the JRSST left the running of the paper to Massingham and the Chairman of the Board of Directors, E.R. Cross, who was Rowntree & Co.'s solicitor and a close friend of Arnold's.[31] Arnold was a member of the Board, but he had little contact with the paper beyond attending the weekly contributors' lunches when he was in London. This situation only changed in August 1916 when E.R. Cross was drowned and Arnold took overall charge of the *Nation* at an especially difficult time. Massingham was relentlessly anti-Lloyd George, especially after the Welshman deposed Asquith in December 1916, while Seebohm Rowntree, who was a Trustee of the JRSST, was a close collaborator of the Prime Minister's. Arnold attempted to steer a middle course between the two, defending Massingham's independence, while urging him to 'avoid all personalities as much as possible' when referring to Lloyd George.[32] Matters became even more fraught in April 1917 when Lloyd George banned overseas sales of the *Nation* on the grounds that it was aiding the enemy.

The newspaper world was, therefore, not an entirely happy field for Arnold Rowntree. During the war the financial position of many of

[28] JRSST, minutes, 29 October 1908, 17 November 1909.

[29] *Letters*, 6–9 November 1911; JRSST, minutes 13 September 1910.

[30] For the Rowntrees and the *Nation*, see A.F. Havighurst, *Radical Journalist: H.W. Massingham* (Cambridge, 1974), pp. 143–144, 153–155, 250–256, 294–302.

[31] JRSST, minutes 29 November 1906.

[32] *Ibid.*, 22 December 1916.

the regional newspapers with which he was associated deteriorated rapidly and by 1920 the situation was desperate. The papers were merged into Westminster Press Ltd, a group headed by Lord Cowdray, a Liberal businessman with exceptionally deep pockets.[33] Arnold remained a Director of the Westminster Press and many of its subsidiary companies until his death, but the papers had passed out of his control. The *Nation* was finally sold in 1923 to a syndicate of Keynes's friends – a prolonged transaction that brought furious criticism from Massingham, who wanted to buy the paper himself.

Local politics

Arnold had been interested in politics since childhood and in the early 1900s he started to play an active role in the Liberal Association in his home city of York, serving as its Secretary 1901–1904 and President 1904–1909. From the first, he was associated with attempts to implement the kind of programme of moral and social reform that was central to John Wilhem Rowntree's vision of the Quaker Renaissance. His main collaborator was his cousin, Seebohm, who had set up a body called the Health and Housing Reform Association to campaign for municipal social reform.[34] Arnold and Seebohm urged council action to help the unemployed and helped prepare and contributed to a series of articles in the *Yorkshire Gazette* (run by Arnold) entitled 'Towards a municipal policy', which outlined how York council could take greater steps to improve its citizens' lives, by, for instance, taking control of the tramways and the gas supply. In the field of 'moral' reform, Seebohm sponsored an anti-gambling organization in York and Rowntree JPs did their best to reduce the number of public houses.

To enact their programme, members of the Rowntree family and their connections started, from 1905 onwards, to gain election to the council and to join Arnold in important positions in the Liberal Association.[35] Their wealth, prestige and clear sense of what they wished to achieve meant they soon effectively controlled the Liberal group on the council and the Association. Leading Liberal councillors after 1905 included J.B. Morrell, James Hogge, who worked for Seebohm Rowntree's anti-gambling organization, K.E.T. Wilkinson, who was married to a cousin of Arnold's, and Sebastian Meyer, a Quaker and

[33] Koss, *Political Press*, pp. 370–371.
[34] For the following: *Yorkshire Herald*, 16 April 1910; *Yorkshire Evening Press*, 12 July, 28 July 1904; D.S. Crichton *et al.*, *Towards a Municipal Policy for York* (York, 1905); B.S. Rowntree, *Betting and Gambling*, pp. 175–176.
[35] R. Hills, *The Inevitable March of Labour? Electoral Politics in York, 1900–1914* (Borthwick Paper no. 89, York, 1996), pp. 12–21; *Yorkshire Herald*, 12 March 1909.

friend of Arnold's from the adult school movement. Oscar Rowntree, Seebohm's brother, became Treasurer of the Liberal Association, and J.B. Morrell succeeded Arnold as President in 1909. This group proved remarkably successful in reviving York Liberalism. They made steady gains from the Tories after 1905 and controlled the council in 1911–1913 with the support of the small Labour group. They also achieved some real successes, especially in winning the local referendum to municipalize the trams in 1909. Thus Arnold had no need to learn his New Liberalism from the party's leadership. He had already been involved in implementing such a programme in York before he became an MP.

MP for York

In some ways Arnold was a fairly obvious choice as Liberal candidate for York. He was a member of a wealthy and prestigious local family, well-known for its service to the city. He was an important figure in the local party and had even served briefly on the executive of the National Liberal Federation in 1904–1905. However, before 1909 he had never given any indication that he wanted to be an MP – after all his life was very full without any additional roles. It was events that year which produced a situation whereby Arnold felt obliged to fight the seat to help the York Liberals out of a difficult situation.

York was a two-member constituency in which each elector was able to cast two votes. In 1906 the seat was shared by a Liberal, Hamar Greenwood, an impecunious Canadian barrister who was widely seen as a Rowntree protégé, and a Conservative, G.D. Faber.[36] Greenwood was the only candidate nominated by the York Liberals and most of them, including Arnold, urged their supporters to use their other vote to back G.H. Stuart, the sole Labour candidate. Though the reluctance of York Liberals to vote for him meant Stuart was defeated, it may well have been expected that another Labour candidate would be selected for the next election. However, the Labour movement fell into serious decline after 1906. Its agent left, its paper closed down and it was reduced to one councillor by 1908.[37] By the summer of 1909, as the People's Budget moved towards the House of Lords and an election became a real possiblity, there was still no Labour candidate in sight. Arnold consulted the chief whip about a second Liberal candidate on

[36] A.S.R. did help to subsidize Greenwood, while Joseph Rowntree attempted to imbue him with suitable principles: A.S.R. to M.K.R., 13 February 1908; Vipont, *Arnold Rowntree*, p. 54. *Yorkshire Evening Press*, 17 January 1906 for A.S.R. urging support for G.H. Stuart.
[37] See Hills, *Politics in York*, pp. 13–14.

16 June 1909, but without any indication he would stand himself. However, no candidate appeared and on 11 September Arnold agonized: 'I fear everything seems pointing to an early election. I wonder what it will be right for me to do, for the crisis is one that calls for sacrifice'. It was clearly not an easy decision for him and it was not announced until 12 November that Arnold had stepped into the breach as Hamar Greenwood's running-mate.[38]

The campaign of January 1910 was desperately closely fought. Faber, the sitting Tory, had retired, but the Conservatives had two strong candidates in J.G. Butcher, who had been MP for York in 1892–1906, and Henry Riley-Smith, the head of John Smith's brewery, based in nearby Tadcaster. Arnold and Greenwood did not just concentrate on the House of Lords' rejection of the Budget. Much of their campaign centred on the issues dear to the heart of the Quaker Renaissance – social reform, temperance, and the reduction of armaments.[39] The result, uniquely for a two-member seat in January 1910, was a draw. All four candidates were within 256 votes of each other, but Arnold and Butcher were elected with Arnold topping the poll by 10 votes. The result was decided by the 136 Tories who voted for Butcher alone and the 130 electors who split their votes between Arnold and Butcher. Possibly the former were 'temperance' Tories unwilling to vote for a brewer, while the latter voted for the two candidates whose names were best-known in York, irrespective of party.

The result in December 1910 was even more unusual. Neither defeated candidate wished to fight the seat again as Greenwood wanted a safer constituency and Riley-Smith was ill.[40] Neither party was confident of holding their existing seat, let alone taking that belonging to the opposition. When it became clear another election was likely in 1910 both local organizations started to explore the possibility of giving the two sitting MPs a walkover. After a good deal of fencing and negotiation this occurred and Arnold was spared a rerun of the agonizingly close finish of January 1910. Though he could not know it, he had secured his place in the Commons for the next eight years.

---

[38] A.S.R. to M.K.R., 16 June, 11 September 1909, letter transcripts, Tessa Cadbury papers, Temp. MS 647, Friends House, London; *Yorkshire Gazette*, 13 November 1909.
[39] See their joint election address, in Candidates Election Addresses, General Election, January 1910, National Liberal Club papers, University of Bristol Library.
[40] *Letters*, 1, 3 March, 6 April, 16, 18 November 1910, 16 May 1911.

Peacetime MP 1910–1914

Arnold was in Parliament out of a sense of duty. He never expressed any interest in holding government office – indeed he often had doubts about going on in politics at all.[41] But he soon blended in with the rest of the rank-and-file on the Liberal backbenches. As a businessman, he belonged to the largest occupational group among Liberal MPs and the one least likely to achieve political office.[42] Entrepreneurs tended to enter the Commons relatively late in life or to have too much to do outside Parliament to concentrate on winning promotion. His Quakerism made him slightly unusual, but there were half a dozen other Quaker Liberal MPs and his denomination had provided over thirty MPs since 1833 so he was part of a long-established tradition.[43] 'Jack' Pease was even a member of Asquith's Cabinet, though a purely nominal Quaker. Arnold already knew a number of Liberal and Labour MPs through his political and business activities and he had one very close friend among them – his brother-in-law, T.E. Harvey.[44]

Arnold's letters give a good picture of his life as a backbench MP up to 1914. His main role was to turn up in the Commons and vote as the whips directed. This was tedious, tiring, and often incomprehensible and Arnold was not unnaturally depressed at the futility of backbench life, especially as parliamentary sittings were becoming longer and Conservative obstructionism more and more vehement. When he could, he escaped to the theatre in the evening – as did many other MPs.[45] But he was not a purely passive MP. His interventions were fairly infrequent – he spoke only eighteen times in 1910–1914 and asked forty-eight questions – and Arnold was well aware that he never really mastered the art of holding the attention of the Commons.[46] But there were a number of interests and concerns he was determined to pursue.

Some of these issues were unavoidable. As MP for York he had to raise occasional local matters and to help with private Bills.[47] However,

[41] *Ibid.*, 18 November 1910 for a particularly heartfelt cry.
[42] Searle, 'Edwardian Liberal Party and business', p. 34 for the view that 38 to 40 per cent of Liberal MPs were still businessmen.
[43] Isichei, *Victorian Quakers*, pp. 202–208.
[44] A.S.R. to M.K.R., 24 June 1909 mentioning meetings with Arthur Henderson, Burns, and Rea at the Commons.
[45] *Letters*, 7 April 1910, 14 March, 19 April, 25 October 1911, 15 February, 14, 18 November 1912, for example.
[46] A.S.R. was less active in the HofC in the pre-1914 period than the average government backbencher. In 1913 he made 5 speeches and asked 9 questions, compared to a mean of 7.5 interventions in debate and 14.3 questions; see M. Rush, *The Role of the Member of Parliament since 1868: From Gentlemen to Players* (Oxford, 2001), pp. 155–156.
[47] *Hansard*, 5th series, XLI, 10 (15 July 1912) for question on Foot and Mouth Disease in the vicinity of York.

his constituency did not loom large in Arnold's parliamentary concerns, despite his slim majority. The local party was well organized and run by his family and close allies and he paid an agent, A.G. Watson, to handle constituents' queries. Arnold also had to defend the interests of his business, but the only really time-consuming issue was the readjustment of duties on cocoa and chocolate in the 1911 Budget. Finally, he sometimes asked questions to help out members of his family, especially when Seebohm Rowntree wanted information for his research.[48]

Most of Arnold's intitiatives as a backbencher, though, arose out of his own interests and concerns. These could be entirely personal, as when on holiday in Eastbourne he met a self-educated coastguard and subsequently asked a Commons question about the contents of coastguards' libraries.[49] But most of his speeches and questions fell into two broad categories. Firstly, Arnold paid some attention to what might be classified as traditional Quaker concerns. One of his relatively rare speeches was in opposition to a bill on conscription introduced by a backbench Tory MP, and Arnold followed in the footsteps of Elizabeth Fry by asking a number of questions on penal reform, especially the imprisonment of debtors.[50] But by far the most substantial part of Arnold's speeches and questions − some 55 to 60 per cent − dealt with social reform. Some of this activity had a constituency motivation, as one of the topics on which Arnold spoke was wages and conditions in the railway industry, whose workers were well represented in the York electorate. But his main contribution was to Lloyd George's National Insurance Act of 1911. Arnold was part of a group of backbench MPs who helped shape and amend the legislation as it went through the Commons, often working in co-operation with Lloyd George.[51] Arnold's particular concern was the Act's provision for women and low-paid workers and he was one of the most active MPs in providing a counterweight to pressures, mainly from the big insurance companies, to cut down benefits for low-paid and casual workers who would be ineligible to join one of the insurance companies or friendly societies administering the Act and would make their contributions to a special Post Office scheme. Arnold then asked the government thirteen questions about the administration of National Insurance, spoke on the subsequent amending bill in 1912–1913 and worked hard on the Chief Whip's committee to publicize and defend National Insurance.[52]

[48] *Hansard*, 5th series, XXXV, 192–193 (5 March 1912) for a question on Belgian light railways.

[49] *Ibid.*, LIX, 1056 (10 March 1914).

[50] *Ibid.*, LI, 1562–1566 (11 April 1913); XLIII, 257 (29 October 1912).

[51] *Letters*, 5, 6, 28 July, 23 October, 1, 2, 7 November 1911.

[52] *Hansard*, 5th series, LV, 1160–1163 (15 July 1913); *Letters*, 27 February, 18 June, 2 July 1912.

Arnold was eager to co-operate with the government's social reforms and generally regarded himself as an enthusiastic supporter of the policies of Asquith's Cabinet. He never considered casting a vote that would result in its defeat. But he was still one of the most rebellious Liberal MPs of 1910–1914. When it was safe to do so, he had no qualms about voting against the government, especially when this involved protesting against arms spending or trying to push the government further on social reform.[53] On these occasions Arnold was happy to co-operate and vote with Labour MPs. Indeed he was an admirer of Ramsay MacDonald and worked closely with Arthur Henderson outside Parliament on religious issues.[54] By any measurement, Arnold was one of the thirty to forty Liberal MPs who constituted the most 'advanced' section of the party, both on traditional radical and social reform issues. His case is a salutary reminder that not all nonconformist businessmen were a drag on the New Liberalism.

But, above all, Arnold's career shows how an MP's outlook was usually formed long before he entered Parliament and how it was difficult for the Commons to radically change those views because it was only ever part of a backbench MP's life. All the time he was an MP, Arnold was a director of a large company and several newspapers, and responsible for running the adult school movement. He was only in London when the Commons was sitting. Even then his mornings were always devoted to his business and NASU, while he attempted to escape to York to see his family and attend to the pressing demands of Rowntree & Co. and local affairs for at least three days each week. Membership of the Commons widened Arnold's circle of friends but did not transform his social life. His closest acquaintances in the Commons were like-minded Liberals, especially Quakers, and he continued to see a good deal of various relatives and Quaker friends in London. It is perhaps indicative that he never acquired a permanent home there. The centre of his life remained in York.

Wartime MP 1914–1918

The coming of war in 1914 transformed Arnold's role as an MP. Overnight he went from being a Liberal backbencher of advanced but unexceptional views to being one of the handful of MPs who were dubbed at best pacifists, at worst traitors. Though he did not lose

[53] A.S.R. participated in the major arms reduction rebellions by Liberal MPs on 13 and 16 March 1911, and 22 and 25 July 1912, as well as voting for minimum wages on 26 March 1912 and 11 February 1913.

[54] A.S.R. to M.K.R., 3 July 1907; *Letters*, 26 March, 18 May 1914.

interest in social reform – indeed his interest in minimum wages,
housing reform and industrial conciliation increased if anything – his
attitude to the war dominated the last four years of his time as an
MP.[55] But that attitude was actually complex. Arnold was both a
Quaker who believed passionately in his denomination's refusal to bear
arms and a radical who had criticized the growth in armaments and
Grey's balance-of-power policies, so it was no surprise that on the night
of 3 August 1914 he declared 'I for one will have nothing to do with
this war'.[56] But he was also a loyal Liberal who believed the Cabinet
had done their best to avoid war. He refused to join in any public
declaration by anti-war MPs, or organizations like the Union of
Democratic Control, that condemned the government's foreign policy.[57]
Moreover, Arnold believed that while the youth of the Empire were
sacrificing their lives for what they saw as a noble ideal, however
misguidedly, those opposed to the war could not justify refusing to
undertake some form of service and self-sacrifice themselves. The
organization that most closely embodied his ideal of non-military service
for pacifists was the Friends' Ambulance Unit (FAU), a group of
volunteers, mostly Quakers, who agreed to go to the Western Front to
undertake nursing and orderly duties.[58] Arnold and his close friends,
Sir George Newman and W.C. Braithwaite, were of central importance
in setting up the FAU and Arnold played a significant role on its
organizing committee throughout the war. This attitude placed Arnold
firmly in the moderate section of Quaker opinion, between those, like
the Cabinet minister J.A. Pease, who were prepared to tacitly endorse
the war and those who saw it as their duty to disrupt the military
machine.

His work with the FAU meant Arnold's commitments outside Parliament had become more hectic than ever. But the years 1916–1918
were also his most active as an MP – he asked 148 questions and made
35 speeches. This was entirely due to the introduction of conscription
in January 1916. Arnold had made clear before the war that he objected
to forcing anyone into the armed forces who had a conscientious
objection to war, not just Quakers.[59] He and T.E. Harvey were probably
the two MPs who were most active in Quaker relief organizations that

[55] *Hansard*, 5th series, LXIX, 1221–1224 (17 February 1915) for minimum wages; *ibid.*,
XCIV, 86–91 (5 June 1917) for industrial conciliation. A.S.R. was also secretary of an all-
party group on housing reform.

[56] *Ibid.*, 5th series, LXV, 1847.

[57] *Letters*, 10 August 1914.

[58] For the FAU see, M. Tatham and J.E. Miles, *The Friends' Ambulance Unit, 1914–19: A
Record* (London, 1919).

[59] *Hansard*, 5th series, LI, 1566 (11 April 1913) on the National Service (Territorial
Forces) Bill.

employed pacifists and they found themselves in the role of spokesmen and intermediaries for those who insisted they would resist conscription.

The government was willing to allow the local tribunals that heard individuals' appeals against conscription to exempt applicants on the grounds of conscientious objection to bearing arms. But T.E. Harvey and Arnold moved the crucial amendment that allowed tribunals the option of directing Conscientious Objectors (COs) to civilian work of national importance, rather than coming under military authority.[60] They knew from their contacts with potential COs that any other option would be unacceptable to many of them. This was probably Arnold's single most important moment as an MP. But it was far from the end of his labours on the matter. The decisions of the tribunals in individual cases led to thousands of disputes and caused immense bitterness throughout 1916–1918.[61] Over 5,000 men were imprisoned for refusing to accept their tribunals' verdict and Arnold, as a known champion of the COs' cause, received a huge amount of mail from these men and their friends and relatives.[62] He did what he could for all of them, whatever their objection to the war, from Jehovah's Witnesses to socialists. Usually, he could only help if the tribunals or the army had broken their own rules, but he was willing to pester ministers tirelessly and ask questions in the House.

Not all COs were grateful for Arnold's efforts. Those who saw it as their duty to refuse any compromise with a state at war, even if it meant imprisonment, like the young Quakers organized in the Friends' Service Committee, or the 'absolutists' in the No-Conscription Fellowship, regarded Arnold's stance as that of a collaborator.[63] On the other hand, his reputation as 'the COs' friend' branded him as unpatriotic in most people's eyes. The political implications of Arnold's position were also complex. At the level of the Commons it meant that while he was disappointed with many of the actions of Asquith's government in 1914–1916, he had no option but generally to align himself with Asquith after the split in the party in December 1916. While he continued to recognize many of Lloyd George's qualities, he could hardly support the man who banned the overseas circulation of the *Nation*, a paper for which he was responsible, or who threatened to extend conscription to Ireland. Arnold voted for Asquith's motion on the Maurice debate in March 1918 – the acid test of Liberal loyalties.

[60] *Ibid.*, LXXVIII, 430 (19 January 1916).

[61] J. Rae, *Conscience and Politics: The British Government and the Conscientious Objector to Military Service, 1916–19* (Oxford, 1970) remains the best examination of this issue.

[62] Some of this correspondence has been preserved in A.S.R.'s papers at Friends House, London, Temp. MS 977/2/2.

[63] T.C. Kennedy, 'Fighting about peace: the No Conscription Fellowship and the British Friends' Service Committee, 1915–1919', *Quaker History*, 69 (1980), pp. 3–22.

As a result, he drew closer to several Asquithian figures like McKenna, Simon and Runciman.[64]

At the local level Arnold was never in danger of being deselected by his constituency party, as T.E. Harvey was in West Leeds, if only because York Liberalism was controlled by his relatives and friends. But there was serious dissension over his attitude to conscription and there could be no doubt that his attitude to the war was deeply unpopular in York.[65] For the first three years of the war he made few public appearances and there had to be real uncertainty about whether he would stand again. Indeed, Arnold said he offered to resign a number of times.[66] But many of his friends, especially J.B. Morrell, the President of York Liberal Association, urged him to stay on and fight the seat again. Arnold delayed his decision and was only re-adopted as Liberal candidate at the last moment on 9 November 1918. He may have been swayed by the opportunity to defend his stand in public. But he could not be under any illusions about the likelihood of winning. York had lost one of its MPs in the 1918 Reform Act and Arnold would have to fight the sitting Tory MP, Butcher, and a Labour candidate for the one remaining seat. As the Tories had won half the vote in 1910, the split in the progressive camp made victory for any Liberal unlikely.

Arnold's election strategy was fairly clear. He was presented mainly as a social reformer, as an MP who had always worked for the rights of women and as a defender of Liberal values. His work with the FAU was mentioned, but not that with COs.[67] Butcher responded by declaring 'Had the men of Britain acted as Mr Rowntree acted, we should to-day have been crushed and enslaved by Germany'.[68] This stance was sufficient for the Conservatives to win a clear victory with 61.5 per cent of the votes. Arnold managed 20.3 per cent – less than half of his share of the vote in 1910, but still enough to beat the Labour candidate. This was a respectable showing in very adverse circumstances and certainly nothing like the disaster that overcame some anti-war MPs in 1918. Sir John Barlow, the only other Quaker MP critical of the war to defend his seat, was reduced to 8.4 per cent of the vote in Frome, a constituency he had first won in 1892. But Arnold was not displeased to be out of

---

[64] *Letters*, 30 May 1916 for McKenna; Simon and Runciman spoke for A.S.R. at the 1918 election; *Yorkshire Gazette*, 14 December 1918.

[65] *Yorkshire Herald*, 15 January 1916 for splits in the local Liberal Party.

[66] *Yorkshire Gazette*, 16 November 1918 for Arnold's acceptance speech after his nomination.

[67] See advertisements in *Yorkshire Evening Press*, 5–12 December 1918, including 'Rowntree stands for generous pensions' and 'Rowntree stands for free trade and no taxes on food'. M.K.R. wrote 'A special appeal to the women voters of York', *Yorkshire Gazette*, 23 November 1918. The same issue had a long feature on Arnold's work with the FAU.

[68] *Yorkshire Evening Press*, 12 December 1918.

the Commons. He never considered standing for Parliament again.[69]

Arnold withdrew from his role in NASU in 1919 and thereafter concentrated on his business career. When Seebohm Rowntree succeeded his father as Chairman of the company in 1923 he relied on Arnold as his deputy. He only stopped playing an active role in Rowntree & Co. in 1931 and kept on his newspaper interests until his death. Arnold remained well respected in York and served in the honorary post of Sheriff in 1931–1932. His main public interest remained his faith and he even served as Vice-Chairman of the FAU when it was reformed in 1939–1945. But his withdrawal from politics was symptomatic of the ending of the great hopes of the Quaker Renaissance. The instruments the young Quakers of the late nineteenth century had chosen to pursue their project of moral and social reform had broken in their hands. The Liberal Party, the high-minded press and the adult school movement were all in serious decline. Their dream of reforming Britain was over.

The letters

Arnold wrote to his wife, Mary, on a regular basis when they were apart, often as much as once a day, describing his activities and movements. Letters also exist for the period 1906–1909, but they have not been reproduced, as they contain little about Arnold's public life. On the other hand, not all the letters seem to have survived, and there are some gaps, especially for the latter half of 1917. The original letters are held at Friends House, London, where they were deposited by Tessa Cadbury, Arnold's eldest daughter. Mrs Cadbury prepared a typescript of the letters containing many useful footnotes identifying family and personal friends. This has been an invaluable aid in putting together the edition, though the text has been constantly checked against the original letters.[70]

The editorial policy adopted has been to reprint everything concerning Arnold's public activities, but only to include material of a personal or family nature where this has some wider relevance. The only substantial piece of text that has been drastically pruned is that dealing with Arnold's visit to Canada in the summer of 1912. Where an entry excludes some words from the original, these are represented as '[...]'. The original punctuation and grammar have been retained, but occasional misspellings, usually of names, have been silently corrected.

[69] Vipont, *Arnold Rowntree*, pp. 80–119 for A.S.R.'s career after 1918.

[70] Copies of Mrs Cadbury's transcript are held at Friends House, London and the Joseph Rowntree Foundation, York.

Arnold had a habit of referring to people well known to his wife by their initials and where this occurs the individual's name is given in full in square brackets. When a person appears for the first time in the text a biographical footnote is provided, except in the case of a handful of individuals who proved impossible to trace.

The letters shed an interesting light on one Edwardian politician's marriage, though in this respect it is deeply disappointing that Mary's letters to Arnold do not seem to have survived. Arnold and Mary had known each other since childhood, as Arnold was a schoolfriend of Mary's brother, T.E. Harvey, at Bootham. The Harveys were a family of Quaker businessmen from Leeds with a long tradition of public work, especially in the fields of education and temperance, so Arnold and Mary's backgrounds were very similar. They married in 1906 and had six children between 1907 and 1921.

The marriage was an extremely happy and close union, based on shared interests. Arnold's family was the centre of his life and he deeply disliked the extended absences from home that attendance at the Commons forced on him. Mary, on the other hand, was deeply interested in social and educational questions and played a significant part in her husband's public life. She presided over the Womens' Liberal Association in York and influenced her husband on a number of questions – in some cases, as with the Criminal Law Amendment Act of 1912, Arnold represented Mary's views to the Commons.[71] They did not disagree on many issues. In particular, Arnold and Mary shared a commitment to improving womens' social conditions and greater equality for women. Arnold was a persistent, if non-violent, supporter of womens' suffrage and also spoke up for equal treatment for women in divorce and in the legal system.[72]

In some ways this was not surprising. Quakerism had a long tradition of allowing women to act as ministers and of public activity by women, most famously Elizabeth Fry. By the early 1900s this had been updated into formal equality of treatment for women in the Society of Friends – in 1918 a woman served as Clerk of Yearly Meeting, the highest position in British Quakerism. Though Quakers were reticent about taking a collective stand for women's suffrage, Arnold's and Mary's views on women's role in society fitted easily into the context of their faith.[73]

The letters are, then, a record of one man's public life. But they are also a testimony to a very happy and close family. After 1918 Arnold Rowntree was one politician who was not sorry to be able to spend more time with his wife and children.

[71] *Letters*, 23 July, 13 November 1912.
[72] *Yorkshire Gazette*, 29 November 1913.
[73] T.C. Kennedy, *British Quakerism, 1860–1920: The Transformation of a Religious Community* (Oxford, 2001), pp. 211–236.

CHAPTER 1

Letters 1910

15 February 1910
National Liberal Club

Just a few lines, darling, to let thee know how this interesting day passed.

I was greeted by old Sir John Brigg,[1] the father of J.J., as I journeyed down to breakfast in the lift and he was most kind and anxious to do anything to help a new member. I breakfasted with Bevan James[2] and advised him to definitely close with the Whiteway offer which evidently is better than anything he can expect to make in York. Then I went off to St James Court and found three very nice furnished sunny rooms which I am quite inclined to engage for 4½ guineas per week. [...] I went off to the 'Nation' meeting and was glad there to meet Ted.[3] Nothing very special – circulation happily increasing but fear we have a somewhat costly action to settle through an unwise article of Archer's.[4] I then had half an hour with Parke[5] and a hasty lunch with Ted at the NLC along with the Nation writers.

The opening of Parliament thou willst read about[6] – I was interested in hearing Burt[7] with his charming brogue and Chaplin[8]

---

[1] Sir John Brigg (1834–1911), Lib. MP Keighley 1895–1911; kt. 1909; and his eldest son John Jeremy Brigg, Lib. cand. Thirsk and Malton 1906, January 1910.

[2] Bevan James, traveller with Rowntree & Co. Whiteways was a large department store.

[3] Thomas Edmund Harvey (1875–1955), eldest bro. of M.K.R.; schoolfriend of A.S.R. and his closest friend and collaborator in HofC. Educated Bootham and Oxford; asst at British Museum 1900–1904; Dep. Warden Toynbee Hall 1904–1906, Warden 1906–1911; LCC 1904–1907; Lib. MP West Leeds January 1910–1918, Dewsbury 1923–1924; Ind. Prog. MP Combined English Univs 1937–1945; PPS E.J. Griffith 1912–1913, C.F.G. Masterman 1913–1914, resigning on outbreak of war.

[4] William Archer (1856–1924), Australian journalist; drama critic of *Nation*.

[5] Ernest Parke (1860–1944), Lib. newspaperman. Managing Ed. and Dir. of *Star* 1891–1908, *Morning Leader* 1892–1912.

[6] *Hansard*, 5th series, 1910, XIV, 3–8 for these speeches on the re-election of The Speaker. This was the first day of the 1910 Parliament and A.S.R.'s first experience of the House of Commons as an MP.

[7] Thomas Burt (1837–1922), Lib. MP Morpeth 1874–1918; PS Bd of Trade 1892–1895; Father of HofC 1910–1918. One of the first two working-class MPs and Sec. Northumberland Miners' Mutual Confident Association 1865–1913.

[8] Henry Chaplin (1840–1923), Con. MP Mid-Lincolnshire 1868–1885, Sleaford 1885–1906, Wimbledon 1907–1916, when cr. Vt Chaplin. Chanc. Duchy of Lancaster

with his pompous friends and then it was quaint seeing Lowther[9] escorted to the chair by both Burt and Chaplin taking him by the hand. I sat between Ted, Lehmann[10] and members who one knew were most kind and cordial at one's appearance inside the House.

I then went with Butcher[11] to see the Speaker and had an interesting talk with him about the cities' rights to the front bench seats! But whilst admitting these existed in the past, he thought that they had certainly lapsed by disusitude (which I was thankful for!)

Since then I have been again to the Leader office to consult Parke over a Northern Echo difficulty and am now going to dine with Cross.[12] I quite hope, darling, to catch the 5.30 train and shall hope to be with thee by 9.30. [...]

16 February 1910
House of Commons

I was so grieved darling to have to wire thee but there were a good many matters at the Leader meeting this morning that we could not settle without first consulting Edward Cadbury[13] and he sent a message pressing me to meet him tonight so I thought on the whole it was the best. [...]

Sherwell[14] has just interrupted and been gossiping about his talk with Dillon[15] – things are all *very* uncertain yet but I think I better not begin to launch out on politics until I see thee.

1885–1886, Pres. Bd of Agriculture 1889–1892, Pres. Local Govt Bd 1895–1900. Archetypal country gentleman, known as 'the Squire'.

[9] James William Lowther (1855–1949), Con. MP Rutland 1883–1885, Penrith 1886–1921; Speaker 1905–1921, when cr. Vt Ullswater.

[10] Rudolf Chambers Lehmann (1856–1929), journalist; Lib. MP Harborough 1906–December 1910.

[11] John George Butcher (1851–1935), Irish-born barrister; Con. MP York 1892–1906, January 1910–1923; Bt 1918; cr. Ld Danesfort 1924.

[12] Elihu Richard Cross (1864–1916), Scarborough solicitor, Clerk to JPs 1895–1913; convert to Quakerism c. 1898, friend and political helper of A.S.R. Performed much legal work for Rowntree & Co., Joseph Rowntree, and his various trusts, of which he was sec. 1906–1916. Chmn of Bd of Dirs of *Nation* 1907–1916; member Land Enquiry 1912–1914, Central Control Bd 1915–1916.

[13] Edward Cadbury (1873–1948), s. of George Cadbury; Dir. Cadbury Bros, Chmn 1932–1944; Chmn Bd of Dirs *Daily News* 1911–1930.

[14] Arthur James Sherwell (1863–1942), Lib. MP Huddersfield November 1906–1918; co-wrote five books on temperance with Joseph Rowntree.

[15] John Dillon (1851–1927), Irish Nat. MP Tipperary 1880–1883, East Mayo 1885–1918; leader of Anti-Parnellites 1896–1900, Irish Nats 1918.

After writing thee last night I dined with E.R.C.[ross] and then tried to see H.L.W.[16] – Greenwood[17] and Con[18] at their respective abodes but failed in all three cases. Today I breakfasted with J.B.M.[19] and spent the morning at the Leader office – lunched with E.R.C.[ross], J.B.M.[orrell] and Hammond[20] here after I had *affirmed*. This afternoon I have been round the House escorted by Rea[21] who has been very good in telling me everything he could.

I had tea with Ted [Harvey] who I am glad to find had secured 2 tickets for the Ladies Gallery for Tuesday so I rather hope thou and Mother[22] will be tempted to come up and then thou canst see the suggested abode. Greenwood is dining with J.B.M.[orrell] and myself at the NLC and then I go off to meet Edward Cadbury, Henry C,[23] Parke and Gardiner (Editor, DN)[24]

[...]

1 March 1910
House of Commons

Just a few lines to darling to let thee know how matters have fared. I had a comfortable journey – we were met by Parke and then settled a few Leader matters in a taxi en route to the NLC. Then

---

[16] Henry Lloyd Wilson (1862–1941), Dir. J. & E. Sturge, Birmingham chemical manufacturers, but devoted his life to Quaker concerns; member Meeting for Sufferings 1889–1919, Council of Woodbrooke 1908–1938; bro. of J.W. Wilson MP.

[17] Hamar Greenwood (1870–1948), Canadian barrister; Lib. MP York 1906–January 1910, Sunderland December 1910–1922, Constitutionalist MP East Walthamstow 1924–1929; US Home Office 1919, Sec. Dept of Overseas Trade 1919–1920, Chief Sec. for Ireland 1920–1922; Bt 1915, cr. Ld Greenwood 1929, Vt 1937.

[18] Constance Margaret Rowntree (nee Naish) (1871–1928), widow of John Wilhelm Rowntree, eldest s. of Joseph Rowntree.

[19] John Bowes Morrell (1873–1963), member of Yorkshire banking family; Dir. Rowntree & Co. 1897–1943; co-dir. with A.S.R. of several regional newspapers; Chmn Westminster Press 1933–1953; prominent figure in York local govt, Councillor Micklegate 1905–1917, Alderman 1917–1945, Ld Mayor, 1914–1915, 1949–1950.

[20] John Lawrence Le Breton Hammond (1872–1949), journalist and historian writing for Liberal newspapers.

[21] Walter Russell Rea (1873–1948), Lib. MP Scarborough 1906–1918, North Bradford 1923–1924, Dewsbury 1931–1935; Lib. whip 1915–1916, Chief Whip 1931–1935; Bt 1935, cr. Ld Rea 1937.

[22] Anna Maria Harvey (nee Whiting) (1851–1934), M.K.R.'s mother.

[23] Henry Tylor Cadbury (1882–1952), s. of George Cadbury; Managing Dir. *Daily News* 1907–1930; Warden of Woodbrooke 1931–1941.

[24] Alfred George Gardiner (1865–1946), Ed. *Daily News* 1902–1919.

went up to the Nation lunch and found Lloyd George[25] there –
happy at the turn events had taken but still expecting an
election in May when the King[26] will refuse the guarantees asked
for!

[...]

Butcher has been discussing a 'May' election and if there is one
would like us to have a walk over in York and says Riley Smith[27] agrees!

[...]

G.N.[28] lunches with me here at 1.30 tomorrow.

Now I must run off to J.E. Ellis[29] and possibly I may write a few
lines later.

2 March 1910
House of Commons

Another day without a division! and I am getting to understand why
folks groan so at the tremendous waste of time. I had a pleasant time
with Newman who was rather full of his visit to the King's levee
yesterday. He says he has accepted Arthur's[30] invitation to come to the
Old Scholars and is going to stay at the school and will give the reading
at the Meeting House on Sunday evening.

[...]

I have had an interesting talk to Dillon today and listened to
bombastic speeches[31] in the House from Beresford[32] and Butcher!

[...]

[25] David Lloyd George (1863–1945), Lib. MP Caernarvon Boroughs 1890–1945, when
cr. Earl Lloyd George; Pres. Bd of Trade 1905–1908, Chanc. of Exchequer 1908–1915,
Min. of Munitions 1915–1916, Sec. of State for War 1916, Prime Minister 1916–1922,
Leader of Lib. Party 1926–1931.

[26] Edward VII (1841–1910), Prince of Wales 1841–1901, King 1901–1910.

[27] Henry Herbert Riley-Smith (1863–1911), Chmn John Smith's brewers of Tadcaster;
unsuccessful Con. cand. York January 1910.

[28] George Newman (1870–1948), Quaker and schoolfriend of A.S.R.; Chief Medical
Officer, Bd of Education 1907–1935; Min. of Health 1919–1935; Hon. Sec. NASU 1898–
1905; Chmn FAU 1914–1919; literary adviser to Ed. of *Friend* 1912–1932, Ed. *Friends
Quarterly Examiner* 1900–1943; kt. 1911.

[29] John Edward Ellis (1841–1910), Lib. MP Rushcliffe 1885–December 1910; US India
Office 1905–1907; Quaker and relative by marriage of A.S.R.

[30] Arthur Rowntree (1861–1949), cousin of A.S.R.; Headmaster, Bootham School, York
1899–1927.

[31] *Hansard*, 5th series, 1910, XIV, 895–896 and 919–927 for Butcher on the Treasury
(Temporary Borrowing) Bill and Beresford on the Supplementary Estimates for the Navy.

[32] Admiral Lord Charles William de la Poer Beresford (1846–1919), Con. MP 1874–
1880, 1885–1889, 1898–1900, 1902–1903, January 1910–1916 in intervals from controversial
Naval career; cr. Ld Beresford, 1916.

3 March 1910
House of Commons – 6.40

[...]

This morning after seeing Essie[33] off I went to the NLC for a short time to read – then walked to the Temple and spent an hour with Greenwood. I didn't tell him what Butcher had said but found him disinclined to come to York again – he thinks that even if he were successful, which he does not think he would be, that still it is not the seat for a man who wants political promotion as he notices it is the men with safe seats who obtain preferment regardless of brains [...]!

[...]

I lunched here with Alden[34] and Gulland[35] – the latter is the whip I like best – a very fine radical. He told me that the letter the Prime Minister used to write every night giving an account of the proceedings of the day for the sovereign died with Victoria and that since that time one of the whips has twice during the course of the evening 'wired' to the King. Last Monday to show the interest the King takes in the present crisis he telephoned down or rather Knollys[36] telephoned for him in between the receipt of the two telegrams to know how things were going on!

The proceedings in the house have been as dull as could be [...].

I shall hope to be home tomorrow shortly after midnight and am happy in the thought of being with thee so soon.

8 March 1910
nearing Hitchin

It was a great disappointment darling to have to run away like this but being unpaired I hardly felt that I could put on one side the Whip's wire so like a good schoolboy I obey my master!

Happily I was long enough at the Works[37] this week to accomplish the chief things I wanted to get done but there is a Board meeting

[33] Sarah Elizabeth Rowntree (1861–1942), A.S.R.'s eldest sister.

[34] Percy Alden (1865–1944), Lib. MP Tottenham 1906–1918, Lab. MP South Tottenham 1923–1924; Warden, Mansfield House 1891–1901; Lab. Councillor West Ham 1892–1901, Dep. Mayor 1898; closely associated with Quakerism from c. 1901, but does not seem to have formally converted; journalist and social worker; kt. 1933.

[35] John William Gulland (1864–1920), Lib. MP Dumfries Burghs 1906–1918; Scottish whip 1909–1915, Chief Whip 1915–1918.

[36] Francis Knollys (1837–1924), Private Sec. to Edward VII 1870–1910, George V 1910–1913; cr. Ld Knollys 1902, Vt 1911.

[37] Cocoa Works of Rowntree & Co. at Haxby Rd, York.

called for Friday morning so I shall try and pair for that day. I also want to get in a School Committee[38] that afternoon as I have had to postpone one I called for tomorrow – then there is the Social on Friday evening.

[...]

I settled up my election expenses today – J.R.[39] kindly gave me £1000 towards them so with J.W.P.'s[40] £25 and H.D.R.'s[41] £100 it means I get off for about £400.

No man has disturbed the quiet of this journey but I have felt lazy and have not read very much. The Liberal Magazine and the illustrated red book on Parliament have kept me going most of the time.

8 March 1910
House of Commons – 10.20

The crucial division was taken late this afternoon and the Government were saved by the labour party not voting for their own amendment! Now there is an amendment to reduce the army by 15,000 men in S. Africa and if it is pressed to a division I shall vote against the government![42] If they are calm I shall try to get a pair on Thursday and come home then.

[...]

15 March 1910
House of Commons

Thank thee darling for thy letter which did not reach St James Court until the 2nd post. The situation here is again terribly disappointing –

[38] A.S.R. was Sec. (later Chmn) of the Cttee of Management of the Quaker schools, Bootham and the Mount, 1903–1945.

[39] Joseph Rowntree (1836–1925), Partner, H.I. Rowntree & Co. 1869–1897; Chmn Rowntree & Co. 1897–1923. Responsible for building the firm into a major force in confectionary manufacturing; propagandist for temperance and housing reform; A.S.R.'s uncle.

[40] John William Procter (1849–1925), agricultural merchant, York Quaker and friend of A.S.R., who succ. Procter as Sec. of Bootham and the Mount schools; JP and ex-member York School Bd.

[41] Helen Doncaster Rowntree (1833–1920), A.S.R.'s stepmother.

[42] Labour put down an amendment to the army estimates, calling on government departments to operate fair wages clauses. They abstained on the vote and the government won 215–152; *Hansard*, 5th series, 1910, XIV, 1317–1350. R.D. Holt moved the amendment on S. Africa, but the matter was not pressed to a vote; *ibid.*, 1378–1382.

nearly all the Liberals feel that this huge increase is not justified[43] and yet owing to the Lords crisis I think most are going to acquiesce in it. If Lough[44] presses his motion to a division I think I shall vote for it. Today I spent the morning at the Nation office, then had lunch with the contributors, a very discouraging opportunity (owing to the situation) and have been here since.

One of the difficulties before us is that the Government are determined to press forward with the Budget despite what the Irish may think and if so, probably will be defeated at that. This division between the Irish [and the] Liberals must be prevented if possible and I have been trying to understand the Irish position through a good talk with T.P. O'Connor.[45] We continue tomorrow afternoon with Massingham.[46]

PS Ted [Harvey] and I went into the little weekly prayer meeting here this afternoon – there were 7 present and Crossley[47] has taken the lead.

16 March 1910
House of Commons – 3.55

[...]

Questions are just over – there were two delightful flashes of humour – after Birrell[48] had been asked by one of the Orangemen whether he would give one day's rest in seven to the Irish police, Jeremiah McVeagh[49] jumped up and asked whether the Hon. member was aware that most of them had 7 days rest in the week!

Another Tory member was giving notice of a motion 'to call attention' to the operation of foreign tariffs in English Trade and to move a *resolution* but instead of saying resolution through nervousness he said *revolution* and was accordingly loudly cheered by Liberal members[50] [...].

[43] A.S.R. is referring to the naval estimates, 1910–1911 of £40 million.
[44] Thomas Lough (1850–1922), Lib. MP West Islington 1892–1918; PS Bd of Education 1905–1908. His motion was to reduce Vote A for the Navy by 3,000 men; *Hansard*, 5th series, 1910, XV, 213–318 for the debate. The matter was pushed to a vote and lost 225–34, with A.S.R. voting in the minority.
[45] Thomas Power O'Connor (1848–1929), Irish Nat. MP Galway 1880–1885, Liverpool Scotland 1885–1929.
[46] Henry William Massingham (1860–1924), Lib. newspaperman; Ed. *Nation* 1907–1923.
[47] Sir William John Crossley (1844–1911), Lib. MP Altrincham 1906–December 1910; Bt 1909.
[48] Augustine Birrell (1850–1933), Lib. MP West Fife 1889–1900, North Bristol 1906–1918; Pres. Bd of Education 1905–1907, Chief Sec. for Ireland 1907–1916.
[49] Jeremiah McVeagh (1870–1932), Irish Nat. MP South Down 1902–1922; noted parliamentary wit; *Hansard*, 5th series, 1910, XV, 358 for this exchange.
[50] *Ibid.*, 363; the unfortunate Conservative was Ion Hamilton Benn (1863–1961), MP Greenwich January 1910–1922; Bt 1920.

Seebohm[51] appeared in the Smoke Room after lunch with Alden. I think he is up for a Temperance Legislation League[52] meeting.

[...] I think considering the four points I had on my mind have been expressed by others, I am satisfied having voted against the Govt. last night, to remain quiet. I am continually doubting whether this is my right place. I know a little about several questions but have not the detailed exact knowledge that is so much needed here. This I think is one of the reasons that keeps me somewhat low in mind. Tonight I am going to Fowell Buxton's[53] to dinner with Noel and Roden[54] so shall post this for thee to get by the first post – thy letter, thanks, was delivered to me in bed this morning! I shall hope to be home on Friday certainly not later than 5.30 but I may possibly come by the 10 if I can get a pair.

17 March 1910
House of Commons – 5.45

[...]
I had an interesting day yesterday after writing to thee – heard Curzon[55] for a short time – then a long talk with T. P. O'Connor and Massingham over the Irish difficulty – then with Elibank[56] the Whip.

[51] Benjamin Seebohm Rowntree (1871–1954), eldest surviving s. of Joseph Rowntree; social investigator, author of *Poverty: A Study of Town Life* (1901) and twenty-five other books and pamphlets; member Land Enquiry 1912–1914; Dir. Welfare Department Ministry of Munitions 1916–1917; member Reconstruction Cttee 1917–1918, Lib. Industrial Inquiry 1926–1928; Dir. Rowntree and Co. 1897–1941, Chmn 1923–1941; close friend of A.S.R.
[52] Temperance Legislation League; organization founded in 1905 to campaign for public ownership of the drink industry, a cause vigorously promoted by Joseph Rowntree.
[53] Sir Thomas Fowell Buxton (1837–1915), Lib. landowner, banker and brewer; MP Lyme Regis 1865–1868; Gov. South Australia 1895–1898; succ. as 3rd Bt 1858.
[54] Sons of Sir T.F. Buxton: Noel Edward Buxton (1869–1948), Lib. MP Whitby 1905–1906, North Norfolk January 1910–1918, Lab. MP North Norfolk 1922–1930; Min. of Agriculture 1924, 1929–1930; cr. Ld Noel-Buxton, 1930. Charles Roden Buxton (1875–1942), Lib. MP Ashburton January–December 1910, Lab. MP Accrington 1922–1923, Elland 1929–1931; convert to Quakerism c. 1917.
[55] George Nathaniel Curzon (1859–1925), Con. MP Southport 1886–1898; US India Office 1891–1892, US Foreign Office 1895–1898, Viceroy of India 1899–1905, Ld Privy Seal, 1915–1916, Pres. Air Bd 1916, Lord Pres. of Council 1916–1919, 1924–1925, Foreign Sec. 1919–1924; cr. Lord Curzon of Kedleston 1898, Earl Curzon 1911, Marquess 1921. *Hansard*, 5th series, 1910, V, 278–296 for his speech on Rosebery's motion to reform the composition of the HofL.
[56] Alexander William Charles Oliphant Murray (1870–1920), styled Master of Elibank as heir to the Scottish peerage of Elibank; Lib. MP Midlothian 1900–1906, January 1910–1912, Peebles and Selkirk 1906–January 1910; Scottish whip 1905–1909, US India Office 1909–1910, Chief Whip 1910–1912, when cr. Ld Murray of Elibank.

Then went off to dinner at the Buxtons with Ted [Harvey] and greatly enjoyed old Sir Thomas and a few minutes chat afterwards with Lady Victoria[57] who is an invalid with rheumatoid arthritis and lies continually on a couch – then back to the House and have a chat with Runciman[58] about the situation. I think the situation is more hopeful but the *cabinet are foolish*. Still I am distinctly more hopeful of the two sides coming to a working agreement. I had a much better night and today spent the morning with Benson[59] over advertizing. Had Greenwood to lunch at the flat and been in the precincts of the house having tea with Harold Spender.[60] Several of us are going shortly to have a talk with the Whip to again urge working absolutely with the Irish – then G.N.[ewman] comes here to dine and is going to stay the night at the flat.

[...]

22 March 1910
House of Commons

[...]
   [...] Liberals here are in better spirits – the resolution[61] pleases them and whilst there is nothing definitely fixed with the Irish there is evidently hope for feeling that an agreement will be arrived at.

I have been in the Lords for a short time this afternoon. Lord Bathurst's[62] peroration was very funny – warning the backwoodsmen not to vote for Rosebery's[63] resolution limiting the hereditary principle – 'Remember your children – down to the third and fourth generation and remember what they will think – I tell you they will turn and rend you!'
   [...]

[57] Lady Victoria Buxton (d. 1916), wife of Sir T.F. Buxton; daughter of first Earl of Gainsborough.
   [58] Walter Runciman (1870–1949), Lib. MP Oldham 1899–1900, Dewsbury 1902–1918, West Swansea 1924–1929, St Ives (Lib. Nat. from 1931), 1929–1937, when cr. Vt Runciman; PS Local Govt Bd 1905–1907, Fin. Sec. to Treasury 1907–1908, Pres. Bd of Education 1908–1911, Pres. Bd of Agriculture 1911–1914, Pres. Bd of Trade 1914–1916, 1931–1937, Ld Pres. of the Council 1938–1939.
   [59] Samuel Herbert Benson (1854–1914), founder of S.H. Benson advertising agency, which handled Rowntree and Co.'s account 1897–1931.
   [60] Harold Spender (1864–1926), Lib. journalist.
   [61] The government tabled its three resolutions on reform of the Lords on 21 March 1910.
   [62] Seymour Henry Bathurst (1864–1943), succ. as 7th Earl Bathurst 1892; diehard peer. A.S.R. was paraphrasing the closing words of his speech on Rosebery's motion to reform the Lords; *Hansard*, 5th series, 1910, V, 469.
   [63] Archibald Philip Primrose (1847–1929), succ. as 5th Earl of Rosebery 1868; US Home Office 1881–1883, Ld Privy Seal 1885, Foreign Sec. 1886, 1892–1894, Prime Minister 1894–1895, Leader Lib. Party 1894–1896.

29 March 1910
House of Commons

[...]
    The debate today has been interesting[64] – Asquith's[65] speech was
quite the best I have heard him give in the House. Balfour's[66] answer
I thought very lame though his agility in raising clever debating points
is always clever. He seemed to me to tire very quickly and I doubt
whether his health is going to last. I am writing now in the House
listening to a somewhat dull speech from Barnes[67] who followed a revolt
on this side of the House from Munro Ferguson.[68]
    [...]

5 April 1910
House of Commons – 6 pm

I haven't very much of interest darling to tell thee. Last night proceedings included dinner with G.N.[ewman] and Percy Alden – after
resisting Butcher who was very friendly and wanted to take me off and
then I heard the three closing speeches of the debate[69] – an excellent
short maiden one from Roden Buxton, a clever but impudent one from

[64] The debate was on the government's motion to create a Committee of the Whole
House to form resolutions on the relations of the Lords and Commons. Asquith declared
the government wished to remove the Lords' veto; Balfour was merely critical of Asquith;
Munro-Ferguson wanted reform of the composition of the Lords, and Barnes declared
for a single chamber; *Hansard*, 5th series, 1910, XV, 1162–1222.
    [65] Herbert Henry Asquith (1852–1928), Lib. MP East Fife 1886–1918, Paisley 1920–
1924; Home Sec. 1892–1895; Chanc. of the Exchequer 1905–1908; Prime Minister 1908–
1916; Leader Lib. Party 1908–1926; cr. Earl of Oxford and Asquith, 1925.
    [66] Arthur James Balfour (1848–1930), Con. MP Hertford 1874–1885, East Manchester
1885–1906, City of London February 1906–May 1922, when cr. Earl of Balfour; Pres.
Local Govt Bd 1885, Sec. for Scotland 1886–1887, Chief Sec. for Ireland 1887–1891, First
Ld of Treasury and Leader HofC 1891–1892, 1895–1905, Prime Minister 1902–1905, Ld
Privy Seal 1902–1903, First Ld of Admiralty 1915–1916, Foreign Sec. 1916–1919, Ld Pres.
of the Council 1919–1922, 1925–1929, Leader Con. Party 1902–1911.
    [67] George Nicoll Barnes (1859–1940), Lab. MP Glasgow, Blackfriars 1906–1918, Co.
Lab. MP Glasgow, Gorbals 1918–1922; Gen. Sec Amalgamated Society of Engineers
1896–1908; Chmn Lab. MPs 1910–1911; Min. of Pensions 1916–1917, War Cabinet 1917–
1920.
    [68] Ronald Crauford Munro-Ferguson (1860–1934), Lib. landowner and partisan of
Rosebery; MP Ross and Cromarty 1884–1885, Leith 1886–1914; Lib. whip 1894–1895,
Gov.-Gen. Australia 1914–1920, Scottish Sec. 1922–1924 in Con. govts; cr. Vt Novar
1920.
    [69] *Hansard*, 5th series, 1910, XVI, 129–160 for these speeches on the Con. amendment
to the Libs' resolutions on the HofL.

Bonar Law[70] and then Lloyd George's reply – good but not absolutely
his best form but still the kind of speech needed in the country. We
didn't get home until after 12 so I took Percy Alden back with me who
had missed his last train.

This morning I have been to the Leader office and Benson's and
lunched with Hobson,[71] Hirst[72] and Masterman[73] at the Nation lunch.
I send thee a photo that was taken last week when Masterman and I
were entering Westminster Palace Yard and which Parke thought rather
good!
[...].

6 April 1910
House of Commons – 5.35 pm

I am writing in the House whilst Austen[74] is replying to Haldane[75] –
G.N.[ewman] came to dinner here last night and Sherwell and Gerald
France[76] joined us. The House sat late, until 1.30 I think, but at 11 pm
I found Butcher and as he wanted to prepare briefs and I wanted to
go to bed we paired. [...] At 8.15 a private members resolution comes
on and if I get a pair I am going with Gilbert[77] and George to see
Galsworthy's[78] 'Justice' at the Duke of York's Theatre which is a very

[70] Andrew Bonar Law (1858–1923), Con. MP Glasgow, Blackfriars 1900–1906, Dulwich
May 1906–December 1910, Bootle 1911–1918, Central Glasgow 1918–1923; PS Bd of
Trade 1902–1905, Sec. of State for Colonies 1915–1916, Chanc. of Exchequer 1916–1919,
Ld Privy Seal 1919–1921, Prime Minister 1922–1923; Leader of Con. Party 1911–1921,
1922–1923.
[71] John Atkinson Hobson (1858–1940), Lib. journalist and economist.
[72] Francis Wrigley Hirst (1873–1953), Lib. journalist; Ed. *The Economist* 1907–1916.
[73] Charles Frederick Gurney Masterman (1873–1927), Lib. journalist; MP North West
Ham 1906–1911, South West Bethnal Green 1911–1914, Rusholme 1923–1924; PS Local
Govt Bd 1908–1909, US Home Office 1909–1912, Fin. Sec. to Treasury 1912–1914,
Chanc. Duchy of Lancaster 1914–1915.
[74] Joseph Austen Chamberlain (1863–1937), LU MP (Unionist from 1912) East Worcestershire 1892–1914, West Birmingham 1914–1937; Civil Ld of Admiralty 1895–1900,
Fin. Sec. to Treasury 1900–1902, Postmaster-General 1902–1903, Chanc. of Exchequer
1903–1905, 1919–1921, Sec. of State India 1915–1917, Min. without Portfolio 1918–1919,
Ld Privy Seal and Leader of Con. Party 1921–1922, Foreign Sec. 1924–1929, First Ld of
Admiralty 1931; KG 1925. Chamberlain was replying to Haldane's speech on the
government's proposals to prevent the Lords delaying money bills in the future; *Hansard*,
5th series, 1910, XVI, 449–479.
[75] Richard Burdon Haldane (1856–1928), Lib. MP Haddingtonshire 1885–1911; Sec. of
State for War 1905–1912, Ld Chanc. 1912–1915, 1924 (in Lab. govt); cr. Vt Haldane 1911.
[76] Gerald Ashburner France (1870–1935), Lib. MP Morley January 1910–1922.
[77] Edwin Gilbert (1859–1933), Quaker; Sec. NASU 1902–1919.
[78] John Galsworthy (1867–1933), author, playwright and (at this time) committed radical
who used his legal training to condemn the punishment of criminals (especially solitary
confinement) in his play, *Justice*.

striking play showing the result of our present method of punishment.
[...]

I had a letter from Bowes [Morrell] this morning saying that
Elmhirst[79] and the Tories he has consulted in York are in favour of a
compromise if the Election comes this year. Bowes & Elmhirst are
exchanging letters promising to use their best efforts with their supporters to induce them to only nominate one candidate so that I think
we may say that unless the Labour people complicate matters we shall
probably get through without a contest. I wonder however every day
whether it is best for me to go on but I suppose we shall be led rightly.

Noel Buxton has just told me the apocryphal story of Asquith and
the King. A. asked for pledges and the King turned round to him –
'Your pledges – take one yourself!' [...].

7 April 1910
House of Commons

Thank thee darling for thine. Since I wrote thee I think my movements
have been as follows – E.G.[ilbert] came to dinner last night, then we
went to see Galsworthy's 'Justice' – a very remarkable play – very sad
but the way in which our present system of punishment absolutely
destroys the victim is wonderfully brought out by absolutely realistic
scenes of prison life. I should suppose the effect of the play will be to
force the attention of thoughtful people to the need for wiser treatment,
especially giving occupation of mind. [...].

[...] W.C.B.[80] is now in the gallery and dines with me here along
with R. [Cross] and J.A. Baker.[81] I have not been able to get hold of
Greenwood yet but perhaps shall before I need post these.
[...]

12 April 1910
House of Commons – 5.45

Balfour is going to speak in a few minutes[82] so I must get a few lines
written to thee darling. [...] We were late last night engaged in defeating

[79] Charles E. Elmhirst, Chmn York Con. Association.
[80] William Charles Braithwaite (1862–1922), Quaker; barrister, banker, and historian
of Quakerism. Old friend of A.S.R. and Chmn NASU 1900–1922.
[81] Joseph Allen Baker (1852–1918), Lib. MP East Finsbury 1905–July 1918; LCC 1895–
1907. Quaker, active in adult school movement and Chmn J. Baker & Sons Ltd who
supplied machinery to Rowntree & Co.
[82] *Hansard*, 5th series, 1910, XVI, 1118–1127 for Balfour's speech on the HofL's veto.

a private member's bill to build a church on an open space in
Piccadilly.[83] This morning I had breakfast with Greenwood at the
Reform Club and was shown over that building afterwards. I spent
some time at Benson's over advertising matters and then came back
to the Reform Club and wrote letters. Lunch with the Nation
contributors and then came on here but up to now there has been
little of interest.

[...]

The enclosed from Mrs Asquith[84] has come – I think it would be
rather interesting for thee to accept!

I have refused the Croydon invitation and half a dozen more today –
I hate doing it but I don't see at present what else I can do. Everything
here is very uncertain still. I fear the Irish difficulty is not yet at an
end.

13 April 1910
House of Commons – 6.15 pm

[...]

I had an interesting invitation to dinner last night. Richard Denman[85]
the member for Carlisle asked me to join him and some friends
including Violet Hodgkin.[86] As the dinner was at the House I accepted
and found Lady Barlow,[87] Mr and Mrs Runciman,[88] Mr Hobhouse,[89]

---

[83] The St James's Vestry Hall (Westminster) Bill proposed allowing Westminster Council
to buy out the Rector of St James's right to use the vestry hall on certain occasions and
to give him permission to use the proceeds to build a mission hall in the churchyard.
The bill was defeated 183–64, with A.S.R. voting in the majority. *Hansard*, 5th series,
1910, XVI, 1007–1024.

[84] Margot Asquith (1864–1945), second wife of H.H. Asquith.

[85] Hon. Richard Douglas Denman (1876–1957), Lib MP Carlisle January 1910–1918,
Lab. (Nat. Lab. from 1931) MP Central Leeds 1929–1945; 2nd Church Estates Commissioner 1931–1943; Bt 1945.

[86] Lucy Violet Hodgkin (1869–1954), daughter of prominent Quaker, Thomas Hodgkin.
Writer and traveller, visited Australia and New Zealand in 1909.

[87] Lady Anna Maria Heywood Barlow (1873–1965), sister of Hon. Richard Denman;
convert to Quakerism c. 1911, virtually continuous member Meeting for Sufferings
and Peace Cttee 1914–1965; Lib. cand. High Peak 1922, Ilkeston 1924; m. 1895 Sir
John Emmott Barlow (1857–1932) Quaker and Lib. MP Frome 1892–1895, 1896–1918;
Bt 1907.

[88] Hilda Runciman (nee Stevenson) (1869–1956), m. 1898 Walter Runciman, Lib. MP
St Ives 1928–1929.

[89] Charles Edward Henry Hobhouse (1862–1941), Lib. MP East Wiltshire 1892–1895,
East Bristol 1900–1918; 2nd Church Estates Commissioner 1906–1907, US India Office
1907–1908, Fin. Sec. to Treasury 1908–1911, Chanc. Duchy of Lancaster 1911–1914,
Postmaster-Gen. 1914–1915; succ. as 4th Bt 1916.

the Sec. of the Treasury, and Simon.[90] I sat between Lady Barlow
and Mrs Runciman and talked chiefly to them. Lady Barlow is very
keen on Friends and a great admirer of Ted [Harvey]'s. She hopes to
be able to give evidence before the Divorce Commission[91] for Friends
because she is anxious to put before them the extraordinary high
ideal of marriage which she feels Friends have and because of the
way the men look upon their women folk as their equals. She has
found that in no other body. She is interestingly keen to see Friends
more boldly come out into the open amongst thoughtful people because
she holds so strongly the future is with them, and she put forward
a view which I have often pondered over and that is why more
spiritually minded women don't join the Society that really gives
to them the position of equality that they should hold and exercise
in any religious body, and then she went on with an interesting
disquisition as to whether women because of the way in which they
were constantly occupying their lives, or at any rate running the
risks of a sacrifice of life, were not really much more spiritually
minded than men. From personal experience I was able to confirm the
view!

Mrs Runciman is the sister of Arthur Stevenson[92] of York and is
very attractive. Afterwards we went to Runciman's private room to
smoke. I had a long talk with Violet Hodgkin who is very *hot* on
Australia.

Oscar[93] called this morning and I had my first lunch at the Reform
Club. There certainly are a very interesting set of folks there. I had
quite a long talk at lunch with Sir George Gibb[94] and afterwards with
Roger Fry[95] (Joan F.'s brother) who is greatly concerned about the
suppression of the duma of Finland by Russia.

This afternoon I went across to Caxton Hall to a meeting of the

[90] Sir John Allsebrook Simon (1873–1954), Lib. MP Walthamstow 1906–1918, Spen
Valley 1922–1940 (Lib. Nat. from 1931); Solicitor-Gen. 1910–1913, Attorney-Gen. 1913–
1915, Home Sec. 1915–1916, 1935–1937, Foreign Sec. 1931–1935, Chanc. of Exchequer
1937–1940, Ld Chanc. 1940–1945, Leader Lib. Nat. Party 1931–1940; kt. 1910, cr. Vt
Simon 1940.

[91] Royal Commission on Divorce and Matrimonial Causes, 1909–1912.

[92] Arthur Stevenson, s. of James Stevenson, chemical manufacturer and Lib. MP South
Shields 1868–1895.

[93] Oscar Rowntree (1879–1947), s. of Joseph Rowntree, Dir. Rowntree & Co.; elected
to York Council 1905 for Castlegate ward, Ld Mayor 1926; Treasurer York Liberal
Association.

[94] Sir George Stegmann Gibb (1850–1925), prominent dir. of various railway companies.
Friend of the Rowntrees from his days in York as Gen. Manager NER 1891–1906; kt.
1904.

[95] Roger Eliot Fry (1866–1934), art critic and painter; Joan Mary Fry (1862–1955).
Members of the Quaker chocolate-manufacturing family from Bristol and children of Sir
Edward Fry.

International Labour Association and heard a good speech of Churchill.[96] His speech last night at the House was excellent.[97]

26 April 1910
National Liberal Club

Thank thee darling for thy letter. I am sorry to hear of the two
resignations from the Women's Liberal. I didn't know Maria Richardson
was becoming such a good old Tory. Appleton[98] stayed with me last
night and this morning I had a conference with 5 travellers at St James
Court and afterwards with Appleton and Crossland[99] at the NLC. As
a result Appleton followed J.R.[owntree] to Torquay to consult with
him. Then followed the Nation lunch. Things are very dull here this
afternoon. I am glad at the thought of escaping on Thursday morning.
I went to the little Prayer Meeting this afternoon and had to take the
reading.

18 May 1910
Kingsley Hotel, London – 7pm

[...]
This morning I spent at St James Court having a long interview
with W.C.B.[raithwaite] and E.R.C.[ross] (who stayed the night with
me) B.S.R.[owntree], G.C.[100] and Henry Cadbury and came fairly
clearly to the conclusion to do nothing at present with the Spectator.[101]

[96] Winston Leonard Spencer Churchill (1874–1965), Con. MP (Lib. from 1904) Oldham
1900–1906, NW Manchester 1906–1908, Dundee 1908–1922; Con. MP Epping 1924–
1945, Woodford 1945–1964; US Colonies 1905–1908, Pres. Bd of Trade 1908–1910, Home
Sec. 1910–1911, First Ld of Admiralty 1911–1915, 1939–1940, Chanc. Duchy of Lancaster
1915, Min. of Munitions 1917–1919, Sec. of State for War 1919–1921, Sec. of State for
Colonies 1921–1922, Chanc. of Exchequer 1924–1929, Prime Minister 1940–1945, 1951–
1955, Leader Con. Party 1940–1955; KG 1953. Churchill spoke to the British Association
for Labour Legislation on his work to promote trades boards and labour exchanges and
on future plans for unemployment insurance.
[97] *Hansard*, 5th series, 1910, XVI, 1127–1141. The speech was on Commons–Lords
relations.
[98] Thomas Appleton, Quaker; factory manager (later Dir.) at Rowntree & Co.
[99] Joseph Crossland, Sec. Sales Cttee at Rowntree and Co.
[100] George Cadbury (1839–1922), partner in Cadbury Bros from 1861, Chmn 1899–
1922; Chmn, Bd of Dirs *Daily News*, 1901–1911.
[101] In 1910 the Cadburys and Rowntrees were being severely criticized in the Con.
press (especially *The Spectator*) for continuing to print betting news in their London evening
paper, the *Star*.

Then we had a conference with the Braithwaites[102] about building
operations at Woodbrooke[103] – and then Cullen about two large German
visits to York like the one last year and finally had Beveridge[104] to
lunch. [...]

I am thoroughly tired of this démarche of national mourning and
after the ceremony on Friday shall be glad to get clear of it all – now
I must be off.

8 June 1910
House of Commons – 5.45

I had a comfortable journey darling last night and this morning spent
most of the time with Parke at the ML office and Henry C.[adbury]
at the DN.

I had lunch with G.N.[ewman] at the Reform Club and as the
house is expected to be up about dinner time I am going out to
the Hatch with him shortly if I can get a pair. This afternoon I
have had talks with Massingham, Alden and Spender. This conference
that is suggested is the King's[105] wish and therefore very difficult to
oppose.[106] All the men I have spoken to are very indignant at the
Spectator articles and are strongly against our taking any notice of
them. The real difficulty is to find some way of preventing
J.R.[owntree] being continually uncomfortable and of pacifying
Friends – otherwise I think this last attack only strengthens one in
the feeling of the importance of standing absolutely firm and going
on unmoved by such argument. I am going to see Edward Cadbury
tomorrow.

[...]

[102] Isaac Braithwaite (1844–1929), Warden of Woodbrooke 1907–1914, and his wife
Mary Snowden Braithwaite (nee Thomas) (1850–1931), American Quaker.

[103] Woodbrooke; Quaker adult education college in Birmingham set up by the Cadburys
in 1903. A.S.R. was on the governing Council and wrote a history of the college in
1923.

[104] William Beveridge (1879–1963), social investigator; Dir. Lab. Exchanges, Bd of
Trade 1909–1916, Ministry of Food 1916–1919; Dir. London School of Economics 1919–
1937, Master of University College, Oxford, 1937–1945; author of Beveridge Report
(1942); Lib. MP Berwick 1944–1945; KCB 1919, cr. Ld Beveridge 1946.

[105] George V (1865–1936), Prince of Wales 1901–1910, King 1910–1936.

[106] When Parliament reassembled on 9 June 1910, Asquith proposed and Balfour
accepted a Constitutional Conference to try and agree on reform of the Lords and so
spare the new King, George V, a constitutional crisis.

12 July 1910
House of Commons – 6 pm

[...]
I spent some time this morning at the Leader office and then read in
the NLC until lunch when I joined the Nation group.

The debate here is going badly against the bill.[107] Churchill has just
brilliantly attacked it for its anti-democratic tendencies and no speeches
in favour absolutely satisfy one. Bad though the Bill is, I shall vote for
it hoping that if it was passed it would be followed by an Electoral
Reform Bill widening the franchise, but it was disconcerting hearing
McLaren[108] one of the leaders of the Bill declare that he was satisfied
with it as a *settlement*!

I believe Balfour is speaking very shortly so I will cease this now and
go into the House.

13 July 1910
House of Commons

[...] I had a pleasant time with Gerty[109] – she brought Lady Gibb[110] to
the House and of course they were both disappointed with the second
vote[111] – but really the cause has made a great step forward. The debate
was of a very high order and genuinely serious and if the women play
their cards well and don't yield to violence they will I think now make
steady progress. The debate was quite the most interesting I have heard
in this house.

This morning I spent some time with Benson – then had an interesting
hour with Henry Cadbury and Crosfield[112] about amalgamation – then

[107] The Parliamentary Franchise (Women) Bill (or 'Conciliation Bill') would have
granted a vote to all women who possessed a household qualification or a £10 occupation
qualification. Many Liberals feared this would enfranchise only wealthy women and
opposed the measure. *Hansard*, 5th series, 1910, XIX, 211–228 for the speeches by
McLaren and Churchill.

[108] Walter Stowe Bright McLaren (1853–1912), Lib. MP Crewe 1886–1895, April 1910–
1912; nephew of John Bright and leading Lib. suffragist; nominal Quaker.

[109] Gertrude Sophia Taylor (1863–1950), sister of A.S.R.; m. 1898 Frederic Taylor, bro.
of E.E. Taylor.

[110] Lady Dorothea Gibb (nee Garrett-Smith), m. 1881 Sir George Gibb.

[111] The 'second vote' on whether the Conciliation Bill should proceed to a Cttee of the
Whole House ended its chances of success and showed a large majority against of 320–
175. *Hansard*, 5th series, 1910, XIX, 329–334.

[112] Bertram Fothergill Crosfield (1882–1951), Quaker; Manager *Daily News*, Managing
Dir. *News Chronicle* 1930–1951; m. 1910 Eleanor Cadbury (1885–1959), daughter of George
Cadbury. The amalgamation discussed was that of the *Morning Leader* and *Daily News*.

lunch with the Buxtons and Whyte[113] here and this afternoon listened
to Runciman's statement with great interest.[114]

Afterwards attended an Armaments Meeting and then dined with
Alden at the Reform Club. It looks from Asquith's statement[115] as if the
House would be practically finished by Bank Holiday so I think we
may look to getting away on Aug. 4th, which is a delightful prospect.

20 July 1910
House of Commons – 6 pm

I am writing in the house whilst Masterman is replying to criticisms
levelled against the Home Office.[116] [...] Shipley Brayshaw[117] came to
breakfast with me this morning to discuss some developments in
connection with his business. Then I spent the rest of the morning at
Bensons over our autumn advertising scheme – had lunch with
Buxton,[118] Ted [Harvey] and Whyte and spent 1½ hours this afternoon
with the Liberal suffrage group discussing the future of the women's
bill. It is very difficult to see what is best to be done and I kept silence!
[...].

The NER strike is very disturbing.[119] I do hope it will not extend to
York – if it does one could hardly leave the country whilst it was on –
but Buxton evidently realises the importance of dealing with the
question, so I hope it may be speedily settled. [...]

21 July 1910
House of Commons

The feature of last night's debate on the Home Office was Churchill's
statement as to his wishes with regard to Prison Reform.[120] It was most
refreshing hearing such a speech and showed what a progressive fertile

[113] Alexander Frederick Whyte (1883–1970), Lib. MP Perth January 1910–1918; PPS
Winston Churchill 1910–1915; kt. 1922.
[114] *Hansard*, 5th series, 1910, XIX, 386–407 on the work of the Bd of Education.
[115] *Ibid.*, 375–376 on the business of the House.
[116] *Ibid.*, 1302–1311.
[117] Shipley Neave Brayshaw (1871–1957), Quaker businessman, founder of Brayshaw
Furnaces and Tools of Stockport.
[118] Sydney Charles Buxton (1853–1934), Lib. MP Peterborough 1883–1885, Poplar
1886–1914; US Colonies 1892–1895, Postmaster-Gen. 1905–1910, Pres. Bd of Trade 1910–
1914, Gov.-Gen. S. Africa 1914–20; cr. Vt Buxton 1914, Earl 1920.
[119] NER strike; a local dispute in Newcastle and Sunderland, 18–22 July 1910.
[120] *Hansard*, 5th series, 1910, XIX, 1343–1354. Among a number of progressive measures
Churchill announced solitary confinement would usually be reduced to one month.

mind Winston has. Thou shoulds't read the speech, darling, if possible. This morning I spent at business amongst other things visiting Heals to order a table like our dining room one for my office. [...] I then lunched with the Webbs[121] – perfectly simple and informal and enjoyed hearing them talk about their report and its prospects.

I shall do my best to catch the 5.30 tomorrow but possibly may miss it but if I do I shall wire thee. I am thinking of pairing for next week but have not quite made up my mind yet – in fact it is difficult to know what is best to do if this strike is going to last.

29 July 1910
Birkdale

[...]
Here is an important letter from Henry C.[adbury] suggesting the early amalgamation of the ML and DN – I fear it will mean a long conference in London on Thursday afternoon – so I shall have to depart that day by the 10!

6 September 1910
Chalfont's[122] – 9.05 pm

[...]
I have little of special interest to report. I had breakfast next door then spent the morning at the board – nothing specially interesting – and in talks with J.B.M.[orrell] and E.R.C.[ross] on another amalgamation scheme that the Cadburys are proposing with regard to the DN, ML. I don't think it will do at all, but we go up tomorrow to town to discuss it with Parke preliminary to a conference with the C[adbury]s on Thursday.

[...] Bowes [Morrell] reports curious proceedings at the committee of the council last night about the new Lord Mayor. All the Tories except Birch's brother[123] voted against a proposal to ask the present Lord Mayor first! And despite the fact that the LM was presiding, Long[124] and others feel no difficulty in expressing the view that they wanted this next year a specially good man! Eventually the Liberals

[121] Sidney (1859–1947) and Beatrice (1858–1943) Webb, Fabians, social investigators and originators of the Minority Report of the Royal Commission on the Poor Law (1909).
[122] Home of A.S.R. in York 1906–1939.
[123] The Ld Mayor of York in 1908–1910 was Alderman James Birch, a Tory plumber. His brother, Frederick Birch, was Con. councillor for Castlegate.
[124] Dr Sanderson Long, Con. councillor Micklegate ward 1908–1911.

left it to a committee of Tories to fight it out! Many of the Tories are
keen on Riley Smith − but Carter[125] has supporters as well as Birch.
[...].

7 September 1910
National Liberal Club

[...] I have fared comfortably today despite some worrying matters, i.e.
G.N.[ewman] forwarded today a letter that Sir Edward Fry[126] had
written for insertion in the Friend on 'Friends and Betting' − H.S.N.[127]
had refused to insert it but it shows that Fry is not content to let the
matter rest and he may burst out again. He thought it was a matter
for bringing the discipline of the Society into action! and reminds his
would be readers that Friends were disowned for owning slaves!
    Cross, Morrell and I travelled up by the 12 o'clock train − very full
to Doncaster with St Leger's spectators and then had a long talk with
T.P. Whittaker[128] at lunch and afterwards. He is one ·of the fiercest
individuals that I know but is very interesting, withal. He thinks that
the complete destruction of the Nation and DN and ML would be a
great gain to the liberal party! We have had a two hours conference
with Parke over the last mad suggestion of the C[adbury]s and tomorrow
thou canst think of us as dealing with the Cadburys. [...]

8 September 1910
GNR Restaurant Car − Train from London to York

[...]
    [...] This morning was given up to conference first with Parke,
afterwards with the Cadburys. The latter have now decided to take
over the whole responsibility of the amalgamation of DN, ML and Star
and as they do not seem to want J.B.M.[orrell] and myself in the

---

[125] Alderman Carter, Tory butcher and the senior alderman who had not yet been Ld
Mayor. He eventually got the job.
    [126] Sir Edward Fry (1827−1918), prominent Quaker; High Court judge 1877−1883, Ld
Justice of Appeal 1883−1892; on Permanent Court of International Arbitration at The
Hague 1900−1912; GCB 1907. He objected to betting news being carried in the *Star*.
    [127] Henry Stanley Newman (1837−1912), Quaker provisions dealer from Leominster,
with long service on Meeting for Sufferings and as Hon. Sec. of Friends' Foreign Mission
Association; Ed. the *Friend* 1892−1912; father of George Newman.
    [128] Sir Thomas Palmer Whittaker (1850−1919), Lib. MP Spen Valley 1892−1919; kt.
1906.

amalgamation I think it looks as if we should be released from office next year.[129] On the whole I expect it is best but I will tell thee all about it when we meet. Our gathering was of the most friendly character. I lunched with J.B.M.[orrell], E.R.C.[ross] and Massingham and spent the afternoon over advertising matters at Bensons and caught the 6.05 train in which at present I am jogging. [...]

14 September 1910
Chalfonts

[...]
[...] I met Winifred[130] but hadn't much gathered talk with her as at the time I was bothered by a woman suffragette pressing the claims of 'Votes for Women' upon me in a way rather to repel than to attract. I think I told thee that I was going to Bradford tomorrow and sometime soon I must go to Sheffield to see H.J. Wilson[131] about one or two matters connected with the Independent. [...]

14 October 1910
St Enoch Star Hotel

I have just come in here for tea darling as I have decided to go to Ure's[132] meeting in St Andrews Hall before returning to Edinboro tonight. I have never seen a great Scotch political gathering and I should like to. I confess to having a great admiration for Ure for the splendid way in which he gives himself ungrudgingly to the advocacy of the land question. [...].
This morning we came here (Glasgow) by an early train and have been interviewing travellers and looking into confectioners windows all day. Owing to very strong local opposition our sales have

[129] The conferences agreed that the *Morning Leader* and *Daily News* would amalgamate and the new paper would share its printing facilities with the *Star*. The Cadburys would own both papers outright.
[130] Helen Winifred Sturge (1866–1941), Headmistress, the Mount School, York 1902– 1926.
[131] Henry Joseph Wilson (1833–1914), not formally a Quaker, but a regular attender at Meetings; Lib. MP Holmfirth 1885–1912 and leading figure in Sheffield Liberalism. The *Sheffield Independent* had been saved from extinction in 1909 with money from A.S.R. and J.B. Morrell.
[132] Alexander Ure (1853–1928), Lib. MP Linlithgow 1895–1913; Scottish Solicitor-Gen. 1905–1909, Ld Advocate 1909–1913, Ld Justice Gen. 1913–1920; cr. Ld Strathclyde 1914; fanatical proponent of the Single Tax.

gone down in this locality and it is clear the place will need special treatment. However, it is good for us to have hard situations to overcome. [...]

29 October 1910
Chalfonts

The chief reason darling for my sudden departure was because of another approach from the Daily Chronicle people about the 'Star' and I thought it best at once to talk the whole thing over with Parke. I also saw Henry C.[adbury] and Bertram [Crosfield]. I also wanted to see Benson and one or two other travellers. [...].

16 November 1910
Reform Club

Quite an interesting day darling though perhaps not much work done. In the morning I went to the ML office and had a talk with Parke and Bowes [Morrell] about paper matters. Then lunched with Bowes and Bertha[133] and then on to the wedding. St Margaret's seemed almost full. I thought the wedding ceremony passed off very well. Florence G.[134] looked very bonny as far as her face was concerned but her dress I considered absurd! Some form of trellis work tunic! which made her look like a fish with scales. As an addition at the back she had a very long train – altogether it looked to me very artificial but was redeemed by being held up by four bonny children in blue – two of whom were Sir John Simon's bairns. I sat with Duncan and Win[135] and Bowes and Bertha [Morrell], and with them [...] went on to the reception which was very crowded. Florence G.[reenwood] asked me twice after thee and wanted remembering to thee and was sorry thou wasn't present. The husband[136] is a small and ugly little man – but I suppose very

[133] Bertha Morrell (1877–1954), wife of J.B. Morrell and daughter of Robert Spence Watson (1837–1911), Quaker solicitor from Newcastle and Pres. Nat. Lib. Federation 1890–1902.
[134] Florence Greenwood, sister of Hamar Greenwood.
[135] Arthur Duncan Naish (1881–1936), Works Manager Rowntree & Co. and bro. of Constance, widow of John Wilhelm Rowntree. Winifred Naish (1884–1915), m. A.D. Naish and daugher of Joseph Rowntree.
[136] Leopold Charles Maurice Stennett Amery (1873–1955), Con. MP Birmingham South 1911–1918, Sparkbrook 1918–1945; US Colonies 1919–1921, P & F Sec. Admiralty 1921–1922, First Ld of Admiralty 1922–1924, Sec. of State Colonies 1924–1929, Sec. of State India 1940–1945.

clever. Amongst others I talked to were Mr and Mrs Ferens[137] who
invited me to stay with them at Hull next week at the Federation
meetings. I told them I wasn't sure if thou would not be going as well
and so the invitation was at once doubled! I must let them know thy
decision later. I then went on to the House of Lords – happily was
able to get Duncan and Win [Naish] entrance and heard the debate
that thou no doubt will read.[138] It seems to me to make a December
election more doubtful but I don't think we can say definitely until
Friday. Meanwhile the Executive meetings of the two York party
organisations that were to be held on Friday are postponed. I had some
talk with Butcher – he evidently wants a compromise in February now
but I doubt whether that is either wise or possible. However Hamar
[Greenwood] is coming to breakfast with Bowes [Morrell] and me
tomorrow morning at the NLC. Since leaving the Lords I have called
and seen G.N.[ewman] and I am expecting him and Harold Spender
to dinner very shortly now.

[...]

18 November 1910
National Liberal Club – *7.35 pm*

Well, this great day is nearly over darling and the Liberal Party are in
great spirits over the PM's declaration[139] which is taken to mean that
he has obtained guarantees from the King and that if a victory is
secured the veto policy succeeds. To me the joy of this pronouncement
has been sadly lessened owing to the awful scenes with the women
outside the house! I did not witness them but the reports that came in
were bad enough. I won't add on this painful question.[140]

[...]

I suppose the agreement at York will now go through. I saw Butcher
for a few minutes and encouraged him not to make any bellicose

[137] Thomas Robinson Ferens (1847–1930), chemical manufacturer and Lib. MP East
Hull 1906–1918; never made a speech in House of Commons. Ettie Ferens (nee Field)
(d. 1922), m. 1873 T.R. Ferens. The National Liberal Federation Annual Conference was
in Hull on 25 November 1910.

[138] *Hansard*, 5th series, 1910, VI, 684–691. Ld Lansdowne, leader of the Con. peers,
made a very conciliatory speech on reform of the HofL, which temporarily raised hopes
of agreement.

[139] Asquith announced the dissolution of Parlt on 18 November 1910. On 16 November,
he had received guarantees from George V that the King would create sufficient peers
to pass a bill reforming the HofL if the Libs won the election.

[140] Demonstration outside the Commons by the Womens Social and Political Union.
It led to 119 arrests and accusations of heavy-handed tactics by the police.

speeches until things are settled – I hate appearing to shirk a fight and yet I can't help feeling that probably from a party point of view it may be wise. On an old register I don't feel sure of York which may I think be shocked by the strength of the govt. proposal.[141]

I have paired for next week with a Tory on the basis of using it myself or passing it on to another – it gives me a free hand and for most of the time I shall be doing better work in the country than in the house acting as a machine. I wish I felt surer of my ground as to whether I am in the right place – the old doubts creep up again when I contemplate the apparent waste of time – and my soul revolts against the bitterness of much of this warfare, and though I do feel the interest of it all I don't like the divorce from thee and those precious bairns. So thou sees I am not altogether in exuberant spirits tonight.

[...]

[141] *Yorkshire Herald*, 23 November 1910 announced that there would only be one Lib. and one Con. candidate for the two York seats.

CHAPTER 2

Letters 1911

7 February 1911
House of Commons

Thank thee darling for thy letter I am so glad to know thou art feeling better but hope that thou willst take things quietly these next few days.

The old doubts of last year are ever more rising up – this indefinite life oppresses me despite its great interest. Last night the debate was poor. Balfour was very clever over Winston [and] the photographer[1] and later in the evening Ramsay MacDonald[2] was good. This afternoon the mixed marriage case (McCann)[3] has been cleverly exposed by Devlin[4] as simply a political dodge and there seems little left of the scandal which has been worked by the Orangemen so much. The morning I spent at the office and with Parke and then lunched with the Nation contributors.

Things seem to be going well politically except the difficulties over the navy estimates and I fear we shall not be able to stop a large increase.

I am stopping tonight at 314 Camden Rd[5] and am sorry I forgot to wire earlier. The debate on the address will not conclude this week so I shall very likely pair on Friday and come home that morning.

[1] In the debate on the Address, Balfour had chided Churchill for his publicity-seeking visit to police operations against some alleged anarchists in the 'Siege of Sidney Street'; 'I understand what the photographer was doing, but what was the Right Hon. Gentleman doing?'; *Hansard*, 5th series, 1911, XXI, 55.

[2] James Ramsay MacDonald (1866–1937), Lab. MP Leicester 1906–1918, Aberavon 1922–1929, Seaham 1929–1935 (Nat. Lab. from 1931), Combined Scottish Univs 1936–1937; Leader Lab. Party 1911–1914, 1922–1931, Prime Minister 1924, 1929–1935, Ld Pres. of the Council 1935–1937.

[3] McCann case; Mr McCann, a Belfast Catholic, left his wife, taking his two young children with him and leaving Mrs McCann, a Presbyterian, no clue to their whereabouts. Unionists claimed this had occurred with the connivance of the local Catholic priests, who wished to ensure the children were brought up as Catholics. The case received much publicity in Ulster at the December 1910 elections.

[4] Joseph Devlin (1872–1934), Irish Nat. MP North Kilkenny 1902–1906, West Belfast 1906–1922, Fermanagh and Tyrone 1929–1934; the leading figure in Irish Nationalism in Belfast.

[5] 314 Camden Rd; home of Hannah Elizabeth Gillett, A.S.R.'s aunt.

15 February 1911
House of Commons

I have interesting news to tell thee darling – last night Ted [Harvey] opened out to me and practically told me he was in love with Irene Thompson[6] and had much enjoyed a weekend there last week and was groaning that he couldn't go down again for a month owing to other engagements.

He spoke to me again this morning and told me he hadn't slept much for thinking about it and so I encouraged him to see Silvanus Thompson soon about the matter and I think after he has told the parents at home this weekend he probably will. He hasn't breathed it to anyone yet so thou and I are the only two who know at present. She will I think do beautifully for him and I have been very happy in the contemplation today of this great restful joy for him. I think he feels that it will mean giving up Toynbee Hall[7] but that I think will be a right step because he feels the strain of oversight there and Parliament.

He was very happy when I told him that I know thou wouldst approve and that it had crossed thy mind after our Sunday at the Newmans.

[...]

2 March 1911
House of Commons

The debate this afternoon has been excellent and compensation for many days of weariness darling.[8] Balfour's vigorous defence of the hereditary system and his admission that he approved of the actions of the House of Lords in refusing the Budget, Education Bill and Licensing Bill and that the reason why he wanted the H of L reforming was to *strengthen* it will do the Tories no good in the country and many of the young Tories looked very unhappy.

I am looking forward to returning tomorrow and unless I hear to the contrary shall not have lunch on the train but hope to have it with thee at York station.

[...]

[6] Alice Irene Thompson (1887–1955), daughter of Prof. Silvanus Phillips Thompson (1851–1916), physicist and Quaker, originally from York; Principal of City and Guilds of London Technical Institute at Finsbury 1885–1916.
[7] T.E. Harvey had been Warden of Toynbee Hall since 1906; he resigned in 1911 after his marriage.
[8] *Hansard*, 5th series, 1911, XXII, 565–581 for Balfour on the 2nd Reading of the Parlt Bill.

14 March 1911
242 St James Court

I have not much news for thee darling except to look forward hopefully with thee to Saturday evening when I have asked Frank Sturge[9] to come to supper. I really think he must be after Edie[10] and I know nothing better for rheumatoid arthritis! However we must possess our souls in peace.

Grey's[11] speech was *most* encouraging last night – whilst it does not undo the harm of the folly caused of the German scare it does give promise of an advance in the future. One of the most encouraging things was the way in which he showed his confidence and belief that this treaty[12] was in the bounds of reasonable possibility if only the nation would rise to it.

Winterton's[13] sniggerings would have riled thee badly. Many members (including Ted [Harvey]) after Grey's speech would have liked Macdonald[14] to have withdrawn his motion but I think he and Ponsonby[15] were right in persisting because Grey's bold stroke does not undo the folly of the past.

I have been to Bensons this morning and then to the Nation lunch. This afternoon I have been writing diligently here. I seem to have got badly into arrears this evening as I have found out that there is a vacant seat at His Majesty's I am going to hear Henry VIII forsaking Haldane and his estimates.

[9] Frank Lionel Player Sturge (1871–1948), schoolmaster at Bootham School 1906–1919, Warden of Woodbrooke 1919–1931.

[10] Edith Maria Rowntree (1870–1955), sister of A.S.R.; m. Frank Sturge 1 August 1911.

[11] Sir Edward Grey (1862–1933), Lib. MP Berwick-on-Tweed 1885–1916, when cr. Vt Grey; PS Foreign Office 1892–1895, Foreign Sec. 1905–1916; succ. as 3rd Bt 1882; KG 1912.

[12] In reply to a backbench motion censuring the increase in arms spending, Grey suggested the government might take up President Taft's suggestion of a wide-ranging Treaty of Arbitration; *Hansard*, 5th series, 1911, XXII, 1977–1992.

[13] Edward Turnour (1883–1962), Con. MP Horsham 1904–1951; US India 1922–1924, 1924–1929, Chanc. Duchy of Lancaster 1937–1939, Paymaster-Gen. 1939; succ. as 6th Ld Winterton in Irish peerage 1907; cr. Ld Turnour in UK peerage 1952.

[14] John Archibald Murray Macdonald (1854–1939), Lib. MP Bow and Bromley 1892–1895, Falkirk 1906–1922.

[15] Arthur Augustus William Harry Ponsonby (1871–1946), Lib. MP Stirling 1908–1918, Lab. MP Sheffield, Brightside 1922–1930, when cr. Ld Ponsonby of Shulbrede; PS Ministry of Transport 1929–1931, Chanc. Duchy of Lancaster 1931, Leader Lab. Party in HofL 1931–1935. Former diplomat and leading back-bench critic of Grey's foreign policy.

16 March 1911
Great Central Railway letter card – nearing Leicester

The Chesterfield folks were very kind to me yesterday. I was met by
Alderman Pearson, a large pottery man employing something like 600
people who have recently come into the movement[16] and who is helping
them with a new building at Whittington. We went off in a motor car
to see the building as they wanted suggestions about its conversion into
a school club. Then after tea with Mr and Mrs Pearson we went to a
meeting in the Town Hall and had I think a very good solid opportunity
with about 300 men and women representatives from 18 different
Derbyshire schools all started within the last six years.

I came back with Harry[17] and enjoyed staying with him and Auntie
[...].

Thank thee darling for thy letter and the Herald. I think my vote
on Monday[18] which I expect to repeat today! will provide the local
Tories with material for many speeches! – [...].

There is the Nation dinner tonight which may be awkward with
the Navy debate going on. Thou sees Hamar [Greenwood]'s
wedding[19] is announced. I think he will be pleased with a nice letter
from thee! [...]

19 April 1911
House of Commons

Thank thee darling for thy letter and further enclosure which I have
handed on to Ted [Harvey]. We signalised our return by an all night
sitting and I scored 19 divisions and returned home about 5 am. [...]

Winterton has just passed and I heard him say to another member
that we are to have another late sitting tomorrow – he should know! I
have not heard anything from Theo and Kitty[20] and am so wondering
whether my wire missed them. With regard to Friday, Ted [Harvey] is
coming by the 10 o'clock train and will catch the 3.00 from York. I

---

[16] The Adult School Movement.

[17] James Henry Doncaster, Sheffield steel manufacturer and s. of Hannah Mary
Doncaster, sister-in-law of A.S.R.'s stepmother.

[18] In the debate on arms increases on 13 March 1911 A.S.R. had voted for Macdonald
and Ponsonby's motion criticizing the government. *Yorkshire Herald*, 15 March 1911
denounced A.S.R. for joining 'the motley crew of faddists and cranks who have "bees in
their bonnets"'.

[19] Hamar Greenwood m. Margery Spencer (1886–1968), 23 May 1911.

[20] Theodore Hotham Rowntree (1867–1949), and his wife, Katherine Lucy (nee Burtt)
(1870–1971), A.S.R.'s brother and sister-in-law. Theodore was Sec. of Rowntree & Co.
1897–1924 and Lib. councillor for Bootham on York Council 1912–1919.

fear I shall not be able to get away from York until 6.55 as I have a
village trust meeting besides a good deal of business.

[...]

Yes it was sad about Lord Carlisle[21] – will't thou write to Dorothy
Howard[22] our condolences – thou knows her better than I do. [...]

Parliament is very dull today – the Army Bill – so I am spending all
my time writing in the Library. This evening there is a private members
motion so Ted [Harvey] and I thought of slipping off to the Little
Theatre – but I expect it will be to bed instead.

24 April 1911
Chalfonts

[...]

I enjoyed my journey up with Seebohm [Rowntree] as companion,
he seems to me better than I have known him for some time and it
must be years since I have had such a gathered talk with him about
business, unemployment, consumption, Quakerism. He has a splendidly
clear mind when he is well. The garden at Chalfonts really is most
beautiful and I am sorry thou can not see the daffodils and hyacinths –
they do much credit to thee and Armes[23] and he will send to the
Workhouse and Hospital at the end of the week large bunches.

[...] I find Friday, May 5th, is the date of the Women's Suffrage
debate[24] and I think I must be there to vote – if so will't thou take my
place at the Wesleyan Bazaar and then come to town by the 4.15 train
and join me there! If thou will't do this for thy little wayward husband
I will run the YMCA by myself on Thursday! Don't let it oppress thee
darling! We had a comfortable board and I got the main lines of our
advertising scheme through for next winter.

25 April 1911
House of Commons

[...]

We sat up last night until three o'clock – the suspension of the 11
o'clock has been moved for tonight so we may be late again.

[21] George James Howard (1843–1911), Lib. MP East Cumberland 1879–1880, 1881–
1885 but LU from 1886; succ. as 9th Earl of Carlisle 1889; landowner and painter.
[22] Lady Dorothy Georgiana Howard, (1881–1968), daughter of 9th Earl of Carlisle; m.
Francis Eden, 6th Ld Henley, 1913.
[23] John W. Armes, gardener at Chalfonts.
[24] The second reading of Sir George Kemp's Women's Enfranchisement Bill. A.S.R.
attended and voted for the measure.

[...]

Asquith has moved the Kangaroo closure today which means that the Chairman has liberty to select the substantial amendments up to a certain point in the bill[25] out of the mass of frivolous ones so probably we shall make quicker progress. [...]

26 April 1911
House of Commons

[...] Both Ted [Harvey] and I are feeling fagged today. These long sittings and the difficulty of getting settled sleep leave one somewhat good for nothing but I shall get a good night when I get back from Sutton and be alright tomorrow. I expect one will get used to it soon. Everything is a matter of habit, but I am more and more impressed with the tremendous strain under which ministers work.

[...]

The gambling meeting seems to have passed off very well yesterday – a very small gathering. Strachey[26] did not speak but Seebohm [Rowntree] had quite an interesting twenty minutes with him.

[...]

Now I think I will go back to the House where an interesting debate is proceeding on the referendum.[27] [...]

1 May 1911
House of Commons

[...] I attended the Board meeting and was able to catch the 12.15 and had a comfortable journey here [...].

Aunt Phoebe[28] will be interested in hearing that the Mansion House Peace meeting according to J.A. Baker was *very* good and the city audience were able to gauge rightly the two speeches. When Asquith rose he was received well but with nothing like the excitement of

---

[25] Parliament Bill, 1911.

[26] John St Loe Strachey (1860–1927), owner and Ed. *The Spectator* 1897–1925. Anti-gambling activist and most vociferous Con. critic of the Cadburys and Rowntrees over the *Star*'s continued coverage of betting news under their ownership.

[27] *Hansard*, 5th series, 1911, XXIV, 1808–1881 for Con. amendment to Parlt Bill providing for a referendum on disputed bills.

[28] Phoebe Doncaster (1847–1924), sister of A.S.R.'s stepmother, Helen Doncaster Rowntree. The meeting at the Guildhall on 28 April 1911 was to promote an arbitration treaty between Britain and the USA. Asquith proposed the motion and Balfour was the seconder.

welcome Balfour received – but when he sat down he was cheered far more loudly than Balfour.

I had ten minutes with two militant women this morning – and broke it to them that I was going to pair instead of vote on Friday – and as they received it quite kindly I have definitely summoned the sub committee for that afternoon.

[...]

4 May 1911
Friends Institute – 138 Bishopsgate, London

After treating thee so badly yesterday I must really try and write thee a gathered letter darling. We were late on Tuesday evening. I didn't get home until after 2 am so yesterday I breakfasted at 10 and then after working at home went to the presentation of plate to the Speaker and Mrs Lowther by members of the House of Commons. It really was a charming ceremony – all the speeches were good, no exaggeration or unnecessary flattery, but the feeling of affection in which old Lowther is held was admirably brought out by Grey, Balfour, Redmond[29] and MacDonald – afterwards the leaders and the plate were photographed by old Sir Benjamin Stone[30] and a second picture contained many of the lesser lights.

The debate yesterday afternoon on the preamble was quite inter-esting – personally I thought MacDonald's speech the best and Ted [Harvey] and I after seeing that the government were perfectly safe voted with the Labour Party against the Govt. so I am a free man respecting a reformed second chamber.[31]

The reason why I didn't write thee yesterday was that I went to a meeting of Liberal Members about 6 pm on the question of the appointment of magistrates and I was summoned from that on the arrival of Mrs Meyer (Seb's sister-in-law I think)[32] and the Hon. Mrs Wilkinson[33] who seemed so greatly upset and disappointed by my

[29] John Edward Redmond (1856–1918), Irish Nat. MP New Ross 1881–1885, N. Wexford 1885–1891, Waterford 1891–1918, Leader Parnellite Nats 1891–1900, Irish Nats 1900–1918.

[30] Sir John Benjamin Stone (1838–1914), Con. MP Birmingham East 1895–January 1910; kt. 1892; official photographer for 1911 Coronation.

[31] A.S.R. (and T.E. Harvey) voted for a Labour amendment to remove the preamble from the Parlt Bill which committed the goverment to reforming the second chamber; *Hansard*, 5th series, 1911, XXV, 445–558 for the debate. The motion was lost 218–47.

[32] Sebastian William Meyer (1856–1946), York Quaker; Lib. Councillor Bootham 1902–1907, alderman from 1907.

[33] Hon. Mrs Caroline Wilkinson (d. 1929), daughter of 3rd Ld Decies; m. 1886 Lt-Col. George Wilkinson of Dringhouses Manor, York. She and Mrs Meyer were Pres. and Hon. Sec. of the York branch of the National Union of Womens' Suffrage Societies.

pairing instead of voting and said the women of York would be, that I promised to seriously consider whether I could alter my arrangements. As thou knows I am very anxious that the women shouldn't feel that I am playing with them, and as I fear they have many disappointments still in front of them I decided last night that if I get a favourable wire from thee this morning I would agree to their request. I have just had thy wire telephoned on to me and saint as thou art thou hast made it possible for me to do what is probably my duty – but which I admit is somewhat grudgingly performed when one holds that a 'pair' would have been as effective. I do hope darling that it will not be difficult to thee or spoil thy day. Chaff Butcher! I have warmly encouraged him to be there and I told him how popular it will make him amongst York women if he goes to York whilst I stay in London.

[...]

I may *possibly* go to see Bernard Shaw's[34] play as the House will rise at 5.30 but if thou wires that thou art coming by the earlier train I shall come and meet thee. I had dinner last night with Ted [Harvey] who was entertaining Joe Wigham[35] and Birley[36] – the latter Ted says has been appointed Warden in his place at Toynbee – We had a most amusing talk with Swift MacNeill[37] afterwards – he is full of good stories and gossip! He is a great admirer of Ted [Harvey]'s and said he was at a country house a short time ago and heard a description of Ted's goodness and character which would have made even St Paul blush! After hearing this account he determined to spot Ted by his face amongst the members. This he did – the only other man he felt any doubt about as to coming up to the description he had heard by the look of his face was Sir John Barran![38] [...]

This morning Needham,[39] Shipley Brayshaw's member came to breakfast with me – a really good fellow – mentally perplexed like thy man as to whether he is in his right place.

Since then I have been to see Henry C[adbury] and Bertram C[rosfield] at the Daily News office about the right line to take at YM. Then I came on here to get some time to write thee preparatory to the Flounders Trust.[40] I think I shall cut the premises committee as I

[34] George Bernard Shaw (1856–1950), Irish playwright; the play was probably *Fanny's First Play* (1911).

[35] Joseph Theodore Wigham (1874–1951), Irish Quaker and doctor.

[36] Maurice Birley, Warden of Toynbee Hall 1911–1914.

[37] John Gordon Swift MacNeill (1849–1926), Irish Nat. MP Donegal South 1887–1918; eminent lawyer, wit, and parliamentary troublemaker.

[38] Sir John Nicholson Barran (1872–1952), Lib. MP Hawick 1909–1918; PPS H. Samuel 1910–1914, Sir E. Grey 1915, H.H. Asquith 1915–1916; succ.as 2nd Bt 1905.

[39] Christopher Thomas Needham (1866–1944), Lib. MP Manchester SW December 1910–1918; kt. 1919.

[40] Flounders Trust; Quaker trust founded to promote the training of teachers.

am anxious to hear George on his insurance proposals. May and Egbert Morland[41] can of course stay at St James Court as long as ever they like.

Just post time – a wonderful *scheme* of Lloyd George, Newman, Roger Clark,[42] Ted [Harvey] and I all dining together tonight. [...]

One of the most awkward issues that A.S.R. had to deal with in the Commons was the vexed question of the duty on imported raw cocoa. This stood at 1d per lb. Cocoa manufacturers claimed this put them at a disadvantage when exporting manufactured cocoa or chocolate, while Conservatives asserted that firms like Rowntree & Co. benefited from a form of protection, because imports of chocolate paid 2d per lb. in duty. The issue was resolved in the 1911 Budget, which allowed cocoa manufacturers to reclaim sums paid in duty when they exported manufactured cocoa and chocolate, while lowering the duty on imported chocolate.

16 May 1911
House of Commons – 3.30 pm

The Budget debate will begin shortly so I think I better get a few lines written to thee now darling lest I am swept away on a flood of cocoa later!

I enjoyed having Arthur [Rowntree], Richard [Cross] and Appleton last night though it didn't conduce to early retirement!

This morning I went wifeless to the great pageant[43] and was really interested. There were several members to keep me company in a frock coat but of course most were in court dress and uniform. With the sun shining it was really a brilliant sight and I confess to prefer seeing such a spectacle in the open air rather than in a vitiated atmosphere at night. The King and Kaiser looked *very* happy and it's a great help to the royal procession having those nice looking children. I sat next to Sir John Dewar[44] an enlightened liberal whisky distiller! and had quite

[41] Dr Egbert Coleby Morland (1874–1955) and his wife Mary Windsor (nee Latchmore) (1873–1948), a school friend and cousin of M.K.R.; Quakers who lived in Switzerland. Egbert was Ed. *The Lancet* 1937–1944.
[42] Roger Clark (1871–1961), Sec. C. & J. Clark Shoes of Street, Somerset; a school friend of A.S.R. and prominent Quaker; Clerk of YM 1920–1928.
[43] On 16 May 1911 George V unveiled the Queen Victoria Memorial outside Buckingham Palace. He was accompanied by Kaiser Wilhelm II, who had arrived the previous day to attend the Coronation.
[44] Sir John Alexander Dewar (1856–1929), Lib. MP Inverness 1900–1916, when cr. Ld Forteviot; Chmn, John Dewar & Sons Ltd; Bt 1907.

a long talk with Sir Robert Hudson.[45] Ada[46] couldn't come so I
wandered about as a widower!

Walter[47] and Appleton are staying up over tonight as we meet the
Customs Appeals tomorrow along with Fry and Cadbury to see whether
we can agree to some scale of non protection duties.

We had an interesting 'Nation' lunch – a good discussion on the
Insurance Bill. Our little committee[48] is meeting daily and I am
beginning to enjoy Parliament!

[...]

Lane Fox[49] says Riley Smith is *very* bad and I fear dying. I told him
how much I liked him and what a loveable man he was. Lane Fox
then said perhaps he might be excused if he told me that Riley Smith
had said the same of me!

The Budget is on the whole satisfactory and certainly Austen [Cham-
berlain]'s reply to George on Cocoa is feeble.[50] I should like to reply
to him but I shall desist as it would only call attention to a subject I
wish to get through as quickly as possible.

31 May 1911

[...] to YM with Con[stance Rowntree] and sat out the Education
Debate and spoke for a minute or two at the Teachers Pension Scheme.
A great many Friends came up to speak to me about Friday's meeting
most kindly. I think Theodore Clark's[51] testimony pleased me the most.
Lunch with W.S. Clark,[52] Con, Roger [Clark] and Bobby Mennell[53] at
the Great Eastern. Then to the House with Con and a hunt for

[45] Sir Robert Arundell Hudson (1864–1927), chief organizer of the Lib. Party in his
roles as Sec. Nat. Lib. Federation 1893–1922, Hon. Sec. Lib. Central Association 1895–
1927; kt. 1906.
[46] Adelaide Constance Newman (nee Thorp) (d. 1946), wife of Sir George Newman;
artist.
[47] Walter Barrow (1867–1954), cousin of George Cadbury; Dir. and lawyer Cadbury
Bros; Lib. member Birmingham Council 1898–1904.
[48] A.S.R. was a member of a committee of back-bench Liberals formed to extend the
scope of Lloyd George's National Insurance bill, particularly in its provisions for women.
They often worked in co-operation with the Chancellor.
[49] George Richard Lane Fox (1870–1947), Con. MP Barkston Ash 1906–1931; PS for
Mines at Board of Trade 1922–1924, 1924–1928; cr. Ld Bingley 1933; Yorkshire landowner.
[50] *Hansard*, 5th series, 1911, XXV, 1866 and 1872–1874 for Lloyd George's announcement
of the changes in cocoa duties and Chamberlain's response.
[51] Theodore Clark, Quaker from Croydon; teacher, later Head of Crohamhurst School.
[52] William Stephens Clark (1839–1925), Quaker businessman; Chairman C. & J. Clark
Shoes of Street, Somerset 1903–1925; father of Roger Clark.
[53] Robert Oscar Mennell (1882–1960), Quaker tea importer; later a leading CO, serving
as Sec. and Treasurer FSC; imprisoned 1917–1919; Lab cand. Surrey E., 1924, 1929.

coronation seats with her. [...] now I am just off to an Insurance Committee. This has finished and thou will be glad to know that I have paired for Friday so shall come home by the 9.50 which will enable me to give that afternoon to business. [...]

1 July 1911
Chalfonts – 9 pm

I have had a happy day at Scarbro with J.R.[owntree] despite several showers. We talked chiefly about the Insurance Bill and business matters. [...]

2 July 1911
Chalfonts – 4.10 pm

I must get a few lines written to thee now darling otherwise I shall miss the post, as Winifred Sturge is coming to tea – to *the* tea in the Dining Room and Mac[54] comes in later to talk about the Drs. and the Insurance Bill.
  [...]

3 July 1911
East Coast Dining Car Express – between England and Scotland – 5 pm

[...]
  I had to leave early this morning after breakfast in order to welcome the Colonial visitors at the Works. We then had our Board meeting – nothing of special interest and then I ran off to the Guildhall to lunch and left them all feeding there in order to catch the 2.22 from York. I have spent the journey in talking to one of the leading Friendly Society men in York and in reading Sidney Webb's severe criticism of the Bill (insurance).
  [...]
  [...] I am trying to induce thee to go to the Garden Party on Friday [...] for a short time and if thou does I hope thou willst make one of thy delightful short speeches. I have asked J.B. M.[orrell] to give the major offering! Thou might say a few words about the increasing social

---

[54] Dr Peter Macdonald (1870–1960), opthalmic surgeon, appointed physician to Rowntree & Co. 1904; m. Agnes Rowntree (1870–1960), eldest daughter of Joseph Rowntree.

consciousness of responsibility one for another – as represented by
modern legislation and the need for most careful thought of all in
framing such legislation. Thou willst help one greatly if thou willst do
this.

[...]

5 July 1911
House of Commons – 9.10 pm

I was sorry darling not to be able to send thee a letter by the early
post but I was sitting through a ticklish discussion on Women's
place in the Insurance Bill.[55] I haven't much news to tell thee. I
spent most of this morning at the Treasury with a deputation to
George on the position of women. An interesting time – we were
led by Lees-Smith[56] *very* well and I think gained several points. I
lunched with Percy Alden and J.W. Wilson[57] at the Reform – the
latter man I am getting really fond of. Gillman[58] is up with me
helping me and now I must go into the House as a new amendment
is being moved.

6 July 1911
House of Commons

[...]
I have little news darling to tell thee. We didn't finish until 1 am last
night but managed to get through Clause 1.[59] This morning I was at
work with Gillman [...] and this afternoon have been in the House
continuously. I hope to get home on Saturday by the train reaching
York at 3.24 and am game for anything with thee and the kiddies until
6.30 when I have to meet a Friendly Society deputation and then I
have a Friendly Society meeting later. [...]

[55] *Hansard*, 5th series, 1911, XXVII, 1196–1216 for debate on Keir Hardie's motion to
include wives in national insurance benefits on the basis of their husbands' contributions.
[56] Hastings Bertrand Lees-Smith (1878–1941), Lib. MP Northampton January 1910–
1918, Lab. MP Keighley 1922–1923, 1924–1931, 1935–1941; Postmaster-Gen. 1929–1931,
Pres. Bd of Education 1931.
[57] John William Wilson (1858–1932), LU (Lib. from 1903) MP North Worcestershire
1895–1918, Stourbridge 1918–1922; Quaker businessman, Dir. Albright & Wilson, phosphorus manufacturers from 1879, Chmn 1915–1932; close collaborator of George Cadbury.
[58] Frederick John Gillman (1866–1949), worked at Rowntree & Co. from mid-1890s
and became A.S.R.'s private sec. c. 1903–1904; convert to Quakerism 1918; succ. A.S.R.
as Hon. Sec. NASU 1919–1924.
[59] Clause 1 of the National Insurance Bill, 1911.

25 July 1911
House of Commons

[...]
Thou willst have read of yesterday's proceedings in the papers.[60]
There is little to add except that it was evidently all organized with the
object of stimulating the feeling in favour of the no-surrender party
and it looks as if now a creation of peers would be necessary – but the
great difficulty is that it probably will not be sufficient to get us over
the Home Rule difficulty.

I spent this morning over advertising matters with Appleton and
Crossland and later went to the Nation lunch. Now after tea I am
going to an Insurance Committee.

28 July 1911
House of Commons

[...] I returned after seeing thee off to the Reform Club and read there,
dining with J.W. Wilson.

This morning Shipley Brayshaw breakfasted with me and told me of
his engagement to Ruth Holmes which however is not to be made
public until Saturday. Needless to say, he seemed very happy.

I was at Committees over the Insurance Bill all this morning [...]
and have been here since, hovering between both houses. The Lords
have turned up in great force. Old Lord Peel[61] was there and Lord
Cross[62] who must be nearer 90 than 80 but the speaking is really very
dull.

[...]

[60] On 24 July 1911 Asquith had been shouted down in the HofC by Con. MPs when
he tried to speak on the Lords' amendments to the Parlt Bill.

[61] Arthur Wellesley Peel (1829–1912), Lib. MP Warwick 1865–April 1895; Sec. Poor
Law Bd 1868–1871, PS Bd of Trade 1871–1873, Chief Whip 1873–1874, US Home Office
1880, Speaker of the House of Commons 1884–1895, when cr. Vt Peel; youngest s. of
Sir Robert Peel.

[62] Richard Assheton Cross (1823–1914), Con. MP Preston 1857–1862, Lancashire SW
1868–1885, Newton 1885–1886, when cr. Vt Cross; Home Sec. 1874–1880, 1885–1886,
Sec. of State India 1886–1892, Ld Privy Seal 1895–1900.

7 August 1911
House of Commons

I have just come out of the House darling after listening to the most
brilliant satirical reply to Smith,[63] Cecil[64] and Co. that was possible by
Ellis Griffith[65] the leader of the Welsh party. The Tories so far have
shown up badly – Balfour was hesitating and feeble and F.E. foolish
when dealing with the Lords, clever when criticising Irish policy, but
Asquith's reply to Balfour was admirable and to my thinking complete
and certainly Griffith has left nothing of F.E.[66]

[...]

8 August 1911
House of Commons

The atmosphere today is oppressively hot and it is hard to keep a
tranquil mind in the passions this bill arouses but I suppose it is all in
one's education to try and preserve a peaceable spirit. [...]

I worked at home this morning and then went to discuss several
matters with G.N.[ewman] at the Board of Education. He has had an
offer from the London County Council of becoming its chief medical
officer and a salary several hundred pounds in advance of that which
he is receiving at present, but I hardly think he will accept as his sphere
of influence is certainly larger where he is now. I lunched with him at
the Reform Club. [...]. This afternoon your friend Cecil has had his
innings and been recommending force as a remedy.[67] Carson[68] has
been very angry whilst Churchill who is acting for the PM was not

[63] Frederick Edwin Smith (1872–1930), Con. MP Liverpool, Walton 1906–1918, West
Derby 1918–1919; Solicitor-Gen. 1915, Attorney-Gen. 1915–1919, Ld Chanc. 1919–1922,
Sec. of State India 1924–1928; kt. 1915, Bt 1918, cr. Ld Birkenhead 1919, Vt 1921, Earl
1922.

[64] Ld Hugh Richard Heathcote Cecil (1869–1956), Con. MP Greenwich 1895–1906,
Oxford Univ. January 1910–1937; cr. Lord Quickswood 1941.

[65] Ellis Griffith (1860–1926), Lib. MP Anglesey 1895–1918, Carmarthen 1923–July 1924;
Chmn Welsh Lib. MPs 1910–1912, US Home Office 1912–1915; Bt 1918.

[66] The debate was a Con. motion of censure on the govt for extracting pledges from
George V to create Lib. peers if the Lords rejected the Parlt Bill; *Hansard*, 5th series,
1911, XXIX, 795–807 (Balfour), 807–817 (Asquith), 817–830 (Smith), 831–839 (Griffith).

[67] *Hansard*, 5th series, 1911, XXIX, 967–999 for Cecil, Carson, and Churchill on the
HofL's amendments to the Parlt Bill.

[68] Sir Edward Henry Carson (1854–1935), LU (Unionist from 1912) MP Trinity College,
Dublin 1892–1918, Belfast, Duncairn 1918–1921, when cr. Ld Carson; Solicitor-Gen.
Ireland 1892, Solicitor-Gen. 1900–1905, Attorney-Gen. 1915, First Ld of Admiralty 1916–
1917, War Cabinet 1917–1918, Leader Irish Unionists 1910–1921; kt. 1900, Ld of Appeal
1921–1929.

very effective. The temperature of the House of Lords was above 80! and the speakings I heard of Lord Crewe[69] very dull!

9 August 1911
House of Commons

An absolutely roasting day darling – I am told the hottest on record but of course I have no chance of checking this at present. I almost envy anyone on the moors! I have decided to come back to York on Friday night if the bill goes through the Lords they will probably have a thanksgiving meeting that night. [...]

I had breakfast this morning with the Greenwoods. Then I went to Benson's to meet Crossland, and am here this afternoon as possibly the Cocoa question may come up in an acute form.

I am glad thou had such a good day at Rievaulx and Byland yesterday. I meant to write but I have just been with Caley[70] for a long time and now it is post time.

PS The House of Lords debate has been most entertaining. The anger of Halsbury[71] and the balancings of the Archbishop[72] most interesting to watch.

15 August 1911
House of Commons

Thank thee darling for thy p.c. Things are comparatively quiet here – members seem happy at having voted themselves £400 per year yesterday, and afterwards all the remaining votes in supply were voted upon without discussion. I think we voted something like £97 million pounds! and scored six divisions! [...]

This morning I worked with him [E.R. Cross] over Insurance Bill

---

[69] Richard Offley Ashley Crewe-Milnes (1858–1945), Liberal peer; Ld Lieutenant of Ireland 1892–1895, Ld Pres. of Council 1905–1908, 1915–1916, Ld Privy Seal 1908–1911, 1912–1915, Leader Lib. Peers 1908–1916, 1936–1944, Sec. of State Colonies 1908–1910, Sec. of State India 1910–1915, Pres. Bd of Education 1916, Amb. to France 1922–1928, Sec. of State for War 1931; succ. as 2nd Ld Houghton 1885, cr. Earl of Crewe 1895, Marquess 1911.

[70] Caley, member of family who controlled A.J. Caley Ltd, biscuit and chocolate manufacturers of Norwich.

[71] Hardinge Stanley Giffard (1823–1921), Con. MP Launceston 1877–1885; Solicitor-Gen. 1875–1880, Ld Chanc. 1885–1886, 1886–1892, 1895–1905; leading diehard peer; kt. 1875, cr. Ld Halsbury 1885, Earl 1898.

[72] William Cosmo Gordon Lang (1864–1945), Bishop of Stepney 1901–1909, Archbishop of York 1909–1928, Archbishop of Canterbury 1928–1942; cr. Ld Lang 1942; *Hansard*, 5th series, 1911, IX, 900–907 for Lang's declaration he would vote for the Parlt Bill.

matters and then after a swim went to the Nation lunch. This afternoon I have introduced a deputation of Chocolate manufacturers to George on the eternal question of duties! He is exceedingly clever and adroit in dealing with such a gathering. It really is amusing to find how angry a man like Caley (a strong Tory protectionist) is with the Tariff Reformer in having forced the government to deal with this question by having blackguarded both them and their supporters with favouritism and then when an alteration in duties is suggested it is not us that the alteration hurts but Caley and others!

I don't see much light yet about returning but think probably it will be Friday as George wants to see some of us on Thursday about Insurance matters. [...]

21 August 1911
Royal Station Hotel, York

[...]
Then I went and had a talk with Philip Burtt[73] here until the Directors Meeting resumed and then went off to the strike committee and sat with them for an hour.[74]

Then to the Lord Mayor to enquire about the use of the military. Then another talk with P. Burtt about the terms and then went on with the proposed terms to the Strike Committee and have spent two hours with them discussing suggested amendments. Now I am going to have a talk with Butterworth[75] and P.B.[urtt] to see whether it is possible to meet some of the points of the Strike Committee – so whatever comes of it I feel that probably it was right to come and act in this way as a go between. My decision as to whether to go to London tomorrow must depend upon developments tonight. I must do whatever seems to help forward a settlement.

As things are at present, I doubt whether we shall come to a settlement tonight especially as the York committee have to be guided by the decision of the London executives.

I will post now darling – thou knowest I hate being away from thee just now but I feel satisfied that it is my duty and that as I have the confidence of the strike committee I must do my best for them.

Just had an hour with Butterworth – I hope hopeful.

[73] Philip Burtt (1862–1931), Dep. Gen. Manager NER 1905–1914; Quaker with wide interests, including publishing and missions to China.
[74] There was a national railway strike on 18–19 August 1911. By the time A.S.R. wrote this letter, it was officially over, but strike action continued in York until 23 August, when a 'no victimization' assurance was given.
[75] Alexander Kaye Butterworth (1854–1946), Gen. Manager NER 1906–1921; kt. 1914.

22 August 1911
Royal Station Hotel, York – 9.50

I have just arrived back darling and everyone is waiting here for the news but the representatives of the Co. and the men sit on and on and one naturally fears that the negotiations are not going as well as one hoped.

I didn't sleep much last night but am feeling quite brisk tonight and have booked a room here. I don't know that I accomplished much in London this morning but by visiting the men and then the Board of Trade helped in this consultation tonight. Nothing very special in Parliament. The Railway Commission is not quite as strong as some hoped. Ramsay MacDonald was very severe on Winston [Churchill] over his use of the military.[76]

I had tea with Ted [Harvey] who is probably going to Leeds next week with Irene and then on to spend the following weekend at Runciman's. [...]

16 October 1911
242 St James Court – 9.45

Just a line darling to let thee know that I have had a comfortable and interesting day. I found Herbert Stead[77] and Fred Taylor[78] on the train and had lunch with them en route. Fred returning from Darlington. I went straight to the Daily News office and had three hours with Bertram [Crosfield], Henry [Cadbury] and Parke – speaking generally the Cadbury group agree to the main outlines of the document and are very grateful to J.R.[owntree] for what he has done.

I then went and had tea with Sherwell and found Addison[79] and

[76] *Hansard*, 5th series, 1911, XXIX, 2291–2293 for Asquith's announcement of a Royal Commission on the railways arbitration scheme set up in 1907, and 2293–2299 for MacDonald.

[77] Francis Herbert Stead (1857–1928), journalist and activist for various good causes, especially old age pensions; Warden Robert Browning Hall, Walworth 1894–1921.

[78] Frederic Taylor (1861–1944), brother of E.E. Taylor and husband of Gertrude Sophia Rowntree, sister of A.S.R.; Sec. Friends' First Day School Association. Helped found West Hill College 1907 and on NASU Council 1899–1923.

[79] Christopher Addison (1869–1951), Lib. MP Shoreditch January 1910–1922; Lab. MP Swindon 1929–1931, 1934–1935; PS Bd of Education 1914–1915, PS Ministry of Munitions 1915–1916, Min. of Munitions 1916–1917; Min. of Reconstruction 1917–1919; Pres. Local Govt Bd 1919; Min. of Health 1919–1921; PS Ministry of Agriculture 1929–1930, Min of Agriculture 1930–1931; Sec. of State Dominions 1945–1947; Sec.of State Commonwealth Relations Office 1947; Ld Privy Seal 1947–1951; Paymaster-Gen. 1948–1949, Ld Pres. of Council 1951, Leader HofL 1945–1951; cr. Ld Addison 1937, Vt 1945; former prof. of anatomy and leading proponent of state health care.

Lees-Smith and talked insurance for some time. Then called on G.N.[ewman] at the Board and then came on here for dinner with Norman Angell[80] – E.R.C.[ross]. I think we shall recommend the Trust[81] to provide Norman Angell with a good secretary so as to help him with his propagandist work. He was most interesting as to the change of view that has come over the Harmsworth people[82] with regard to Germany and believes he has unconsciously converted them largely to his view.

Now I must set to work with Richard [Cross] in amending the Fry document.

I do hope thou hast got on well with the women Liberals. I should have enjoyed hearing thee.

*

23 October 1911
Board of Education

I am here waiting for G.N.[ewman] with Percy Alden. We have just come from an interview with Lloyd George which has in many ways been more satisfactory than I expected. I think we are going to get a 50 per cent grant for local authorities to deal with tuberculosis in thorough fashion and I hope we may get this properly managed by the Sanitary Authority rather than by the Health Committee. But we are meeting him again tomorrow and if we get these two things and something for the children I shall support him through thick and thin. But the whole performance is extraordinarily casual and thou would be amused and grieved at the way in which government is run. George says there are changes in the government imminent and if Burns[83] leaves the LGB there is much greater hope for wise co-operation between the LGB and the authorities running the Insurance Bill.

G.N.[ewman] says we must be off. I go with him to work up a policy for tomorrow. [...]

---

[80] Ralph Norman Angell (1872–1967), Lab. MP North Bradford 1929–1931; kt. 1931; journalist, author of *The Great Illusion* (1910), which argued war could not benefit any of the European Powers.

[81] Joseph Rowntree Social Service Trust, founded 1904. On 19 December 1911 the Trust agreed to provide Angell with £500 for a secretary and office in London.

[82] Primarily Alfred Charles William Harmsworth, 1st Ld Northcliffe (1865–1923), owner of *The Times* and *Daily Mail*. Angell worked for Northcliffe as Gen. Manager in Paris for the *Daily Mail*.

[83] John Burns (1858–1943), Lib. MP Battersea 1892–1918; Pres. Local Govt Bd 1905–1914, Pres. Bd of Trade 1914.

24 October 1911
St James Court – 1 pm

[...] I worked with G.N.[ewman] till lateish. He told me in confidence about the Cabinet changes – he knew all about it because Runciman had of course to let one or two know – G.N.[ewman] had to send a faked telegram to Morant[84] who was in Rome and has come suddenly back to welcome his great chief! At that time it was expected that Burns would go to the Home Office and McKenna[85] take the LGB but some hitch has occurred over that transference. The telegram ran – Winnie [Churchill] is to sail ships, Johnnie [Burns] goes home and Reggie [McKenna] follows him, Walter [Runciman] grows turnips and Lancaster [Pease] goes to school – or something to that effect. Morant made everything out except Lancaster! It is a disappointing shuffle I think. Pease[86] is painfully weak – quite unfit for any office and if Burns had only gone to the Home Office it would have meant much easier working of the Insurance Bill (for Burns is still deadly jealous of George) and also a more hopeful prospect for Poor Law Reform. I hope Winston [Churchill] will do better at the Admiralty but I have me doubts!

I came in with George [Newman] this morning and have been working here. [...] I am inclined not to let my flat as I seem so often to want it for committees. I am expecting several members of our committee to lunch any time now.

(Later) Sherwell, Alden, Lees Smith and Newman came to lunch and we are just off to see the Chancellor again on the subject of married women.

Ted [Harvey] seems well. I am arranging to go to him for tomorrow and the day after. Just been to the Chancellor and had a very good interview. I think a grant for medical treatment of children will now be given.

The insurance bill has just begun so –

[84] Sir Robert Laurie Morant (1863–1920), PUS Board of Education 1903–1911, Chmn Nat. Health Insurance Commissioners 1912–1919, PUS Ministry of Health 1919–1920; KCB 1907.

[85] Reginald McKenna (1863–1943), Lib. MP North Monmouthshire 1895–1918; Fin. Sec. to Treasury 1905–1907, Pres. Bd of Education 1907–1908, First Ld of Admiralty 1908–1911, Home Sec. 1911–1915, Chanc. of Exchequer 1915–1916.

[86] Joseph Albert Pease (1860–1943), Lib. MP Tyneside 1892–1900, Saffron Walden 1901–January 1910, Rotherham March 1910–1917, when cr. Ld Gainford; Lib. whip 1905–1908, Chief Whip 1908–1911, Chanc. Duchy of Lancaster 1910–1911, Pres. Board of Education 1911–1915, Postmaster-Gen. 1915–1916; second Quaker to reach Cabinet.

25 October 1911
House of Commons

[...] I am in distinctly better spirits about the Insurance Bill – L.G. has now agreed to put medical treatment for children in the bill (in private). Sherwell, Newman were at lunch at the Treasury today discussing it. He is also going to give us practically what we want with regard to sanatoria so I am voting with the Government today on the closure much as I regret the necessity. Balfour's speech was really very effective as well as Healy[87] against. J.M. Robertson[88] has just told me he has been offered the Undersecretaryship at the Board of Trade which is an *excellent* appointment. One other private piece of information – Burns is going shortly to make the notification of consumption *compulsory* which will immensely help matters forward. I was going to ask him a question but he wants me to desist lest opposition should be aroused. The House was up soon after 9 last night so I went to the Savoy for a short time with Richard [Cross] to see 'Samuran' a famous German production in dumb show. I thought it rather disappointing. [...]

I go with Ted [Harvey] tonight but have decided to keep on the flat. I think really it will be more restful.

26 October 1911
House of Commons

There is little to report darling. We were late last night so I did not go back with Ted [Harvey] but went to the flat. This morning I spent three hours with Benson then did some work with Gillman and have been at the House since, listening to a dull debate on the grouping of the small societies which the government have devised as a method whereby small societies can be approved.[89] I think they have met a real difficulty very well. I quite hope I shall catch the 5.30 tomorrow.

[87] Timothy Michael Healy (1855–1931), Irish Nat. MP Wexford 1880–1883, Monaghan 1883–1885, S. Derry 1885–1886, N. Longford 1887–1892, N. Louth 1892–December 1910, N.E. Cork 1911–1918. *Hansard*, 5th series, 1911, XXX, 121–135 and 159–169 for Balfour and Healy's speeches on the allocation of time for debating National Insurance.

[88] John MacKinnon Robertson (1856–1933), Lib. MP Tyneside 1906–1918; PS Bd of Trade 1911–1915; a secularist.

[89] *Hansard*, 5th series, 1911, XXX, 307–318 for Lloyd George's announcement of a new amendment to his National Insurance Bill to this effect.

30 October 1911
House of Commons

Just a line darling to let thee know that I got comfortably through my Kentish Town engagement. It wasn't a very easy audience. Mostly women folk but many came up to me afterwards to express unity with what I said. [...] Then I came to the House and have spent most of the time inside but the debate has been largely technical. Tomorrow the Post Office contributors are discussed. George is going to accept an amendment limiting the operation of that part of the act to 1914 so that will force legislation in their parliament. [...]

31 October 1911
242 St James Court

[...]
I have been working here this morning, thinking over a defence of Lloyd George for his post office contributors plan which comes up for debate tonight.[90] [...]

1 November 1911
242 St James Court

[...]
[...] We had a good debate last night on the Deposit contibutors. Sherwell spoke splendidly and practically all our Committee spoke afterwards at the request of Lloyd George pressing for wider treatment for consumption and the Medical Treatment of children.[91] Lloyd George replies this afternoon and we are hoping he will accede to the request.
[...]
Nothing of much further interest to report. George was quite sympathetic to our speeches of yesterday and we are evidently going to get our grant for children.

[90] *Hansard*, 5th series, 1911, XXX, 798–801 and 815–817 for T.E. Harvey and A.S.R.'s defence of the post-office scheme for those too low-paid to join a Friendly Society under the National Insurance proposals.
[91] If this is correct, the committee consisted of Sherwell, T.E. Harvey, E.W. Davies, W.A. Chapple, Alden, A.S.R., and Addison.

2 November 1911
House of Commons

Thanks for thy letter darling. Thou would see that George promised to deal with children yesterday and consequently our little group is much pleased. Our little demonstration on Tuesday night was at his request to show there was feeling behind the demand. I think the York election results are really very encouraging, but show the increased support that men give to labour after a strike.[92] Bowes [Morrell]'s election was a near squeak. The liberals evidently split whilst the labour folk plumped. The result should at any rate ensure a fair division with regard to committees between parties.

I spent the morning at the DN with the Cadburys, etc. over the best way of dealing with the Star and then had lunch with G.N.[ewman] at the Reform Club. He says (very private) that George wants him to be one of the Insurance Commissioners but now that he is going to get a grant for medical treatment he naturally is not very keen to go. He also says Pease has begun well – working very hard and very anxious to help forward G.N.[ewman]'s work. [...]

The controversy in the Society of Friends caused by the carrying of betting news in the Star *newspaper refused to subside. The matter was aired once again at an adjourned Yearly Meeting on 6–9 November 1911. The meeting appointed a committee to 'enter into sympathetic conference' with the Cadbury and Rowntree families. The committee's deliberations were lengthy and it finally reported only in May 1914. It reaffirmed Quaker opposition to gambling, 'earnestly desire[d]' an end to such news in the press, and urged all Quakers to work to eradicate gambling. This did not satisfy the critics, but the committee's existence at least did something to take some of the heat out of the argument.*

6 November 1911
House of Commons – 6.10

I think I better get off a few lines to thee now darling otherwise I shall be submerged as I am expecting Parke, Richard [Cross], Shipley Brayshaw and Harry Wilson here later at intervals.

[...]

---

[92] In 1911 there had been strikes in York at Leetham's flour mills and the York Glass Co., as well as the railways. Labour won two seats from the Conservatives and the Liberals gained one, depriving the Conservatives of an overall majority. In Micklegate the result was J.F. Glew (Lab.) 1,428; J.B. Morrell (Lib.) 1,186; D.S. Long (Con.) 1,003.

The Cadburys house at Wind's Point[93] is charming, right at the end of the Malvern hills with a wonderful view right across to the Bristol channel to the south and the Radnorshire beacon to the north. I had a long talk with Mr and Mrs G.C.[adbury], Edward [Cadbury] and Henry [Cadbury] over all this question and as a result we are letting our critics know that if they like to consult with us about this question composed of half their friends and half ours we shall offer no objection and if that committee felt quite clear that it was wisest for the Cs to sell the Star I don't think they would refuse.

I think Elsie Cadbury[94] is feeling the whole question very much. [...] Still they were very nice and G.C.[adbury] amuses me greatly.

[...]

7 November 1911
House of Commons – 6.30

[...] Addison and I are off very shortly to see the Chancellor on the question of sanatoria. The discussion at the YM comes off tomorrow at 10 am. I expect T. Hodgkin[95] will bring forward the proposal for a committee of 10 to sympathetically consult and I hope we shall be spared a very lengthy discussion. Joshua[96] afterwards will probably suggest inserting some words about the influence of the press into the paragraphs but that is perfectly right and Richard [Cross] has been with Joshua this morning agreeing I hope on some sound form of words. Whatever happens I feel I have done my best to prepare the ground and to prevent any explosion. I have just received a wire from G.C.[adbury] saying he is not coming up which is also a relief to me. The Friends in the house here – J.W. Wilson, Percy Alden and Jos. A. Baker are *very* angry with the whole agitation and would like to speak some straight words.

---

[93] Country house about four miles from Malvern, acquired by George Cadbury and his brother Richard as a retreat for the Cadbury family.

[94] Elizabeth Mary Cadbury (1858–1951), second wife of George Cadbury; Lib. cand. Birmingham, King's Norton 1923; DBE 1934.

[95] Thomas Hodgkin (1831–1913), leading Quaker; banker and writer on historical topics.

[96] Joshua Rowntree (1844–1915), Lib. MP Scarborough 1886–1892; cousin of A.S.R. Ed. the *Friend* 1871–1875, first Warden of Woodbrooke 1903–1904.

8 November 1911
House of Commons

I asked Richard [Cross] darling to call on thee this evening and to let
thee know the result of the YM discussion. I did not think it was a
very satisfactory opportunity that is the general discussion on the
advices but I felt thankful that we had arranged beforehand for this
committee and that as far as we were concerned we had done everything
we could to prevent a really fierce debate which might have done real
harm. I think also it was a good plan getting T. Hodgkin to introduce
the question. H.L.W[ilson] has acted throughout as a most devoted
Friend and as a splendid '*go-between*'.

Friends do not really understand the problem and this experience
may make them *think* as they have not done before.

Insurance is flat today – everybody is thinking of Balfour's coup and
speculating on the new Leader. The choice seems to be between Austen
and Long.[97] [...]

9 November 1911
House of Commons

[...]
Harry Wilson has just been here. He says the following 9 Friends
have been appointed – W.H.F. Alexander, Rd. Beck, A.H. Brown,
W.C.B.[raithwaite], Alfred F. Fox, T. Hodgkin, H.J. Morland, R.A.
Penny and H.L.W.[ilson][98] as the committee to sympathetically consult
with us. I expect we shall have quite a pleasant time but I fear it will
consume a large amount of *time* but such is life!

[...]
I had lunch with G.N.[ewman] and he gave me a very interesting
account of his experience last Sunday with Lloyd George when he took

[97] Walter Hume Long (1854–1924), Con. MP N. Wiltshire 1880–1892, Liverpool, West
Derby 1893–1900, S. Bristol 1900–1906, Co. Dublin, S. 1906–January 1910, Strand
January 1910–1921, when cr. Vt Long of Wraxall; PS Local Govt Bd 1886–1892, Pres.
Bd of Agriculture 1895–1900, Pres. Local Govt Bd 1900–1905, 1915–1916, Chief Sec. for
Ireland 1905, Sec. of State Colonies 1916–1919, First Ld of Admiralty 1919–1921. In fact,
Andrew Bonar Law succeeded Balfour as Conservative leader.

[98] William Henry Fisher Alexander (1855–1941), insurance broker; member Meeting
for Sufferings 1898–1909, 1923–1941. Richard Beck (1858–1945), merchant's clerk from
Southampton. Alfred Henry Brown (1860–1932), fin. manager in an engineering works;
member Meeting for Sufferings 1923–1930. Alfred Francis Fox (1867–1947), London
solicitor. Harold John Morland (1869–1939), Partner Price, Waterhouse & Co. 1907–1932;
Clerk of YM 1928–1934. Robert Alfred Penny (1863–1935), shipping business on the
south coast; Asst Clerk of YM.

him to the home for cripples that we visited a few weeks ago, but I will tell thee about this tomorrow.

Hamar [Greenwood] told me last night that he would want a midwife in June and that he wanted to call the boy '*York Greenwood*' but his wife always put down his suggestions and wouldn't hear of it! I told her the advantage of York as a name was that it would fit either sex.[99]

[...]

21 November 1911
House of Lords

Cheer up darling, don't be afraid I have not been elevated to this august house, I am simply waiting to see the Chancellor's secretary on the subject of magistrates. We sat late last night not reaching home until after 2 am but I had a good night and am quite fresh today.

I spent the morning with Henry [Cadbury] and Bertram [Crosfield] and afterwards with Parke, lunching with him and hearing a very interesting account of his 6 mos imprisonment in 1890 for libelling Lord Euston.[100] Parke had charged him with visiting some place of evil resort which there is no doubt he did but he got a conviction on some quibble despite the effort of Lockwood[101] and Asquith who were pleading for Parke. Parke managed to get 6 months of his time cancelled owing to the clever way in which he managed to starve himself – at least existing on 6 oz of bread and some tea each day. But he had six months of it!

[...]

I am not quite so happy about the Conference tomorrow because G.C.[adbury] insists on coming and wants to speak first of course the difficulty with the dear man is that no one knows what he may say. However I hope we shall pull through alright.

[...]

[99] The child was a girl and was christened Angela Margo Hamar Greenwood.

[100] Henry James FitzRoy, Earl of Euston (1848–1912), eldest s. of 7th Duke of Grafton, but predeceased his father.

[101] Sir Frank Lockwood (1846–1897), Lib. MP York 1885–1897; Solicitor-Gen. 1894–1895; kt. 1894.

23 November 1911
House of Commons

[...] I was at the office all the morning interviewing travellers and this
afternoon have spent a considerable amount of time with Dawson of
Kirbymoorside over the Insurance Bill. I have now just come from an
interesting meeting of Liberal and Labour men at the Suffrage question
at which Lloyd George has been present. I believe he is most absolutely
sincere in his desire to get some enfranchised on a broad and democratic
basis and a great effort is going to be made in revivifying the Peoples'
Suffrage Federation[102] and make it into a really effective fighting
organisation backed by 200 members of Parliament.

23 November 1911
Thackeray Hotel – 11.30 pm

I have just got back from the House darling. The debate was not very
satisfactory and I was forced in the end into voting against the
government and with the labour people but finally we got a unanimous
vote asking the Government to arrange a meeting between the directors
and the men.[103] I am glad to find that Henderson[104] and Thomas[105] are
quite satisfied and feel that a meeting is now inevitable and if so no
strike will take place.

I spoke for a minute or two but gave way for George who wanted
to explain the government attitude.

The Conference seems now quite a thing of the past – everything
went off well and we were all preserved in a spirit of love and
unity and quite enjoyed ourselves! After prayer from T.H.[odgkin]
and G.C.[adbury] the latter spoke of his connection with the DN.

---

[102] People's Suffrage Federation; an umbrella organization founded in 1909 by the
Women's Trade Union League, the Women's Co-operative Guild and the Womens'
Labour League to campaign for the enfranchisement of all adults, rather than of women
under the existing suffrage law.
[103] *Hansard*, 5th series, 1911, XXXI, 1311–1312. A.S.R. seconded a motion urging the
rail companies to recognize the unions.
[104] Arthur Henderson (1863–1935), Lab. MP Barnard Castle 1903–1918, Widnes 1919–
1922, E. Newcastle January–December 1923, Burnley 1924–1931, Clay Cross 1933–
October 1935; Pres. Bd of Education 1915–1916, War Cabinet 1916–1917, Home Sec.
1924, Foreign Sec. 1929–1931, Leader Lab. Party 1908–1910, 1914–1917, 1931–1932, Sec.
Lab. Party 1912–1935.
[105] James Henry Thomas (1874–1949), Lab. MP (Nat. Lab. from 1931) Derby January
1910–1936; Sec. of State Colonies 1924, 1935–1936, Ld Privy Seal 1929–1930, Sec. of
State Dominions 1930–1935. Leading figure in the Nat. Union of Railwaymen, of which
he was Sec. 1918–1931.

I then consumed the rest of the time until lunch with my matters. After an excellent lunch I continued, followed by Cross, Bertram [Crosfield] and Edward [Cadbury]. The first result was that we got our case well presented. The friends were I think genuinely interested and sympathetic and we decided to have a weekend at Uffculme[106] Dec. 16 and 17 to really see if we together could construct a definite policy for dealing with the whole question. It has baffled the best minds up to now.

We adjourned at 4.30 and when Richard [Cross], Ernest,[107] W.C.B.[raithwaite] and I were having tea together afterwards we were much amused by a sleepy man walking in and asking if Sir Edward Fry was present! We answered no and then he said is Mr Rowntree? It then transpired he was a Yorkshire Post representative wanting news of what was done! Some papers would have given I should think many thousand pounds to know all the revelations that were made. G.N.[ewman] was here last night – he is still being pressed by George to become an Insurance Commissioner. [...]

Farewell darling one. I feel relieved the Conference is so well over and don't think there is now any fear of serious mischief being done. They certainly desire to help and there is the most perfect spirit of tolerance amongst us and real freedom.

If thou wants to hear more ring up E.E.T.[aylor] at the Works.

29 November 1911
en route to Manchester

[...] The Meetings last night were a great success – one big one of 3500 and two overflows. The Liberals at Sunderland are very confident and certainly Greenwood seems catching on. There is a good story of an interjection at one of Joynson-Hicks's[108] meetings. He had been saying he was in favour of devolution because then Redmond would go back

---

[106] Uffculme; home in Birmingham of Barrow Cadbury, nephew of George Cadbury. Lent to the Adult School movement 1907–1914.

[107] Ernest Edwin Taylor (1869–1955), Quaker historian; close friend of A.S.R. and Sec. North of England Newspaper Co. 1906–1921, Westminster Press 1921–1933; Hon. Sec. JRSST and Charitable Trust 1916–1936. His bro., Frederic, m. A.S.R.'s sister, Gertrude, in 1898.

[108] William Joynson-Hicks (1865–1932), Con. MP North West Manchester 1908–January 1910, Brentford 1911–1918, Twickenham 1918–1929, when cr. Vt Brentford; PS Overseas Trade 1922–1923, Postmaster-Gen. 1923, Fin. Sec. to Treasury 1923, Min. of Health 1923–1924, Home Sec. 1924–1929. Had been unsuccessful Con. cand. Sunderland December 1910; Bt 1919.

to Ireland, Lloyd George to Wales – and then the voice shouted 'and Samuel,[109] Samuel to Jerusalem!'

Greenwood had tea with Mrs Asquith a day or so before leaving town. She was in very good spirits and said that the King was very friendly with Herbert [Asquith] – he had got satisfactory guarantees and then to show his friendship with democracy he invited Asquith, Lloyd George and Winston [Churchill] with their wives to the palace for this last weekend. She also said that it was quite the thing now at court to talk liberal!

[...]

I have been round by Hartlepool and spoke to a somewhat critical audience there. Furness[110] is having a hard fight and there seems a frightful amount of distress there. [...]

6 December 1911
House of Commons

A comfortable journey darling and I reached the House in time to hear George's slashing onslaught greatly cheered by the liberals.[111] I think perhaps it was a little too much overdone. I have seen T.P.[O'Connor] and he wants to come to us despite the dry house! and guessed that was the difficulty! The Finance Bill will not come on in committee stage until Monday so that means my departure first thing that day. [...]

I have arranged a private interview with George tomorrow afternoon.

7 December 1911
House of Commons

Last night's final scenes were very exciting, the Tories didn't at all know what to do about voting when the 3rd reading was firstly put but

[109] Herbert Louis Samuel (1870–1963), Lib. MP Cleveland 1902–1918, Darwen 1929–1935; US Home Office 1905–1909, Chanc. Duchy of Lancaster 1909–1910, Postmaster-Gen. 1910–1914, 1915–1916, Pres. Local Govt Bd 1914–1915, Home Sec. 1916, 1931–1932, High Commissioner in Palestine 1920–1925, Leader Lib. Party 1931–1935; GBE 1920, cr. Vt Samuel 1937. First practising Jew to hold Cabinet office.
[110] Stephen Wilson Furness (1872–1914), Lib. MP Hartlepool June 1910–1914; Bt 1913.
[111] Lloyd George's contribution to the Third Reading of the National Insurance Bill, 1911 was a sustained attack on a misleading pamphlet on the Bill produced by Lord Robert Cecil.

thou would see that practically all of them abstained.[112] Bonar Law's
speech was very clever – much better than Balfour would have done,
but as Asquith said, if all he stated was true it was a reason for dividing
against the bill not for a reasoned amendment.

[...]

I have just seen Elibank darling and he cannot come until the night
train so he is going to the hotel and will come to us to breakfast.[113]
Illingworth[114] expects to come with me by the 5.30. I have seen George
this afternoon but the Cabinet will not alter their decision about the
Cocoa duties which are now going to be taken on Monday afternoon.
I am going to dine with Ted and Irene [Harvey] here. Now it is post
time.

11 December 1911
House of Commons

Just a line darling to let thee know that I had a pleasant journey with
T.P.[O'Connor] and Leif Jones.[115] The former I think really enjoyed
his stay with us.

I didn't take part in the amusing debate this afternoon[116] – they tried
hard to draw me but whatever I said would have been misrepresented
and I think I was wise in holding my peace – at any rate several
members have congratulated me on my wisdom.

12 December 1911
House of Commons

I have not much to report, darling. I dined last night with G.N.[ewman]
and J.A. Baker here and then we were late – happily I got away at 12

[112] On the Third Reading of the National Insurance Bill, 1911 only eleven Conservatives
voted against the Bill.

[113] The Yorkshire Liberal Federation organized a Home Rule demonstration at the
Festival Concert Room in York on 9 December 1911. T.P. O'Connor was the main
speaker and he and Elibank took the opportunity to meet Yorkshire Libs and reassure
them about the government's intentions.

[114] Percy Holden Illingworth (1869–1915), Lib. MP Shipley 1906–1915; junior whip
1910–1912, Chief Whip 1912–1915.

[115] Leifchild Stratten Jones (1862–1939), Lib. MP Appleby 1905–January 1910, Rushcliffe,
December 1910–1918, Camborne 1923–1924, 1929–1931; Pres. United Kingdom Alliance
1906–1932; cr. Ld Rhayader 1932.

[116] The debate on the changes to the cocoa duty during the committee stages of the
Finance Bill; *Hansard*, 5th series, 1911, XXXII, 1947–1990.

but most had to stay until 4 am. Dr Messer[117] and his boy had breakfast with me at the Thackeray and then I went off to our office. Lunch at the NLC with the Nation people and have dined again with G.N.[ewman] at the Reform tonight. He is evidently getting great influence over Pease who takes him into his closest confidence and who is *very* anxious to do well and keenly anxious to work. Thou willst notice in the papers tomorrow the appointment of Selby-Bigge[118] in Morant's place. G.N.[ewman] thinks on the whole it is the best appointment.

I have paired again for tonight from 11 pm and am off with Ted [Harvey] to Hammersmith.

[...]

14 December 1911
Queens Hotel, Birmingham – 8 pm

[...]
This morning I had a very interesting talk with C.P. Scott[119] of the Manchester Guardian about the newspaper problem and felt great unity with his view and spirit.

I had Parke to lunch at the Reform and talked further with him on the question and after a short time at the House escaped and came here by the express [...].

I expect Richard [Cross] and Ernest Taylor tomorrow afternoon to talk over the case we are to put before the committee and then in the evening I meet along with Richard [Cross] and Walter Barrow several Adult School men to discuss with them the right attitude to adopt towards the Insurance Bill.

[...]

[117] Dr Messer, Medical Officer of Health and active figure in the Adult School movement.
[118] Lewis Amherst Selby-Bigge (1860–1951), PUS Bd of Education 1911–1925; KCB 1913, Bt 1919.
[119] Charles Prestwich Scott (1846–1932), Lib. MP Leigh 1895–1905; Ed. *Manchester Guardian* 1872–1929.

CHAPTER 3

Letters 1912

14 February 1912
House of Commons

The house is 'up' darling – I am shortly going off to the Reform Club with Dr Addison for dinner and then I shall go on to the 'Miracle'.

Asquith was wonderful today and there is little left of Bonar Law.[1] All he says about Germany is most encouraging, and the way in which he drew from him what he meant with respect to the Insurance Bill is of course splendid material for liberals. All our men are very happy over the turn of events and the Govt will do well to force the Tories to make good their charge of corruption. The Tories are now wanting 'a new leader'.

The function in the Lords was tame and sombre – but the King looked very well and sunburnt but he has an unpleasant rough voice.

I enjoyed my visit to Newcastle – we had a good meeting and the people were all very kind. I stayed with Wedgwood[2] at his mother's house – a beautiful old dame living in an old country farm mansion.

[...]

15 February 1912
House of Commons – 5.15

I am writing in a meeting of Liberal women and Liberal MPs discussing Women's suffrage, having just reached the House from Benson's where I have spent the whole day over advertising matters. [...] I went to the

---

[1] *Hansard*, 5th series, 1912, XXXIV, 28–38. Asquith's speech on the Address praised Haldane's mission to Berlin for exploratory talks with the German government, as well as drawing from Bonar Law the admission that he would repeal the National Insurance Act. Asquith also challenged Bonar Law to prove his allegations that Liberals were receiving preferential treatment in appointments to the civil service.

[2] Josiah Clement Wedgwood (1872–1943), Lib. MP (Lab. from 1919) Newcastle-under-Lyme 1906–1942, when cr. Ld Wedgwood; Chanc. Duchy of Lancaster 1924. His mother was Emily Catherine Wedgwood (1840–1920) and her house was Barlaston Lea.

'Miracle' last night with Whitehouse[3] and was very much impressed with it though it is rather gruesome in some places. Uncle John Edmund[4] was there and I walked back with him. I fear I shall not reach home tomorrow until after 9.00 pm as I have to meet several of our travellers tomorrow afternoon.

A national ballot of the Miners' Federation on 18 January 1912 had produced an overwhelming majority for a national strike to secure a minimum wage. The government attempted to mediate from 20 February onwards, but the strike began on 1 March and was not called off until 4 April 1912.

27 February 1912
House of Commons – 6.15 pm

I am writing darling in a meeting of the broad franchise MPs[5] and am hoping that by this time thou art safely at Southport and hast had a happy journey with the bairns.

I have had a fairly active day first with Henry Cadbury and Bertram Crosfield at the DN, then a business conference at Benson's, lunch with the Nation board and this afternoon an Insurance Committee[6] besides this one which is now going on.

I am having quite an interesting dinner party tonight – Ted, Irene [Harvey], Arthur,[7] Dr Addison, Phil,[8] Mr Wiles[9] and his daughter. The reports tonight respecting the strike are more hopeful but the miners are very cautious in saying yet what the result will be but I gather the government is taking a very decided line in urging the minimum wage upon the owners.

I fear I have no further news and it is almost impossible to write anything whilst the discussion goes forward.

[3] John Howard Whitehouse (1873–1955), Lib. MP Mid-Lanarkshire January 1910–1918; PPS Lloyd George 1913–1915; employed Cadbury Bros. 1894–1903; resident at Toynbee Hall 1905–1908, where a mutual passion for Ruskin cemented a close friendship with T.E. Harvey; became a Quaker c. 1917; founder and Headmaster Bembridge School 1919–1954.
[4] John Edmund Whiting (1853–1932), brother of M.K.R.'s mother; head of family firm, Hotham & Whiting. Much involved in temperance and foreign mission work.
[5] MPs who favoured universal adult suffrage, rather than the enfranchisement of women under the existing voting qualifications.
[6] National Insurance Cttee, Lib. Party organization set up by the Chief Whip, the Master of Elibank, to promote the popularity of National Insurance.
[7] Arthur Bevington Gillett (1875–1954), A.S.R.'s first cousin; partner in Gillett & Co., bankers in Banbury.
[8] Philip Harvey, brother of M.K.R.; farmer.
[9] Thomas Wiles (1861–1951), Lib. MP South Islington 1906–1918; PPS T. McKinnon Wood 1911–1912.

28 February 1912
House of Commons – 5.50

We all seem living in a state of great tension not knowing what the next hour may bring forth. I have just seen Brace,[10] one of the miner's leaders, and he reports badly of the way in which negotiations are going and yet he says he expects a turn soon. He says Asquith has been doing splendidly in manner and matter. I think I have felt the suspense more because our advertising scheme which we were going to launch on Friday is valueless if there is going to be a strike and so all arrangements have had to be made conditionally which has of course made it more difficult.[11] We had a pleasant dinner party last night darling and happily all to ourselves in a private room and I think Arthur [Gillett] and Phil [Harvey] enjoyed it. Gladys Wiles, her father tells me is down with fever today – the result I suppose of a vegetarian meal! Arthur stayed the night with me [...].

This morning I spent at Bensons, had lunch with Mr Parke at the Reform Club to talk over paper matters and this evening as there is a private members motion on I think I may perhaps go to 'Bunty' as I feel to need a change. [...]

[...]

The Tories are lying frightfully over the Insurance Bill. I have just seen a circular they are distributing in Manchester which says amongst other things the Insurance Bill 'halves the present benefits Friendly Societies give'.

29 February 1912
House of Commons – 6 pm

I hope thou hast not been too anxious darling over the coal strike. I really don't think thou need fear as to any difficulty in returning. I have just seen one of the miners' leaders who says the PM is doing wonderfully in the negotiations and he has laid it down that a minority of coal owners *cannot* be allowed to hold up for any length of time the whole industry of the country and if they do not give in voluntarily they will be forced to by act of Parliament.

The government are however right I think in exhausting every effort

---

[10] William Brace (1865–1947), Lab. MP South Glamorgan 1906–1920; US Home Office 1915–1919; Pres. South Wales Miners' Federation 1911–1919.
[11] In February 1912 Rowntree & Co. opened a new campaign to promote Elect cocoa and chocolate, offering the public a 6d chocolate bar in return for a cocoa coupon and a 2d stamp.

to secure peace without legislation if that is possible. A stoppage of a few days will do no very serious harm because of the enormous stocks held all over the country and now that people know the strong line the PM has taken they are hopeful that a settlement will be reached. [...]

Frank [Sturge] is in the gallery and I must take him now to feed as he leaves for York shortly. [...]

1 March 1912
242 St James Ct – 6.40 pm

We have all left the House darling in very bad spirits – for the moment the negotiations have collapsed owing to the miners refusing to accept anything but their schedule of fixed rates of pay. This is all the more disappointing because before everything was going so well and it seemed as if Asquith was going to succeed. As a matter of fact I don't think there is much to be said against the miners' schedule but of course it is almost impossible for the government to accept it without at any rate first of all having evidence on both sides. I hope between now and Monday some way may be found to overcome this difficulty. At any rate we must try and peacefully and confidently live through it all. I am sure thou need not feel worried about being landed at Southport – stocks of coal held by the Railway Companies will certainly last out a fortnight as a limited service. I believe a month and this will be settled as far as England is concerned, much before that I still look to next week!

[...]

This move of the miners will I fear turn public opinion against them.

2 March 1912
Mount Villas

The dinner last night darling was a great success and I think Phil [Harvey] greatly enjoyed it.[12] Redmond's speech was excellent, in fact all the speeches were good but the failure of the Govt. to come to terms with the men took away from the sparkle of such an occasion – and of course people were very angry with these mad women[13] who

[12] On 1 March 1912 the Eighty Club held a dinner in Redmond's honour at the Hotel Cecil to mark the start of the Irish Home Rule Bill's parliamentary odyssey.

[13] The Women's Social and Political Union had resumed its violent campaign for women's suffrage on 1 March 1912 by smashing hundreds of windows in West End shops (and at 10 Downing St).

are really ruining their cause. The effect that this wild agitation is having on members I think most serious. [...]

After tea I am going down to this gathering of Liberal secretaries at Bowes [Morrell]'s house [...].

[...]

There is no further news to report about the strike. I expect we shall have to wait a few days before we see much change. If as the week progresses it looks as if things are getting worse it occurs to me that perhaps thou wouldst feel happier to reach Leeds say this day week and then I could join thee sometime on Sunday or possibly to tea on Saturday. [...]

4 March 1912
Doncaster Waiting Room – 5.40

I am finding these days somewhat exercising darling and at times feel it somewhat difficult to know exactly the right path to take. At the Works things are not altogether easy owing to the Elect difficulty now increased owing to the anxiety of the strike. My private affairs somewhat muddled owing to the collapse of Gillman who goes off to Devizes tomorrow for a month and also Miss Heslop[14] – then there are one's duties in London indefinite and yet just at this time one hardly likes to be away – and then the claims of family ties which do pull very strongly but which I know thou realizes are difficult for me to meet – and thou art most good and generous in excusing my deficiencies.

[...] I don't think I have much news to report – one's day was taken up at the Works with ordinary matters. I don't remember hearing anything of special interest.

There was an appeal from Miss Harrison[15] for Miss Feldwick[16] and I have sent her £10 with love from thee and me and encouraged Mamma to send her the same. The two enclosed letters have come for thee – the begging one is difficult I thought perhaps thou would get Miss Dale's[17] help so I have put her address on it.

I expect to find Seebohm [Rowntree] tonight at the flat and shall hope to get a good talk with him. He says Lydia[18] is having an operation tomorrow – she has not been right since the last baby appeared.

[...]

[14] Miss Heslop, A.S.R.'s secretary at the Cocoa Works.
[15] Emma Lucy Harrison (1844–1915), Headmistress, the Mount School 1890–1902.
[16] Miss Feldwick (1844?–1914), former housekeeper and matron the Mount School; retd 1912.
[17] Miss Dale, York social worker connected to the Bedern Mission.
[18] Lydia Rowntree (nee Potter) (1870–1944), m. Seebohm Rowntree 1897.

Thank thee darling for thy letter [...] I am feeling somewhat dull and done this week – this strike hangs heavily on one. I don't know how the prime movers in the negotiations manage to keep up. Spender was telling me he spent some time yesterday with George because they heard rumours that the suffragettes were going to shoot him and he never takes the slightest care of himself and he found him cheerful and confident, but Spender added he always does face a storm with courage and spirit. Seebohm [Rowntree] didn't stay with me last night after all as he felt he must get back to Lydia to support her in the operation that was taking place this morning. We had an hour together after his lecture. There is little to report of today's proceedings. I worked at home this morning – lunched with the Nation staff and then have been in the precincts of the house this afternoon wishing all the time I was at Southport!

I am going off shortly to dinner with George and Ada [Newman] at Ashley Gardens taking Addison along with me.

[...]

6 March 1912
House of Commons

I have been writing diligently darling and now the post goes in a few minutes. I went to dine with G.N.[ewman] yesterday and he bucked me up somewhat and I was glad to hear about the way in which the Tuberculosis Committee is setting to work. Then we walked back here to be greeted with the S. Manchester result,[19] which is distinctly worse than expected – very damaging. It prevented me sleeping much! but I am better today and had a happy breakfast party with the Greenwoods and Hogge.[20] Then went to the office and lunched at the Reform and have been writing here this afternoon. I think I shall shortly go off on the spree for the evening with Percy Alden returning here in time to vote on Wedgwood's land values resolution.[21] I don't quite see the right thing to do yet about coming to Southport but will wire or write tomorrow. There is a more hopeful view about this afternoon but though negotiations are proceeding there is nothing to build on as yet.

[19] The Liberals lost the seat of South Manchester in a by-election on 5 March 1912 on an 11 per cent swing.

[20] James Myles Hogge (1873–1928), Lib. MP East Edinburgh 1912–1924; Lib. whip 1919–1923. Worked closely with the Rowntrees in York, especially as sec. local Anti-Gambling League; councillor for Castlegate ward 1907–1913 and leading Lib. member of York Council.

[21] *Hansard*, 5th series, 1912, XXXV, 464–502 for Wedgwood's motion on site value rating. It was not carried to a vote.

[...] Gilbert comes to me tonight and G.N.[ewman] comes in for breakfast.

12 March 1912
House of Commons

The train last night was very crowded and Richard [Cross] and I had to find seats in the 3rd class diner, the first was absolutely full. Still we were not very late and found T.H.A.[ppleton] waiting for us on arrival. He looks very well and brown and reports J.R.[owntree] as being in good spirits and very vigorous. It has been very hot and fine every day he has been there with the exception of the Sabbath when he went to Scotch Kirk and found that dry enough.

We talked business matters until nearly 1 am and then were rewarded with good nights. My morning was spent in letter writing and a conference with Parke – then I lunched with the Nation group and have been at the House since. I have attended a meeting of liberal and labour MPs respecting the conciliation bill[22] and am really alarmed at the critical position in which the bill stands at the present time – but thou better not open up that subject to Hettie![23]

This evening Drysdale Woodcock,[24] future MP for Southport, is dining with me here so that he may talk to Sherwell and to Richard [Cross] on future licensing prospects and give his views to them.
[...]
Ted [Harvey] tells me he is in Leeds on Thursday and Friday of this week and is hoping I believe to stay at the Grove so I am rejoicing in thinking thou will't have his company. Poor boy, he is somewhat perplexed today by understanding that he may possibly be asked to be junior whip vice Haworth![25] and if he is it will be very difficult to know what answer to give. I can hardly imagine Ted pressing MPs to vote against their consciences! But of course probably someone else will be asked and I should in many ways feel thankful if Ted was spared the difficulty of making this choice.
[...]

[22] The Parliamentary Franchise (Women) Bill, which proposed to enfranchise women under the existing voting system, was defeated on its Second Reading on 28 March 1912.
[23] Henrietta Louisa Rowntree (1864–1936), widow of A.S.R.'s brother, James Edward Rowntree (1869–1904).
[24] Hubert Bayley Drysdale Woodcock (1867–1957), barrister and unsuccessful Lib. cand. Canterbury January 1910, Southport December 1910, Chatham 1918.
[25] Sir Arthur Adlington Haworth (1865–1944), Lib. MP South Manchester 1906–1912; Bt 1911. Lost his seat when he sought re-election after appointment as a junior whip.

20 March 1912
House of Commons

The position is again serious darling as the miners federation by a majority have refused to accept the Government's bill and insist on the H. of C. inserting the schedule which I believe is quite impossible.[26]

There is gloom and depression here as a result – but somehow I feel we shall pull through and it certainly does one good to be with W.C.B.[raithwaite] [...].

I have had three hours talk with J.R.[owntree] this morning at my rooms – chiefly on paper developments. He is splendidly well and cheerful – as Sherwell has just told me, the only cheerful person today over the coal strike that he has met – has greatly enjoyed Cannes which I gather has answered nicely for Auntie[27] and as usual with such splendid judgement and counsel. He says he saw Chamberlain[28] at Cannes looking better than last year. Some visitor at their hotel had heard Chamberlain talking and saying that the right thing to do to end the strike was to shoot D.A. Thomas![29]

W.C.B.[raithwaite] dined with me last night. I showed him a sight which would hardly be possible in any other country – D.A. Thomas laughing, talking to Ramsay MacDonald and T.P. O'Connor embracing D.A. Thomas and counselling him as to the way he should walk!

21 March 1912
House of Commons

I am sitting in the House listening to Sir Alfred Mond[30] discoursing, but if I am going to get a letter off to thee darling tonight I must write whilst in the House.

---

[26] On 19 March 1912 Asquith had introduced the Coal Mines (Minimum Wage) Bill in an attempt to settle the strike. The Union rejected it, on the grounds that it did not include their demand for a minimum of 5s per day for men and 2s per day for boys.

[27] Emma Antoinette Rowntree (nee Seebohm) (1846–1924), second wife of Joseph Rowntree.

[28] Joseph Chamberlain (1836–1914), Lib. MP Birmingham 1876–1885, West Birmingham 1885–1914 (LU from 1886); Pres. Bd of Trade 1880–1885, Pres. Local Govt Bd 1886, Sec. of State Colonies 1895–1903. Incapacitated by a stroke 1906.

[29] David Alfred Thomas (1856–1918), Lib. MP Merthyr Tydfil 1888–January 1910, Cardiff January–December 1910; Pres. Local Govt Bd 1916–1917, Food Controller 1917–1918; cr. Ld Rhondda 1916, Vt 1918; leading South Wales coal owner and merchant.

[30] Sir Alfred Moritz Mond (1868–1930), Lib. MP Chester 1906–January 1910, Swansea January 1910–1918, West Swansea 1918–1923, Carmarthenshire August 1924–1928 (Con. from 1926); First Commissioner of Works 1916–1921, Min. of Health 1921–1922; Bt 1910, cr. Ld Melchett 1928. Mond was speaking on the Coal Mines (Minimum Wage) Bill.

The debate this afternoon has been very interesting – the difference between Balfour and Bonar Law is *very* wide and the House greatly enjoyed his speech though he seemed in a difficult position and I felt really was very doubtful of the policy he was recommending.[31] The feeling here is that if the Government would accept the minimum of 5/- for men, 2/- for boys, the miners would accept the bill and advise return to work. But the Govt. are hesitating.

I went to R.J. Campbell's[32] midday service this morning and greatly enjoyed his sermon on God is our life and length of days. Afterwards I went down to Spear and Pond's to lunch with the expectation of seeing Parke and came upon Fred Taylor and J.W. Hoyland[33] lunching and joined them.

Hewins[34] the new member for Hereford is now lecturing the House, not a very successful maiden effort.

[...]

25 March 1912
On East Coast Dining Car Express between England and Scotland

Essie [Sarah Elizabeth Rowntree] met me at York this morning, darling, and went up with me to the Works. Mamma had meant to come but was not very well as she had a dizzy bout yesterday. I think thou should telephone her tomorrow if thou feels like it and buck her up a little. Essie gave a good account of Hilda[35] and the bairn and said Frank Sturge thought that none of the Bootham masters were going to apply for the Leighton Park[36] post. He thought Unwin[37] had been privately approached but they are all frightened of Leighton Park's long list of ruined reputations!

[31] In the Second Reading debate on the Coal Mines (Minimum Wage) Bill, Balfour advocated its rejection, while Bonar Law on 19 March had not gone so far.

[32] Revd Reginald John Campbell (1867–1956), famous Congregational minister at the City Temple Church 1903–1915, and exponent of the liberal New Theology; converted to Anglicanism 1916.

[33] John William Hoyland (1855–1927), brother-in-law of George Cadbury and Warden of Kingsmead, a college for missionaries founded by Cadbury.

[34] William Albert Samuel Hewins (1865–1931), Con. MP Hereford 1912–1918; US Colonies 1917–1919; Dir. London School of Economics 1895–1903, Tooke Prof. of Economic Science and Statistics, King's College London 1897–1903; Sec. Tariff Commission 1903–1917.

[35] Hilda Mallinson Rowntree (1874–1968), youngest sister of A.S.R.; married to Henry Isaac Robson (1873–1964). Both were medical missionaries in India.

[36] Leighton Park, Quaker public school for boys at Reading.

[37] Ernest Ewart Unwin (1881–1944), biology master at Bootham School; he took the job at Leighton Park, but emigrated to Tasmania in the 1920s.

I had a busy morning at the Works – at the Board Meeting we decided to raise our labourers minimum wage as quickly as we could to 28/-.

We managed to get that 160 tons of coal last week and with the economies that we effected think we can go on for another fortnight at any rate, which is a relief.

[...]

[...] Farewell darling – we are nearing London and I am hoping that there may be better news about the strike.

27 March 1912
242 St James Ct

After talking to thee this morning I went back to bed for two hours and then as it was a beautiful morning, after arranging to lunch with G.N.[ewman], I strolled out into Hyde Park and walked as far as the Albert Hall. The signs of spring were cheering, the hyacinths and daffodils most beautiful and there seemed thousands of people abroad showing no signs of being affected by this strike. I carefully scanned a few of the side streets, darling, to see whether there were any houses vacant that looked attractive but saw nothing suitable but I increasingly feel that if it is my duty to keep in Parliament we must make some fresh arrangement about living. I don't believe it can be right my being practically divorced from thee and the kiddies because though the time we are together at home is comparatively short yet one or two hours makes all the difference.

Yesterday was very interesting though very sad and I still have the feeling that Asquith, after securing virtual agreement on the big issues between masters and men failed in a comparatively small point – but there is no doubt that the general view of the party is that it would not have done to yield to the Labour Party's request for insertion of the 5 & 2. Asquith was really very much moved in his speech in the House and was most agreeable to us in private conversation.[38]

The future is uncertain but I feel now that probably we shall see the English miners working in a fortnight.

I had lunch with G.N.[ewman], very bright and cheering as usual, and since then have been reading and writing here as there was little on at the House of importance. I am now (6.15) going there and expect to meet Seebohm [Rowntree] for dinner.

[...]

[38] *Hansard*, 5th series, 1912, XXXVI, 231–234.

16 April 1912
242 St James Court

[...] Parke met me at the station. I fear from what he says there is difficulty between him and one or two of the Daily News people. They really are *very* stupid over some things. On reaching London I heard of course of this awful loss of life which I had disbelieved previously and which completely staggers me.[39] One thing certainly impresses me that in that barbarian assembly it wasn't the millionaire that was first saved but women and children – that one fact speaks volumes.

I went to the Nation lunch to see some of the folk. I want to arrange a long weekend at Scalby[40] or some place in May with Hobson, Hobhouse,[41] J.R.[owntree], B.S.R.[owntree] and others to come to close quarters respecting the question of the minimum wage and how to meet the just demands of labour to a fair share of the wealth of the country.[42]

At the House several members have specially asked after thee. Runciman was most solicitous. I haven't heard much of the debate being busy with other matters [...].

17 April 1912
242 St James Court, SW

[...]
[...]The debate closed with a most rasping and offensive though able speech from Bonar Law and the House afterwards was too excited to listen to Birrell.[43]

---

[39] The sinking of the *Titanic*, 15 April 1912.

[40] Scalby, residential home for Quaker conferences near Scarborough; originally the home of John Wilhelm Rowntree.

[41] Leonard Trelawny Hobhouse (1865–1929), social philosopher and journalist for Lib. newspapers, including the *Nation*.

[42] The outcome of this idea was the memorandum sent to Lloyd George on 20 May 1912 by A.S.R., Seebohm and Joseph Rowntree, E.R. Cross, H.W. Massingham, J.A. Hobson, L.T. Hobhouse and Percy Alden. It argued for a general extension of the principle of the minimum wage and was an important formative influence on Lloyd George's Land Campaign.

[43] *Hansard*, 5th series, 1912, XXXVII, 285–301 and 301–310 for the closing speeches by Bonar Law and Birrell on 16 April 1912 on the First Reading of the Home Rule Bill.

24 April 1912
House of Commons

I had a comfortable journey darling – the train was full of corporation officials and gas co. directors coming up for the Committee.[44] I entertained the LM, Town Clerk and three others to tea this afternoon. Since then I have been in the Liberal Insurance Committee. Elibank and the leading officials are much pleased at the suggested posters and illustrated book I have got Bensons to prepare and are I think going to adopt them. I have ordered a horse tomorrow for a trot so shall experiment in Rotten Row!

[...]

29 April 1912
House of Commons

Just a line darling to let thee know that I had a comfortable journey travelling most of the way with J.A. Pease and having quite a good chat with him. I was in the gov. committee for two hours and since then have been talking over Insurance matters with Lees Smith. The Town Clerk has promised to let me give my evidence tomorrow so I quite hope I shall get home tomorrow night probably by the 8 o'clock train.

30 May 1912
Tyn-Llwy-Dan, Ty-Croes, Anglesey[45]

I found Joe Eddington[46] at the station awaiting me last night on arrival at Bodorgan darling and Mr Williams[47] drove us back here – a drive of about four miles which we reached about 10 pm. .

Sir George Meyrick[48] owns most of the land about here but Mr Williams has about 250 acres of freehold squeezed in between Meyrick's land and it is upon this land (which is the farm at which Frederic

---

[44] A private bill, the York United Gas Bill, was due to be considered by a select cttee in the House of Lords. The gas co. wanted to extend its operations over a further seven miles. The Libs on the Council opposed this, as it would make it more difficult to municipalize the company.

[45] Holiday home of George and Ada Newman.

[46] Joseph Clark Eddington (1872–1931), Quaker; high-class furniture maker.

[47] Owen Williams, son of the owner of Tyn-Llwy-Dan.

[48] Sir George Augustus Eliott Tapps-Gervis-Meyrick, Bt (1855–1928), owned 17,000 acres; JP and Dep. Lieutenant in Anglesey; succ. as 4th Bt 1896.

Seebohm[49] stayed and from which he studied and wrote on the Welsh tribal system) that the White Huts are erected. They are of the simplest character – the whole establishment costing I think about £100. [...]

[...]

Joe [Eddington] and Carol[50] seem to have settled things up two days ago, but the intention has evidently been of long duration and they certainly don't seem like a newly engaged couple. George [Newman] and Janet[51] are merry as usual. Ada [Newman] and Carol seem to run the domestic side of the establishment with much success.

[...]

31 May 1912
Tyn-Llwy-Dan

The letters came at 8 am. I was glad to get thine darling and also the shoes. After writing thee yesterday, George [Newman], Joe [Eddington] and I walked across the moor to Aberffraw to shop. It is a little town of 500 inhabitants – many living in wretched hovels because their great landlord Sir George Meyrick who owns practically half of Anglesey will not sell any of his land for new houses. The man I talked to told me there were six of them in the family – he had two sleeping rooms and paid 1/6 for the house, received 10/- wage and victuals as farm labourer – couldn't get any allotment because of Meyrick's refusal to let or sell land, and yet tried to be happy! I believe public opinion would support almost any action to compel these landlords to do their duty in letting or selling land when needed for the development of such towns. [...]

1 June 1912
Tyn-Llwy-Dan

[...] I have received a letter from Seebohm [Rowntree] saying that the Conference[52] arranged for Tuesday is postponed so I think probably I shall not go up to London next week at all.

[...]

---

[49] Frederic Seebohm (1833–1912), bro. of Joseph Rowntree's first wife, Julia Elizabeth Seebohm (1841–1863); banker, author, among many other historical works, of *The Tribal System in Wales* (1895).

[50] Caroline Elizabeth Newman (1876–1950), sister of George Newman; she finally married Eddington in 1913.

[51] Dr Janet Mary Campbell (d. 1954), Senior Medical Officer at Bd of Education; DBE 1924.

[52] Conference on the future of the Adult School movement.

10 June 1912
St James Court

I may not have another opportunity darling of sending thee a line
today so whilst I am waiting for the conference members to turn up I
will begin to write. It was good seeing thee at the station but there was
little time to say much. Scalby has really been a remarkable time but
it leaves several very urgent and large problems for solution. It is clear
that Gilbert is not up to the general organisation of the movement and
of course neither Fullwood nor Boyd[53] are equal to it so it seems as if
we should have to find someone else. If so it seems to point to getting
the really biggest man we can. I don't know whether Currie Martin[54]
would be at all likely but G.N.[ewman] and I were having a great talk
on the way up and incline to the view that probably the time has come
now to stop playing with the movement and secure leaders who shall
effectively build on the magnificent foundations that have been laid.
Parliament seems at present to be going almost faster than the people
are prepared for. I mean that all the measures to be adequately carried
out make a tremendous call on voluntary labour and that the difficulty
of supplying these calls is owing to the absence of really *educated* men
and women. The Adult School with its religious basis, with its call to
service through education, seems the channel through which democracy
might be touched if only we had effective organisation and leaders. It
is pathetic to hear of the collapses in different parts of the country and
the ineffective work being done because of the absence of the right
leaders.

But I will talk to thee about all this later. Seebohm [Rowntree] has
just arrived and is expecting Roden Buxton and Massingham and
Alden.

11 June 1912
House of Commons – 7.50 pm

I wasn't able darling to get a letter off by the first post as I was occupied
with others after 7. Seebohm [Rowntree] and Richard [Cross] stayed
with me last night and we had quite a satisfactory preliminary conference
with some housing authorities and an interesting professor from the

[53] Ebenezer John Fullwood, Asst Sec. NASU 1907–1933. David Parker Boyd (1857–
1935), shared this post 1906–1917. Boyd was a convert to Quakerism.
[54] George Currie Martin (d. 1937), Congregational minister and missionary; Supervisor
Lecture Services NASU 1912–1930. His salary was paid by the Joseph Rowntree
Charitable Trust.

University of Liege dined with us. This morning we talked before
breakfast and then I spent the morning with Seebohm preparing for
this afternoon. We had lunch with the Nation authorities and then had
another gathering of our Scalby conference which ended earlier than
we expected owing to Seebohm's careful preparations beforehand.
Seebohm and Richard left by the 6 o'clock train but then I had a good
talk with J.R.[owntree] about the development I outlined to you
yesterday. He has now come on with me to the House and is sitting
behind me now listening to Birrell. We are very shortly going to dine
with Ted [Harvey] and Silvester Horne.[55] I believe it was 25 years since
J.R.[owntree] was in the House and I am so glad to have him. Bonar
Law is now speaking so he has done well to hear Asquith, Birrell and
Bonar Law in the short time he has been in.[56] Massingham has been
on to see George since our Conference[57] and he has invited us all to
breakfast at Downing Street next Tuesday.

18 June 1912
House of Commons

We had quite a satisfactory conference yesterday darling and an
interesting breakfast at Downing Street this morning. Besides our group
there were Rufus Isaacs,[58] Elibank, Simon, C.P. Scott, Hemmerde,[59]
Buxton and others. We had I thought an interesting conversation.
George is very keen to go in for a sweeping land and housing policy
and a small committee was appointed to initiate investigations in certain
directions. I rather hope Seebohm [Rowntree] will take the lead in this
though Acland[60] was appointed Chairman. It was most refreshing to
see George's desire to have the problem adequately tackled though I
was disappointed that he seemed doubtful whether anything drastic

---

[55] Revd Charles Silvester Horne (1865–1914), Lib. MP Ipswich January 1910–1914;
famous Congregational minister and leading figure in Brotherhood movement.

[56] *Hansard*, 5th series, 1912, XXXIX, 774–777 (Birrell), 777–781 (Bonar Law) on the Irish
Home Rule Bill in cttee. Asquith had spoken earlier (715–717) on the order to commit
the Bill to cttee.

[57] The conference that produced the memorandum of 20 May 1912 to Lloyd George.

[58] Sir Rufus Daniel Isaacs (1860–1935), Lib. MP Reading 1904–1913; Solicitor-Gen.
1910, Attorney-Gen. 1910–1913, Ld Chief Justice 1913–1921, Viceroy of India 1921–1926,
Foreign Sec. 1931; kt. 1910, cr. Ld Reading 1914, Vt 1916, Earl 1917, Marquess 1926.
Intimate friend of Lloyd George.

[59] Edward George Hemmerde (1871–1948), Lib. MP East Denbighshire August 1906–
December 1910, North West Norfolk 1912–1918, Lab. MP Crewe 1922–1924; fanatical
land taxer.

[60] Arthur Herbert Dyke Acland (1847–1926), Lib. MP Rotherham 1885–1899; Vice-
Pres. Cttee of Council on Education 1892–1895; succ. as 13th Bt 1919.

could be done until after another General Election but there is no doubt that he at any rate is in earnest about the matter.

Afterwards I worked with Percy Alden over the Insurance paper – lunched at the Nation and then have been here since with the exception of a call at the Liberal Insurance Committee office. [...]

19 June 1912
House of Commons

[...]
I spent the morning at St James Court – then conferring with Seebohm [Rowntree] (and Lydia has landed up at my flat to stay a few days as all hotels seem full!) and then I went to Marylebone to see the Revd Morrison[61] and his schools. He is the liberal churchman who writes for the Nation and he had pressed me for some time to go and see his work. I stayed to lunch with him and his son-in-law, the son of Sir Albert Spicer,[62] was there with his little child and then afterwards went to Martin Bros and spent £25 in buying crockery! [...]

Since then I have been here and am shortly going to vote for a second chamber for Ireland! – much against the grain.[63]

[...]
Just off to Roden Buxton's to dinner.

2 July 1912
House of Commons

I am writing, darling, in a meeting of MPs and representatives of various women's societies discussing tactics over amendments to the Franchise Bill.[64] I have little to report to thee as I have had a somewhat dull day.

[61] Revd William Douglas Morrison (1852–1943), clergyman and journalist, especially on the subject of prison reform, in *Daily Chronicle* and *Nation*. Rector of Crown living of Marylebone 1908–1941.
[62] Sir Albert Spicer (1847–1934), Lib. MP Monmouth Boroughs 1892–1900, Central Hackney 1906–1918; Bt 1906. His eldest s., Dykes Spicer (1880–1966), married Alice Morrison 1910.
[63] *Hansard*, 5th series, 1912, XXXIX, 1700–1746 for the debate on a motion by two Lib. backbenchers against a second chamber for the Irish Parliament. A.S.R. voted against as the Conservatives backed the motion.
[64] The government had introduced a Franchise and Registration Bill on 6 June 1912. It was intended that the Bill could be amended so as to include women within the new franchise.

[...] I spent most of the morning over Insurance matters at Bensons and lunched at the Reform Club with Hannah G.[65]

[...]

3 July 1912
House of Commons

[...] I found Seebohm [Rowntree] and Richard [Cross] at my rooms on my return last night and today they have had a satisfactory opportunity with L.G. L.G. is much impressed with Seebohm's efficiency.

I visited Parke and Henry Cadbury at the DN offices this morning. On the whole the amalgamation[66] has gone through better than they expected and the circulation of the DN keeps about ½ million.

I had lunch with Seebohm and several of his land group including Heath[67] (of Woodbrooke) who has I understand been appointed to be paid secretary of the committee this afternoon.

[...]

Ted [Harvey] has agreed to become private Sec. to Ellis Griffith – his first step towards the official politician!

10 July 1912
242 St James Ct

We have just finished the first part of our committee[68] darling – W.C.B.[raithwaite] and I have got to draft the report which I must get at directly. I have been to the H. of C. for my letters. I therefore must not enlarge now except to say that we unite in feeling we must obtain the help of competent men to give their time to helping the leaders up and down the country, men of the type of Hibbert[69] to teach the teachers.

Thou willst be glad to know that neither Parke nor Cousin Janet[70]

[65] Hannah Elizabeth Gillett (nee Rowntree) (1840–1931), aunt of A.S.R.
[66] The *Daily News* and *Morning Leader* had finally amalgamated in May 1912, under the sole ownership of the Cadburys.
[67] John St George Currie Heath (1882–1918), Lecturer Woodbrooke 1906–1912, Sec. Lloyd George's Land Enquiry 1912–1914, Warden Toynbee Hall 1914–1917; convert to Quakerism 1910.
[68] Cttee on reforming the administration of the Adult School movement.
[69] Gerald Kenway Hibbert (1872–1957), first warden Swarthmore settlement at Leeds 1909–1919, Head of Ackworth School 1919–1930, Reader at Woodbrooke 1930–1945; convert to Quakerism 1909.
[70] Dr Janet Campbell.

can come to us for Sunday. I am glad but believe it was right to ask them.

I have let the flat from tomorrow so have to clear out by 12 o'clock!

Tomorrow night I stay with G.N.[ewman] at the Hatch to talk over America and the details of our Conference today.

11 July 1912
The Reform Club

I feel fairly happy in the retrospect of yesterday's conference darling, and after dinner with E.E.T.[aylor] and W.C.B.[raithwaite] the latter and I spent the evening in drafting and report of the day's proceedings. I think the most important recommendations was that we considered the time had come when if we could get the right man we should appoint an Educational Secretary with possibly six or eight men and women under him who should give themselves to the kind of work Hibbert is doing in intensive work amongst leaders and potential leaders.

Everything depends upon getting just the right man as General Educational Secretary – a person who by his power and personality will be continually driving new men of power into the movement by visits to Universities, Boarding Schools, etc. – and today I have had Currie Martin to lunch with the thought in mind. He is free at the moment and evidently drawn to the concern but of course will want some days to dwell on the concern.

I am going to the PM's Garden Party for a few minutes this afternoon and then hope to catch the 5.20 train at Euston with G.N.[ewman] to talk over details of this new move and Canada.

It is very hot today and I feel quite unhappy in a frock coat and top hat.

[...]

15 July 1912
nearing London

I have had a comfortable but hot journey, darling, with Richard [Cross] and Walter Rea reading and gossiping most of the way. I hope to have Arnold Viccars[71] to dinner and as there is no division

---

[71] Arnold Viccars; important figure in the Adult Schools movement, from Leicester. Served as Convenor of the Lesson Handbook Compilation Cttee 1910–1936.

tonight shall try to get to Olive's[72] in decent time.

Oscar [Rowntree] was back at business looking well and very merry but he evidently doesn't consider himself quite well yet [...] Seebohm [Rowntree] was not at the Board as he and Lydia are up in town this week – the latter undergoing treatment I believe again. I didn't hear much authentic news about Hilda Westrope's wedding but it evidently was *very* sudden and performed before she had left Seebohm's employ. I am sorry for Mr and Mrs Westrope[73] as such mad proceedings of course encourage gossip.

[...] I have to see Wethered[74] at 3.45 (I will wire when I know) and am a little weakening about Windsor. Walter Rea says he does not like it nearly so much as the Buckingham Palace opportunity.

Lloyd George's speech[75] is excellent and if thou hast not read it I think thou wouldst enjoy doing so – there is a good account in today's 'Manchester Guardian'.

22 July 1912
House of Commons

I had a comfortable journey darling and have heard Winston [Churchill], Balfour, Asquith and MacDonald on Navy policy. These naval debates are sorry opportunities – paganism pure and unabashed is rampant. It seems impossible to know how this mad campaign of shipbuilding will end.
[...]

23 July 1912
en route to Birmingham

Here I am speeding to Birmingham darling to see if I can forward the scheme I have in my mind. It seemed my only chance. I went off with

---

[72] Olive Hope Rowntree, cousin of A.S.R.'s from Scarborough branch of the family. Lived in London with her brother, Ernest Rowntree.

[73] Richard Westrope (1856–1941), former Congregational minister, known as 'Brother Richard' from his 1d edition of the classics, 'Brother Richard's Bookshelf'. First Warden York Educational Settlement 1909–1921. His daughter, Hilda Westrope, was a secretary at Rowntree & Co.

[74] Ernest Handel Cossham Wethered (1878–1975), barrister, active in Adult School movement in Bristol; Circuit Court Judge 1934–1950.

[75] Lloyd George's speech at Kennington Theatre on 13 July 1912 celebrated the inauguration of National Insurance on 15 July with a slashing attack on the Conservatives and *The Times* for their opposition to the measure.

Ted [Harvey] last night to late supper at Hammersmith hoping not to return to the House but I didn't feel quite comfortable to leave those labour fellows alone to vote against the increased Navy and so I returned to vote with the small minority of 42.[76]

I had a good night and enjoyed being with Ted and Irene [Harvey] and the comforts of their home. This morning I went to Hampstead with a few other MPs to see the garden suburb and was greatly interested in the advances there and the proposals for the future.

I lunched with G.N.[ewman] and Currie Martin at the Reform. I think probably Currie Martin is right for us but I cannot quite make up my mind.

Rufus[77] has written to say he will come to the Rockies. I find G.N.[ewman] is just a little fearful of whether he will be commandeered to start a National Health Service of Doctors if as expected they adhere to their stupid boycott!

The two points thou mentioned to me about the White Slave Traffic Bill[78] are being carefully considered by members and there is going to be an effort made to alter the bill in report.

[...]

I hope thou hast fared well at today's Liberal Meetings. [...]

24 July 1912
en route to London

I am just returning darling after an interesting visit to Selly Oaks.[79] I dined with the Wilsons at Selly Wood last night and finding it convenient agreed to sleep there as well. After dinner I went and had a long and interesting talk with Tom Bryan[80] and then on my return stayed up and chatted with Harry [Wilson] until midnight. [...] After breakfast I went to Woodbrooke to spend a little time with the Adult School

[76] On 22 July 1912, twenty-two Liberals, including A.S.R., voted for a Labour amendment criticizing the increased Navy estimates. *Hansard*, 5th series, 1912, XLI, 835–948 for the debate.

[77] Rufus Matthew Jones (1863–1948), leading American Quaker and close friend of A.S.R; Prof. of Philosophy at Haverford College, Pennsylvania.

[78] White Slave Traffic Bill, popular name of the Criminal Law Amendment Bill, 1912. This was a private member's bill which the government took over. It tightened up the law on prostitution.

[79] Selly Oaks; collective name of five educational colleges in Birmingham founded by George Cadbury.

[80] Tom Bryan (1865–1917), first warden of Fircroft, a working men's college and part of the Selly Oaks group, 1909–1917; convert to Quakerism.

settlers there at present. Had talks with Rendel[81] – he may look in and see thee on Friday en route to Norway.

Brother Richard [Westrope] very loveable but feeling I fear still acutely Hilda's vagaries (I believe it might do Mrs Westrope good if thou could pay her a friendly call of sympathy.) I heard one of the lectures, then took part in a drilling class by a Swedish lady and was glad to hear one of Ernest Dodgshun's[82] lectures on the influence of poetry. [...] I then said a few words to them and fled in a taxi to lunch at Barrow Cadbury's[83] and had a talk with him and caught the 2.45 away and am travelling with William C.[84]

(Later) Have arrived safely home after an interview with G.N.[ewman] at the Board of Education.

25 July 1912
House of Commons

It has been a dismal week here darling with these naval votes and discussion and very difficult to know what should be done. So I am greatly rejoicing in the thought of getting into a home atmosphere tomorrow! I fear I shall not be with thee however before 9.20 as I have a business conference in the morning and must stay here for the afternoon. The German visit[85] went off well this morning and I feel increasingly that this kind of interchange of visit must be encouraged and largely extended.

Whyte has just been to tell me that the wife of the American that took my flat committed suicide last night in the flat! I fear the announcement will puzzle some friends who don't know I've moved from 242!

Dear love to the kiddies and Mamma. I may go to Scarbro with

[81] Dr James Rendel Harris (1852–1941), eminent Orientalist and theologian; Fellow of Clare College, Cambridge 1875–1882, lectured in USA 1882–1893, Lecturer in Palaeography, Univ. of Cambridge 1893–1903. Dir of Studies Woodbrooke 1903–1918, Curator John Rylands Library 1918–1925; convert to Quakerism mid-1880s.
[82] Ernest Dodgshun (1876–1944), Quaker; lecturer in adult education; Hon. Sec. NASU 1924–1944.
[83] Barrow Cadbury (1862–1958), nephew of George Cadbury; Dir. Cadbury Bros., Chmn 1922–1932. Inspirer of West Hill, a college for training Sunday school teachers and part of the Selly Oaks group; Hon. Treasurer NASU 1907–1922.
[84] William Adlington Cadbury (1867–1957), brother of Barrow Cadbury; Dir. Cadbury Bros; elected to Birmingham Council 1911 for King's Norton, Ld Mayor Birmingham 1919–1921.
[85] In 1912, 100 English Adult School members visited Germany, while a similar number of Germans from Frankfurt and Dusseldorf visited England and stayed in the homes of Adult School members.

J.R.[owntree] on Saturday. I am arranging with Cousin Ernest[86] for Monday.

25 July 1912
House of Commons

I forgot to mention darling I have spent some time over the point of the 'special constable' thou mentioned to me and seen some ladies and the Home Sec. about it.[87]

I am getting an amendment put down reinstating the previous words and it will receive the Home Sec.'s backing on report stage.

I tried to get in tonight but just failed, I was next to be called but Walter Long got up 10 minutes before his time.

29 July 1912
House of Commons

I had a quiet journey up darling travelling by myself most of the way but as things turned out it was quite unnecessary to hurry as we had a majority of over 150 on the first division![88] But you never can tell. In a few minutes I am expecting the Leeds contingent to tea. Baron de Forest[89] has been talking to me this afternoon in a way which would have made Hettie [Rowntree] stare.

He is very much upset with Churchill and thinks that it is necessary to form a party of radicals who shall steadily work together for peace – persistently vote against the Govt. in their naval estimates, accept no honours, titles or anything and if necessary even vote against the govt. in critical divisions! I am not sure about the latter policy until Home Rule is through – but his policy is interesting coming from *him*.

[86] Michael Ernest Sadler (1861–1943), eminent educationist; Sec. Oxford Univ. Extension Cttee 1885–1895, Dir. of Special Enquiries, Bd of Education 1895–1903, Prof. Manchester University 1903–1911, Vice-Chanc. Leeds Univ. 1911–1923, Master University College, Oxford 1923–1934; KCSI 1919. His wife was a cousin of M.K.R.

[87] One controversial element of the Criminal Law Amendment Bill was which rank and type of police officer should be able to make arrests under its provisions. A.S.R. was not able to produce an amendment to cover special constables.

[88] The first vote on 29 July 1912 on 'business of the House' produced a government majority of 253–94. *Hansard*, 5th series, 1912, XLI, 1669–1672.

[89] Baron Maurice Arnold de Forest (1879–1968), Lib. MP North West Ham 1911–1918.

30 July 1912
House of Commons

I am writing during the process of an Anglo[-German] Friendship Committee darling. I was at the office this morning and then went to the Nation lunch. Poor H.W.M.[assingham] is greatly disturbed with recent events in the House. Charles Roberts[90] says he is not going to take his motion tonight on the Opium Traffic to a division so I am going off with G.N.[ewman] tonight to arrange our tour and I will deal with the matters you refer to in thy letter.

I have paired for Thursday morning so I shall be in York that night and hope to see Mamma. I feel at present like cutting the Friday banquet and coming to Barmoor[91] but I may feel the call of duty more strongly when I get to York! We managed ten divisions last night! and Ted [Harvey] and I returned home with Birrell. Birrell said that Balfour remarked the other day, referring to Bonar Law's strong language 'It always used to be the custom for those in opposition to suppose that sometime they will assume office!'

[...]

On 17 August 1912 A.S.R. sailed from Liverpool to Canada on a two-month tour of North America, accompanied by George Newman. The visit was a combination of holiday, business trip, social investigation, and chance to meet Quaker friends living across the Atlantic. Only a brief selection of his letters home are published as most were taken up with descriptions of the sights he encountered on his travels.

17 August 1912
en route – Manchester to Liverpool

[...] I signed another will with Richard [Cross] included as executor and had a talk with him on the telephone last night. He is very busy with the land enquiry and will I fear get a very short holiday. He is finding several liberals very nervous about the land campaign.

---

[90] Charles Henry Roberts (1865–1959), Lib. MP Lincoln 1906–1918, Derby 1922–1923; US India Office 1914–1915, Lib. whip 1915–1916. *Hansard*, 5th series, 1912, XLI, 1926–1933 for his speech on the Indian budget debate.

[91] Barmoor, Hutton-le-Hole; country home of Harvey family on Yorkshire moors.

17 August 1912
on board SS Megantic – 2.15

[...] I have already met several MPs – Bird (custard),[92] Macmaster,[93] a
Tory Canadian, Munro Ferguson, a friend of Lord Rosebery, and a
Mr Wheler.[94] I understand there are more.

19 August 1912
on board SS Megantic

[...]
Today we have been more in evidence amongst our neighbours and
have had considerable conversation with Bird and Macmaster, two
Tory members of the H of C. Macmaster is much the best of the two –
a King's Counsel practising both in the Canadian and English Courts
and is making his 76th voyage! He is able to help George about his
Canadian enquiries.

23 August 1912

[...] Our talks with our MPs continue – Hamersley[95] improves distinctly – custard powder Bird is very amusing [...].

26 August 1912
The Windsor Hotel, Montreal

[...]
We have had an interesting day – in the morning I spent some time
with the Editor of the Montreal Herald, the liberal paper here, talking
over several questions while G.N.[ewman] discussed medicine and
witnessed operations at the Great Victoria Hospital. Dr Chipman[96]

[92] Alfred Frederick Bird (1849–1922), Con. MP West Wolverhampton January 1910–
February 1922; Chmn Alfred Bird & Sons Ltd, manufacturing chemists; kt. 1920, Bt
1922.
[93] Donald Macmaster (1846–1922), Con. MP Chertsey January 1910–March 1922; called
to Canadian bar 1871, English bar 1906; Member Canadian HofC 1882–1886; Bt 1921.
[94] Granville Charles Hastings Wheler (1872–1927), Con. MP Faversham January 1910–
1927; Bt 1925.
[95] Alfred St George Hamersley (1848–1929), Con. MP Woodstock January 1910–1918;
barrister, practising at Canadian and New Zealand bar.
[96] Dr Chipman, Canadian surgeon, based at McGill University.

invited us to lunch at the Crack Club and there we came across more MPs travelling with a large party [...]. Thy friend Lord Winterton was amongst the number. [...]

31 August 1912
nearing Regina

[...]
We had a most interesting day at Winnipeg yesterday, of which I hope to write in journal form today. I feel now to understand the emigration problem much better than I have done before and am greatly impressed with the wise paternal care the Canadian government exercise over immigrants and now that I know personally the two chief officers in Winnipeg and the way in which they act I shall have much greater confidence in recommending the right type of family to try their fortunes in this country. It is indeed a country of extraordinary hope and promise.
[...]

7 September 1912
Lake Louise Chalet, Laggan, Alberta

[...]
[...] I think we together have some work to do for other children and I agree with G.N.[ewman] in thinking that the Liberal party wants to deal with the question of Education far more seriously than it has done so far, and whilst owing to the lack of a university training I cannot do much in connection with higher education, I feel I might be able to help forward along with thee a movement for a healthier and safer education of young children and this, of course, must begin with the training of mothers in the way we were speaking of a few weeks ago.
[...]

1 October 1912
Carnegie Foundation for the Advancement of Teaching, 576 Fifth Avenue, New York

[...]
G.N.[ewman] is hard at work at the telephone here fixing up

appointments for today and tomorrow. His friend Waldorf Astor,[97] the member for Plymouth, has appeared on the scene and I believe is coming with us to some of the places, so probably I shall vanish shortly to Mt Kisco[98] being unable to compete with American Millionaires.

Would thou or Gillman send me to the boat at Liverpool (I expect this won't reach thee in time to send to Queenstown) copies of papers giving reports of Parliament so that I can read up on my way home and would thou also tell Gillman to send me any general papers, etc., which want attention on my return and which require reading first. [...]

23 October 1912
House of Commons

[...] I have spent most of the afternoon in talking to members – a necessary task on one's first appearance.

The general view seems to be that the government are much stronger than they were and Home Rule is thought to be going very well. I gather that the Government action over the Drs[99] is considered very generous and that it is quite expected that they will now fall into line.

The outlook in the East is thought to be very serious and evidently very few think that the Allies can win.[100]

[...]

24 October 1912
House of Commons – 7.30

[...] I enjoyed staying with Ted [Harvey] last night. He seems I find increasingly doubtful as to whether he should stay in Parliament. I

[97] Hon. Waldorf Astor (1879–1952), Con. MP Plymouth December 1910–1919, when succ. as 2nd Vt Astor; PS Ministry of Food 1918–1919, Local Govt Bd 1919, Min. of Health 1919–1921. Member of fabulously wealthy Astor dynasty of New York.

[98] Mt Kisco, home of James Wood (1839–1925), prominent New York Quaker; Clerk of New York YM and Clerk of Five Year Meeting 1907.

[99] The British Medical Association had refused to co-operate with the National Insurance scheme until their demands were met. On 22 October 1912 Lloyd George made a further offer to the BMA, suggesting GPs should be paid 8s 6d per patient per year, including 1s 6d for medicines. If this was rejected, the Chancellor hinted at the attractions of a national medical service.

[100] Between 8–18 October 1912 the allied Balkan states of Montenegro, Bulgaria, Serbia, and Greece declared war on Turkey, whom they easily defeated over the following two months.

don't quite know what has arisen lately to make him feel as doubtful as I am!

This afternoon I have spent with Barrow Cadbury, Arnold Viccars and Edwin Gilbert – and we have I think decided that the Gilberts shall go to New Zealand early in January. Hogge tells me tonight he has been asked to be Lord Mayor! I have mildly discouraged him!

Richard Cross has come so I must go off and have dinner with him.

Thank thee darling for copying my notes. I haven't had time to look at them again but I feel fairly clear as to what I shall say.

G.N.[ewman] came in to lunch – thou willst have heard of his Father's death – he has gone off tonight to make the funeral arrangements. Last Tuesday he was called in to the committee of the cabinet to advise as to what should be done over the Drs difficulty. G.N.[ewman] is somewhat flattered that his suggestions were accepted.

25 October 1912
Reform Club

[...] I was glad to see Richard [Cross] again, he evidently enjoys his new land work though he feels fagged. He is wondering whether he shouldn't come to York to live.

[...]

What a great victory the Bulgarians have scored.

[...]

28 October 1912
House of Commons

I had a comfortable journey darling back to town and was met by Gillman who has been working here this afternoon. Our little office over the way is not quite ready yet but will be in a day or two and Alden writes that he hopes to be back at work sometime this week.

Illingworth's speech which thou hast read looks as if we should be here fairly continuously for 10 months and then we have a period of respite.[101]

I wonder if it would be best for us to try a furnished house next year. I should feel much more settled if I could see thee and the kiddies

[101] At Bradford Liberal Club on 26 October 1912 Illingworth had announced there would be 'very little leisure for any member of the House of Commons' until late in 1913, but no autumn session would be required that year.

day by day. Even if it was only for a short time, but then I don't want
to be selfish and for thee to feel less happy than thou art at Chalfonts
and to be bereft of friends, neither do I want to do anything to bring
the kiddies into an atmosphere less likely to be good for their health –
but possibly London might suit Tessa[102] better than York.

I think that Bristol emphasizes many of the difficulties I am
feeling about the Adult School Movement in the country – lack of
leaders – absence of clear perception as to what we are aiming at
and a cooling towards the movement by Friends. We badly need a
vigorous lead and here is the Honorary Secretary sticking to the
office and not giving it.

[...]

29 October 1912
Gort Lodge, The Avenue, Clifton, Bristol

[...]
With thy help I got through the meeting this morning very comfortably and the people seem to have felt it to be a good time. It was
very wet and the Hall was consequently not quite full but considering
the weather it was really a very wonderful gathering.

Afterwards I went up with Wethered to his schoolroom on the Downs
and met about a dozen of his keenest men and had an interesting
'fireside'. He (Wethered) is really a very remarkable product and his
dedication to this work is wonderful. I am sorry there don't seem more
Friends in the movement at present. [...]

[...]

31 October 1912
House of Commons

[...] I have felt very fit today after a longer night and this morning
spent the time with Starmer[103] over Newspaper matters and then with
Benson over advertising. This afternoon I have been in the House most
of the time as I wasn't quite sure about the wisdom of this proportional

[102] Elizabeth Harvey ('Tessa') Rowntree, second child and eldest daughter of A.S.R.
and M.K.R., b. 1909.
[103] Charles Walter Starmer (1870–1933), Gen. Manager North of England Newspaper
Co. Ltd.; partner with J.B. Morrell in a number of other newspapers, all of which merged
into the Westminster Press in 1921; Mayor of Darlington 1907–1908, Lib. MP Cleveland
1923–1924; kt. 1917.

representation amendment but I think I am now reconciled to it.[104]
Bonar Law's crude and somewhat coarse criticisms of Asquith are just
what are needed to make Asquith supreme in reply – he is lethargic
and needs a good dig.

I have also spent a little time over the Criminal Law Amendment
Act – the great danger is obstruction, so useless amendments have to
be cleared away beforehand.

I hope I shall catch the 5.45 tomorrow to Leeds and be up with
thee before 10 but if I see we are going to sit late I shall have to
go to York but I think we shall rise in decent time and finish the
Bill some night.

[...]

7 November 1912
The Reform Club

Thank thee darling for thy letters. Today I have accomplished several
small commissions that I have been waiting to get done. I first saw
Fred Rowntree[105] about the bath at Bootham and the right method of
proceeding in connection with architects, etc. as Robt. Mennell wants
me to go and help them next week at their committee.

G.N.[ewman] came to lunch to talk over the Friend and Quaker
literature generally. I am not quite sure whether I told thee that
practically all the Quaker journals are wanting new Editors – The
Friend, B.[ritish] Friend, One and All, American Friend and F.[riends]
Q.[uarterly] E.[xaminer], so that it seems the whole question of the
policy of Friends in connection with Quaker literature wants facing.
(This of course is private!) After lunch I looked over one or two
furnished houses so as to be able to talk to thee! but nothing suitable.

Now (5.30) Ron[106] is here and has been having tea with me so that
we might talk over Devonshire House[107] and now as there is no division
until 10.30 I am going up with him to Camden Rd. to see Aunt Hannah
[Gillett] whom I have not seen for years! I hope I shall get a pair for
tomorrow but I have not heard yet whether one has been secured.

[104] Birrell moved a government amendment to the Home Rule Bill providing for the
election of the Irish Senate by proportional representation; *Hansard,* 5th series, 1912,
XLIII, 621–706.
[105] Frederick Rowntree (1860–1927), cousin of A.S.R. from Scarborough branch of the
family; an architect.
[106] Joseph Rowntree Gillett (1874–1940), first cousin of A.S.R.; partner in Gillett Bros
Discount Co.; Pres. London Union of Adult Schools 1911–1920, NASU 1925–1926.
[107] Devonshire House, Bishopsgate St, London; headquarters of English Society of
Friends.

Unless I wire to the contrary I shall be in York at 1.40. I fear we shall
be late tonight so am staying at the Club.

    [...]

*On the night of 11 November 1912 the government was defeated in a snap division
on a financial amendment to the Irish Home Rule Bill by 228–206. On 13
November Asquith opened the debate to rescind this vote, but the sitting was
suspended by The Speaker after serious disorder in the House of Commons. On 14
November The Speaker suggested Asquith and Bonar Law confer to resolve the
matter and the House of Commons adjourned until 18 November. When the
Commons met again, Asquith moved a new financial resolution to supersede the one
the Conservatives had carried on 11 November, rather than directly reversing that
night's vote.*

13 November 1912
House of Commons

Thank thee darling for thy letter. The general feeling here I think I
told thee yesterday was that the *whips* were chiefly to blame and so we
poor fellows who were not present were hardly blamed at all.

The whips were warned and they went to a division gaily thinking
they had a majority. There were men on our side who would have
talked for hours if it had been thought necessary and if they had been
told to.

I had dinner last night with Gulland and Greenwood and it was
most amusing to hear Greenwood lecturing Gulland – for a wonder
Greenwood was in the division so he could play the heavy Father!

There is a most welcome letter today from Barbara[108] saying the way
is now opening out for her to give her whole time to Adult School
work – this greatly clears the air and means I think that the Office
must be moved to London – but she is coming to see me tomorrow
morning and Viccars tomorrow afternoon.

I share thy feeling largely about Clause III[109] but the difficulty about
altering in the way suggested is that it might have led to real hardship
to the women who are privately carrying on this business in their own
homes and who after all must have a home. I send thee the report of

[108] Barbara McKenzie, Convenor of the Women's Cttee of NASU 1906–1911, 1913–
1915.
[109] The original Criminal Law Amendment Act 1885 contained a loophole. A block of
flats could not be defined as a brothel, even if most or all of its apartments were occupied
by prostitutes. Clause III of the 1912 Bill had been intended to deal with this situation,
but it was withdrawn on 5 November because of the reasons outlined by A.S.R.

the debate. I think if thou reads what Lyttleton[110] and Lee[111] say thou willst understand the difficulty of doing it in the way proposed. [...]

Asquith's simple direct way of getting over the difficulty is much approved here. I have ordered Redmond a bed at the Station Hotel.

5.40 – Just off to G.N.[ewman]. This afternoon has been one of the days when one has enjoyed being a member. Asquith's speech was a perfect model.

14 November 1912
National Liberal Club

Before thee receives this darling thou willst probably have heard that the Speaker has intervened and that the House has adjourned until Monday. I hope it may prove to be the right thing but most of our folks are sadly down and look upon it as a bad example of partizanship.

[...] I had a jolly time last night with G.N.[ewman] and party – the house is delightful and I really was not sorry to miss the disgraceful scenes in the House! I left just after the division.

Today I have had long conferences over the future of the Adult Schools movement – this morning with Barbara [McKenzie] and lunch with G.N.[ewman] and Barbara and this afternoon with Viccars and B.[arbara]. I think we see our way fairly clearly but I will talk to thee about it this weekend.

I am lunching shortly with Richard [Cross] and then may possibly go to the theatre. I feel I want a change of occupation and thought.

18 November 1912
National Liberal Club

The House is a curious place darling and sadly annoys a business man. Here we are at 7 pm finished for the night.

The Tories made no opposition to the new proposals of the Government and the Financial resolution as amended by the Banbury proposal was negatived without a division.[112]

[110] Hon. Alfred Lyttleton (1857–1913), Con. MP Warwick 1895–1906, St George's, Hanover Square June 1906–1913; Sec. of State Colonies 1903–1905.

[111] Arthur Hamilton Lee (1868–1947), Con. MP South Hampshire 1900–July 1918; Civil Ld of Admiralty 1903–1905, PS Ministry of Munitions 1915–1916, Min. of Agriculture 1919–1921, First Ld of Admiralty 1921–1922; cr. Ld Lee of Fareham 1918, Vt 1922. Originator of the Criminal Law Amendment Bill.

[112] The Conservative resolution had been proposed by Sir Frederick George Banbury (1850–1936), Con. MP Peckham 1892–1906, City of London June 1906–1924; Bt 1902, cr. Ld Banbury of Southam 1924.

Tomorrow a new resolution will be submitted and we shall have the 'committee stage' then and the 'report' on Wednesday and by Thursday be in committee again on the Home Rule Bill as we ought to have been last Tuesday had not the defeat occurred. I suppose the reason why the Tories allowed the first part of Asquith's new proposal to go through unchallenged was because they desired people to think them *so* reasonable when only the Government follows a rational course! The general opinion amongst liberals is that there would have been exactly the same row if this plan had been proposed first. However, as we are free, I am going off to the Comedy to see Graham Moffat's new play 'A Scrape of the Pen'.[113]

I had a pleasant journey – lunched with Sir Wm Priestley[114] en route and then *walked* to the House. Tomorrow I see Edwin Gilbert in the morning and W.C.B.[raithwaite] in the evening.

19 November 1912
House of Commons – *8.10 pm*

I have little to report to thee darling. I enjoyed 'The Scrape of the Pen' last night but wished all the time that thou was with me. It is not as good however as 'Bunty'.

Richard [Cross] came into the club afterwards and I had breakfast with him this morning. Then I worked with Gillman and Gilbert until this afternoon – when I have been a good deal in the House listening to the debate of the Financial clause of the Bill about which I have felt somewhat doubtful.[115] Now I am expecting W.C.B.[raithwaite] anytime to dinner and if possible I must try and get to the 'Nation' reception later.

[...]

20 November 1912
House of Commons

I spent this morning darling with Barbara [McKenzie] and G.N.[ewman] and Gillman over the new organization arrangements. I then went to see two or three furnished houses in the Bayswater

---

[113] Graham Moffat (1866–1951), Scottish playwright and actor/producer. Author of *Bunty Pulls the Strings* (1911) and *A Scrape o' the Pen* (1912).

[114] Sir William Edwin Briggs Priestley (1859–1932), Lib. MP East Bradford 1906–1918; kt. 1909.

[115] The Irish Home Rule Bill.

region and think that there are one or two that would suit us there. W.C.B.[raithwaite] dined with me last night but I was not able to get to the 'Nation' reception as we were uncertain when the division would be taken. I found Seebohm [Rowntree] and Richard [Cross] at the Club on my return and I think we have virtually decided that Richard shall give his whole time to the J.R. Trust giving more time than now to the 'Nation' which would mean that he would live in York and come up to London definitely once a week.[116]

W.C.B.[raithwaite] says that Stephen Hobhouse[117] is going out to Constantinople to help Miss Burgess[118] and that Rendel [Harris] is also probably going to Turkey in the interests of Armenians.

I think I have decided to go to the Woodbrooke Council on Friday. I want to see Fullwood and Barrow Cadbury. I haven't been to a Council meeting for over a year and I think I can get a pair and I should like to talk over these Adult School arrangements with Henry L. Wilson. If I went I should probably stay Friday night and return by the first train on Saturday morning if as I suppose the Runcimans are not coming on Friday night – of course if I hear they are I must drop Selly Wood.

I am sorry to hear rather bad accounts of Bolton[119] – if that is lost I fear the government will feel shaky.

21 November 1912
House of Commons

I hope thou art comfortably through thy Women's Liberal meeting darling. I have little to report to thee tonight as I have had an uneventful day though I enjoyed my breakfast with Hamar [Greenwood]. His house in Onslow Gardens is a very comfortable one leading straight on to a large green used by all the dwellers in the street. Mrs G. was suffering from anaemia so was not at breakfast though I visited her afterwards in her bedroom and she seemed fairly blooming. The little girl Angela seems very healthy but did not bear much resemblance to Hamar. G.N.[ewman] joined me at lunch at the Reform Club and this

[116] E.R. Cross gave up his post as Clerk to the Justices of the Peace in Scarborough in 1913 and moved to York.

[117] Stephen Henry Hobhouse (1881–1961), s. of a LU MP and nephew of Beatrice Webb. Converted to Quakerism 1909 and gave up civil-service career to become a social worker; went to Balkans to help American Red Cross 1912–1913; founded Emergency Cttee to help aliens in Britain 1914; imprisoned as a CO 1916–1917.

[118] Ann Mary Burgess (1862–1943), Quaker. Worked in Constantinople 1888–1922 with the Medical Mission for Armenians.

[119] The Liberals retained the Bolton seat in a by-election on 23 November 1912.

afternoon I have been with Crossland practically the whole time over advertizing matters. I had dinner last night with Ted and Irene [Harvey] who were entertaining Juliet Reckitt and her brother Albert.[120] Juliet asked specially after thee – wasn't she in love with Ted at one period in her life?

I have got a pair for tomorrow so shall go to Birmingham. I am trying to get one for Monday as there is a great deal of work at York which I want to get done. I feel uncertain about tomorrow night yet but will communicate with thee from Birmingham.

27 November 1912
The Reform Club

Thank thee darling for thine this morning. Yesterday was a great day for divisions – 25 I think – of which I managed 24 so that I shall consider the 'pairing' season might begin again shortly. I am trying to get one for Friday but it is doubtful if I shall succeed. We are expecting to be up all night on Thursday over the Welsh Church timetables. Ernest [Taylor] came to breakfast with me this morning and we had a good talk over America and Quaker periodicals – as thou knows, the Friend, B.[ritish] Friend, Q.[uarterly] Examiner are all in a state of flux. We then walked on together to Eastcheap (R. & Co's office) and had long meetings of the Sheffield and Darlington papers.[121] Both have done distinctly better this last year and next I think Sheffield will pay its way. This afternoon after a visit to the House I have been to see the house in Thurloe Square and the one in Charles Street. I like the former much the best. It belongs to Lady Sullivan[122] and is very simply furnished and the square in front would be famous for the kiddies. I rather fear however that she does not want to let it for more than 3 months from the middle of January so that might not fit in with our recent thought. However thou must see both – but Thurloe Square is *much* more our style and would be an excellent place to try how we liked married life in London. I fear I may have made a mistake over letting St James Court. Miss Berry is off since I 'rose the rent' but I have let it for 3 weeks at 5 guineas from tomorrow.

I have just come in here for a few minutes to get a meat tea before

[120] Juliet Emily Reckitt (1870–1955) and her brother Albert Leopold Reckitt (1877–1947), Quakers. Members of the family who controlled Reckitt & Sons, starch manufacturers of Hull.

[121] Sheffield paper, *Sheffield Independent*; Darlington paper, *Northern Echo*. By the end of 1913 the *Independent* was in profit and the *Echo*'s losses had been reduced to under £500.

[122] Lady Agnes Sullivan, widow of Admiral Sir Francis Sullivan, Bt. Lived at 23 Thurloe Square.

divisions begin again at 7.30 at the House. Tomorrow I have lunch with George – dinner at the House with G.N.[ewman], W.C.B.[raithwaite] and G.C. Jun.[123] over the future of Fircroft and then an important meeting at the offices of the National Council to talk over our future.
[...]

10 December 1912
House of Commons

I have little to report darling. Bradshaw[124] from Leicester came to me last night and I have been interested in hearing from him about all his prison work. It really is rather wonderful what a comparatively uneducated man can accomplish with a real concern. The Commissioners of the Prisons trust him absolutely and are in monthly consultation with him. I spent practically all the morning writing at the Reform Club and this afternoon have had Fred Taylor here talking over 'West Hill' matters in connection with some help he wants from the Trust and at a committee about Armaments especially in view of the Canadian offer[125] – which really brings great risks along with it.

Now (7.30) 5 divisions are just beginning so I fear I shall be late in getting to Gerty [Taylor] who I expect at 8 pm.
[...]
Thou wilt be interested in an answer by Burns to a question about Pensions I asked him which will appear in tomorrow's paper.[126]

11 December 1912
House of Commons

[...]
This morning W.C.B.[raithwaite], G.N.[ewman] and I had a long

---

[123] George Cadbury, Jr (1878–1954), s. of George Cadbury; Managing Dir. Cadbury Bros 1899–1943; founder of Fircroft College. Elected as a Liberal to Birmingham City Council 1911 for Selly Oak ward; Alderman 1921–1927.

[124] Joseph J. Bradshaw, prison reformer who was inspired by the Adult School movement. Prominent in the Central Association for Discharged Prisoners and the Borstal Association.

[125] In July 1912 the Canadian government had agreed to build three Dreadnoughts as their contribution to Imperial defence and a Bill to this effect was introduced to the Canadian House of Commons in December 1912.

[126] *Hansard*, 5th series, 1912, XLV, 276 for A.S.R.'s question on the amount of poor relief the introduction of pensions had saved in York.

talk about Quaker literature with special reference to the future of the
Friend and B[ritish] F[riend].[127] G.C.[adbury] didn't turn up but is
coming tomorrow instead.

I then had an hour's talk with W.C.B.[raithwaite] in the park and
lunched with him and G.N.[ewman] at the Reform Club.

[...]

The last address of Percy Alden that I have is Meyer's Victoria
Hotel, Beaulieu, but I think very likely he is on his way home now. I
think I would send to 'The Outlook' Woodford Green and ask them
to forward.

We are going to have a weary night of divisions at 10.30 there will
be 21! Each taking 10 minutes and now 8 pm we are in the midst of 7.
The opposition is dividing steadily against concessions they have asked
for.

31 December 1912

Thank thee darling for thine. I have had an interesting and busy day.
First looking at offices. I think I have decided practically to engage
rooms for the National Council at the Central Buildings, Westminster
(in the Wesleyan block.)

Then Barbara [McKenzie] came to lunch and we had a long
talk over future organisation. I went over with her the document
and was glad to find her in warm agreement. When I reached here
I found Elizabeth and Tyler Fox[128] waiting for me and found the
latter in much agony of spirit over the question of going on to the
panel and the difficulty of the pledge. After bringing him in touch
with Dr Addison I think he saw the light and will go on with a
clear conscience.

I then had a long talk with Heath about our new Educational
campaign and have dined with Molteno[129] who wanted to talk over
armaments and the policy we should pursue. Liberals here are very
perky over the woes of our opponents and the divisions amongst the
Tories are no doubt *very* serious. We must however not crow too much –
we may easily be plunged ourselves into difficulties though at present
we seem 'on top'.

[127] The *British Friend* was wound up in 1913. A.S.R. became a Trustee of the *Friend*
1913–1945.

[128] Dr Joseph Tyler Fox (1885–1949), fifth generation of his Quaker family to be a
doctor; m. to daughter of Edwin Gilbert. He was concerned about co-operating with the
National Insurance scheme.

[129] Percy Alport Molteno (1861–1937), Lib. MP Dumfriesshire 1906–1918 and leading
anti-armaments campaigner.

CHAPTER 4

Letters 1913

15 January 1913
242 St James Court

[...]

Maurice Whitlow[1] wanted to see me about Home Mission[2] matters and so as I badly wanted exercise, I took him on a walk in the morning in the park. I then went to G.N.[ewman]'s to lunch to meet Barbara [McKenzie] – then to a Centenary Peace Committee[3] with Earl Grey[4] in the chair – then heard Balfour and Asquith at the house. A.J.B.[alfour] very poor; Asquith admirable.[5] Returned here to write [...] – I think Gillman will have the card for the Sheriff's dance – please ask him for it. I should think we should go for about an hour about 10 pm. Talk – drink coffee – smile and then, when I see thee looking bored, come away.

21 January 1913
House of Commons

I had a comfortable journey, darling, despite the crush. I had lunch with Cousin Maria[6] and travelled with her until Retford – then we separated – I read and slept for the rest of the journey.

I am now in an Armaments Committee – am expecting W.C.B.[raithwaite] directly – [...].

[1] Maurice Whitlow (1875–1959), Sec. Friends' Home Mission and Extension Cttee 1915–1920; later joined Salvation Army.

[2] Home Missions; an evangelical Quaker movement that provided full-time ministers for congregations.

[3] The Peace Cttee of YM was preparing celebrations to mark a century of peace between the USA and Britain.

[4] Albert Henry George Grey (1851–1917), Lib. MP South Northumberland 1880–1885, Tyneside 1885–1886 (LU 1886); Gov.-Gen. Canada 1904–1911; succ. as 4th Earl Grey 1894.

[5] *Hansard*, 5th series, 1913, XLVI, 2103–2129 for Balfour and Asquith on the Third Reading of the Home Rule Bill.

[6] Maria Ellis (nee Rowntree) (1845–1941), cousin of A.S.R. from Scarborough branch of family; m. 1867 J.E. Ellis, MP for Rushcliffe.

22 January 1913
House of Commons

[...] I had a pleasant dinner with W.C.B.[raithwaite] and G.N.[ewman] last night and today worked in the morning – had lunch with Sir George Paish[7] and Mr Acworth[8] and the authorities on Railway matters concerning my amendment.[9]

This afternoon have had a committee about Armenian matters and had a talk with John Robson.[10] I am quite looking to see thee at the station at 1.40 on Friday and will then come round to the Meeting House with thee. [...]

27 January 1913
House of Commons

I left, darling, by an early train and was here in time for questions – the position with regards to the Women's question is very serious and the withdrawal of the bill means, too, that unless the government keeps in two years more after May, we shall not get a plural voting bill either.[11] I think probably the government have done as well as could be expected for the women, but I'm doubtful whether private members will be able to sufficiently agree amongst themselves to carry a bill through all its stages – that is another of the great difficulties. The question not only cuts across Parties but the Suffragist party is divided into three or four parts – however, we must keep hopeful and do our best.

I am telling J.R.[owntree] we can now take tickets for February 14

[7] Sir George Paish (1867–1957), Fellow Royal Statistical Society; Ed. *Statist* 1900–1916, member departmental cttee of Bd of Trade on Railway Accounts and Statistics 1906–1908; kt. 1912.

[8] William Mitchell Acworth (1850–1925), barrister, company dir. and member of numerous cttees of inquiry into railways around the world; Con. cand. Keighley 1906, January 1910, 1911; kt. 1921.

[9] The Railways (No 2) Bill was approaching its Second Reading. On 30 January A.S.R. made a speech calling for lower charges and higher wages on the railways and demanding a commission of inquiry into the railway companies; *Hansard*, 5th series, 1913, XLVII, 1599–1604.

[10] John Herbert Robson (1875–1965), Quaker textile manufacturer from Huddersfield active in the Adult School movement.

[11] The government's Franchise and Registration Bill was withdrawn after The Speaker ruled on 27 January 1913 that any amendment to the Bill to include women's suffrage would alter the nature of the original Bill and make it out of order. Pro-suffrage backbenchers were offered government time to introduce their own Bill and the government proceeded with a measure to abolish plural voting. *Hansard*, 5th series, 1913, XLVII, 1019–1030 for Asquith's explanation.

for both of us. Asquith's speech was really a very strong condemnation
of the speaker!

28 January 1913
House of Commons

I have little to tell thee, darling, of interest. The House today is in
a quiet chastened mood – the liberals, of course, very much
disappointed at the loss of the Plural Voting Bill as well as the
women's amendments.

I find that Acland,[12] Dickinson[13] and others consider the chance of
the Private bill next session as fairly hopeful and the best the government
could do under the circumstances, but it is a poor best and I hear this
afternoon that the militants are again very active which, of course, will
hinder and not help.

I am very sorry not to be with thee tomorrow and Thursday but as
I had made engagements for these days and especially as I have to get
up the facts with regard to the Railway Bill, I cannot pair I fear until
Friday. I quite hope to get to York that day at 1.40. Wilt thou lunch
with me at the Station Hotel and then come with me to the Leeman
Road Church Bazaar which I have promised to look in at if at all
possible?

I was working at my flat this morning with Gillman and have today
taken offices for the National Council and myself at the Central Hall,
Westminster. I went to lunch with the Nation contributors and was
glad to find Massingham much happier than I expected and Brailsford[14]
and Nevinson[15] calmer than I had dared to hope. Now I am going into
the House of Lords to hear the Archbishop for a few minutes.[16] Please
give my salutations to the visitors and say how very sorry I am to miss
them.

[12] Francis Dyke Acland (1874–1939), Lib. MP Richmond 1906–January 1910, Camborne
December 1910–1922, Tiverton 1923–1924, North Cornwall 1932–1939; Fin. Sec. to War
Office 1908–1911, US Foreign Office 1911–1915, Fin. Sec. to Treasury 1915, PS Bd of
Agriculture 1915–1916; succ. as 14th Bt 1926.

[13] Willoughby Hyett Dickinson (1859–1943), Lib. MP North St Pancras 1906–1918;
KBE 1918, cr. Ld Dickinson 1930.

[14] Henry Noel Brailsford (1873–1958), Lib. journalist and sec. of the Conciliation Cttee
which aimed to unite pro-suffrage MPs in all parties.

[15] Henry Woodd Nevinson (1856–1941), Lib. journalist and ardent pro-suffragist.

[16] *Hansard*, 5th series, 1913, XIII, 547–555 for the Archbishop of York's explanation of
why he would vote against the Second Reading of the Irish Home Rule Bill.

29 January 1913
House of Commons

[...]

Afterwards, I worked at home and then had lunch with Sir George Paish and Alden. I believe the Railway Bill will come on tomorrow after all. If so, I think probably I shall pair for Monday.

Herbert Wood[17] is here for an Armenian Committee and I have asked him to dine with me tonight.

I am sorry to hear from E.R.C.[ross] who has arrived today that Mrs Frank Hirst[18] is one of the women who has been arrested. I fear it must be the result of Frank Hirst being too strong on the other side.

I hope the QM Peace Conference has gone well today.

11 February 1913
en route to London

We are nearing London and if I am to send thee anything I must write now. I have had a comfortable journey correcting my Adult School memorandum most of the way but at tea time Sydney Leetham[19] came and evidently seemed to want to talk and strange to relate, we had a most interesting and friendly discussion on Socialism – Evolution of Society – Wages & Quakerism. He is a great admirer of Rufus Jones' works – and Free Masonry. He really is a very interesting man and it is only another indication of the good there is in all men and how careful you should be not to judge too hardly.

He considers the Early Quaker view of the Inner Light the greatest religious conception there has ever been!
[...]

7 March 1913
242 St James Court

This is the first letter, darling, written in my new office which is very nice and certainly more suitable than the previous one, though it has

[17] Herbert George Wood (1879–1963), Quaker theologian and teacher; Warden of Wood-brooke 1914–1918, Dir. of Studies 1915–1941, Prof. of Theology Birmingham Univ. 1941–1946.
[18] Helena Hirst, m. F.W. Hirst 1903; great-niece of Richard Cobden. Arrested during suffragette march on HofC 28 January 1913.
[19] Sydney Leetham, York businessman, head of Leetham's flour mills, which were notorious for their low wages. He and A.S.R. had a long-running dispute in the January 1910 election about the effect of a tax on imports of corn.

not such a view. The two National Council offices are also looking very well; and I think folks will be pleased with the move which will, I trust, tend to better work being accomplished. I had a quiet journey up here and have been at a travellers' conference all this afternoon and now I must wend my way to G.N.[ewman]'s where I am dining. Gillman, Fullwood, Boyd and Miss Heslop are all working here to get things straight and I think all promises well for the morrow.

[...]

10 March 1913
House of Commons

I was sorry, darling, the telephone was so bad this morning that we were hardly able to get any talk. I have been working at different matters but came in to hear the King read his address in a rasping, raucous voice – There were very few Lords – they don't turn up like they used to before the Parliament Act.

I think Sunday's conference was really very good.[20] G.N.[ewman] and Wethered especially were in great form and the secretaries really enjoyed the chance of getting together. I believe we ought to do far more of this kind of cooperative entertaining of those who are really doing the work of the schools.

I just got to hear Asquith's speech which was excellent and I am now returning to my flat to read several papers that have been wanting attention for some time.

24 March 1913
Friends First Day Adult School, Shewell Road, Sir Isaacs Walk, Colchester

Ted seems nicely.

Mary Glaisyer's[21] death, no doubt, influenced our gathering and deepened it. Barbara [McKenzie] would like a Women's Fircroft to arise as a testimony to her.

I had a comfortable jouney, darling, reading most of the way, Holmes 'What Is and What Might Be'[22] which I think thou would enjoy – it is

---

[20] Conference of the National Council and officers of NASU on 9 March 1913.
[21] Ellen Mary Glaisyer (1873–1913), Huddersfield Quaker and noted temperance worker; Convenor Women's Cttee NASU 1911–1913.
[22] Edmond Gore Alexander Holmes (1850–1936), Inspector of Elementary Schools for England 1875–1910, and author, among many other works, of *What Is and What Might Be: A Study of Education in General and Elementary Education in Particular* (1911).

a very severe criticism of modern educational methods tracing back
the origin of the repressive method in the West to the dual conception
of God and especially to the view of the child being born with a large
measure of original sin. This view has meant that the the natural
unfolding and developing of the child has been suppressed because
nature was divorced from God until something had happened – the
acceptance of the view of atonement in the form of a dogma. This is
all worked out very well. If Father[23] has not seen the book, I think he
would like to.

[...]

*In April 1912 three ministers, Lloyd George, Rufus Isaacs, and the Master of
Elibank had bought shares in the American Marconi Company, on the suggestion
of Godfrey Isaacs, the Company's managing director and the brother of Rufus Isaacs.
At this time the English Marconi Company (a separate but closely connected concern)
had just signed a substantial government contract and rumours of impropriety started
to circulate. A select committee was appointed to look into the Marconi contract in
October 1912 and Rufus Isaacs gave evidence on 25–27 March 1913. The committee
divided on party lines and its government majority cleared the ministers of any
wrongdoing. Not surprisingly, this failed to satisfy the Conservatives and the issue
helped to severely dent the reputation of the ministers concerned.*

26 March 1913
House of Commons

Thou wilst see from the papers, darling, that we have had great scenes
tonight in the House.[24] The Tories who were evidently in a majority
of 4 or 8 when the first division was expected were greatly chagrined
at Booth[25] finding a way through the Chairman's ruling and talking
until more Liberals had arrived. Happily I was there from the first –
though truth compels me to add it was the first snap I have been in.

I had a good gallop this morning in the park and then worked at
the office all the morning and have been forced to stay here steadily
since.

I fear the ministers' connections with the American Marconi Co. are
going to do us harm – the House has rung today with cries of Marconi
[...].

[23] William Harvey (1848–1928), father of M.K.R; retd linen and silk manufacturer and
prominent Leeds Quaker, active in the Adult School movement.
[24] The debate on the cttee stage of the Consolidated Fund (No. 1) Bill; *Hansard*, 5th
series, 1913, L, 1673–1688.
[25] Frederick Handel Booth (1867–1947), Lib. MP Pontefract December 1910–1918.

9 April 1913
National Council of Adult School Unions, 1 Central Building, Tothill Street,
Westminster, SW

I think I better write now, darling, or I may be driven at the end. I managed to pair last night for 90 minutes and so was able to have a nice quiet dinner with Mamma, Frank and Edie [Sturge]. [...] After dinner, Frank came with me to the House. This morning I have spent most of the time with J.R.[owntree] talking over recent developments – prior to a meeting of the Charitable Trust on Monday; [...].

[...]

10 April 1913
House of Commons

[...]
I have had a busy day – a good ride before breakfast. Afterwards preparing my speech for tomorrow[26] – then a long talk with Alden about the British Institute of Social Service[27] and its future.

Then working here in preparation of the officers' meeting tonight and other matters. I should like to have been at the Education debate in the House but that is impossible.

[...]

15 April 1913
House of Commons

[...]
We reached town comfortably last night though the train was very crowded. I had a ride this morning, the park most lovely in its new foliage. Worked at the office afterwards and lunched (a very good one) with the Speaker along with 30 others and a gathering of Liberal MPs who do not attend the levee. He was very cordial and traced on my hand the course of the injury to his wrist.

Tonight we are expecting to go late over this bill legalizing the collection of taxes owing to Gibson Bowles successful action in the

---

[26] *Hansard,* 5th series, 1913, LI, 1562–1566 for A.S.R.'s speech against the Second Reading of the National Service (Territorial Forces) Bill, a Conservative bill to introduce compulsory military training.
[27] Alden was Hon. Sec. of the British Institute of Social Service (founded 1905), an organization closely linked to the Friends' Social Union.

courts.[28] In three minutes I am expecting Newman and Mansbridge[29] to talk over Fircroft proposals and the best way of uniting the WEA & Adult Schools in that kind of work.

22 April 1913
House of Commons

I had quite a comfortable time at the Manor House, darling. W.A. Cadbury joined us after dinner. We had a good talk about the future of the Friend and discussed names of suitable Trustees and nothing is definitely settled but I hope to get a talk with W.C.B.[raithwaite] on Thursday and will tell thee at the end of the week how matters progress.

I travelled to town this morning with Mrs C.[adbury] & the pretty daughter, spent 2 hours with Brother Richard [Westrope], then lunched with Mrs McKenzie, heard the Chancellor and then having had an interesting hour with Temple,[30] Mansbridge and G.N.[ewman] have come to a very satisfactory agreement about the Fircroft Council. I think we shall get the closest cooperation.

The House is in early so I hope to be able to get to the farewell Mansbridge supper.

22 April 1913
House of Commons

I am writing in the flat, darling, just before lunch when I am expecting Paish and Alden to discuss further the matter to be presented to the PM this day week in connection with Railways. It is very hot and spring like or rather summer like.

I have been on a jolly ride with Philip Morrell[31] in the park which is looking most beautiful in its new plumage. I enjoyed too the supper

[28] The Provisional Collection of Taxes Bill, 1913 was required to correct the decision in Bowles v. Bank of England that collecting new taxes in advance of the Finance Act becoming law each year was a violation of the Bill of Rights. The action had been brought by Thomas Gibson Bowles (1843–1922), Con. MP Kings Lynn 1892–1906, Lib. MP Kings Lynn January–December 1910.

[29] Albert Mansbridge (1876–1952), founder of the Workers Educational Association and its first Sec. 1903–1915. Fircroft was run by a committee of representatives of the WEA, the Adult Schools, trade unions and the co-operative movement.

[30] Revd William Temple (1881–1944), Headmaster of Repton 1910–1914 and Pres. of the WEA 1908–1924, Rector St James's Piccadilly 1914–1918, Bishop of Manchester 1921–1929, Archbishop of York 1929–1942, Archbishop of Canterbury 1942–1944.

[31] Philip Edward Morrell (1870–1943), Lib. MP Henley 1906–January 1910, Burnley December 1910–1918.

to Mansbridge last night. Sir Robert Morant proposed Mansbridge's health. A.L. Smith of Balliol[32] 'National Education' coupled with Lord Haldane's name in a very witty speech announcing first of all that he had been commanded by the President (Temple) 'to draw the badger' then Haldane spoke excellently on the atmosphere of the place and the fine speech Mansbridge had made evidently influenced him and it was fine hearing him declaring that there was something of the ideal in every man and that it could be drawn if properly appealed to. The Bishop of Oxford[33] too spoke very well and one or two working men so that it was really rather a unique gathering. I am off to Bournemouth at 4 pm and return tomorrow night for an education dinner to Pease. [...]

I hope QM has gone off well, darling, and that thou wilt get comfortably back to Hutton.

3 June 1913
House of Commons

I have little interesting to tell thee today, darling. I worked at the office this morning, lunched with the Nation staff and, this afternoon, have had a long talk with Mansbridge – very satisfactory and all pointing to much closer working with the WEA.

The House is up at 7 and I am hoping to have dinner with Gerty [Taylor] at the flat and then take her to 'Milestones'. [...]

11 June 1913
House of Commons

[...]
Encouraged by thee, I spoke this afternoon and though I felt it to be a ragged performance, several members seemed pleased.[34] I finished up voting against the government when I saw the Tories were not

---

[32] Arthur Lionel Smith (1850–1924), Dean of Balliol College, Oxford 1907–1916, Master 1916–1924. Passionately committed to university extension movement.

[33] Charles Gore (1853–1932), Bishop of Worcester 1902–1904, Birmingham 1905–1911, Oxford 1911–1919.

[34] *Hansard,* 5th series, 1913, LIII, 1661–1666 for A.S.R.'s speech on the Second Reading of the Finance Bill in favour of a Labour amendment to reduce food taxes and raise direct taxes. The amendment was lost 256–38 with 14 Liberals, including A.S.R., in the minority.

going to. The big incident thou will't read about, I fear it may mean the closing of the Gallery.[35]

17 June 1913
House of Commons

I had a comfortable journey, darling, and went across to the Nation lunch on arrival. Then to the office where Gerty [Taylor] visited me. [...] I am dining tonight with the Armaments group who are entertaining Lord Loreburn.[36] My chief concern this afternoon has been to get one or two of Lloyd George's friends to encourage him to make an ample apology tomorrow if he and Isaacs do that they will I am sure regain much of what they have lost. Addison has had a talk with G.N.[ewman] over the telephone – I am much more hopeful now of the right thing being done.

18 June 1913
House of Commons

It has been a most interesting day, darling – T.W. Russell[37] says the most impressive debate he has heard during his 30 years in Parliament – I thought Rufus [Isaacs] was excellent from his standpoint and whilst George was himself, I think it was a tactical mistake for the Tories as he did over the corruption charge.[38] It would have been much better to let one of his colleagues do that. Still the Tories are very unhappy. After the handsome admission of indiscretion, I feel absolutely no difficulty in voting for the government amendment and am inclined to think the party will weather this storm. I am now listening to Banbury [...].

I will try and get a pair for June 27 and have written to Forster Todd[39] to tell him to fix 4.15 or 4 for the opening of the Bandstand.

[35] A male suffragist in the Strangers' Gallery threw a bag of flour at Asquith and the Chamber was scattered with leaflets urging MPs to 'Remember Miss Davison'.
[36] Robert Threshie Reid (1846–1923), Lib. MP Hereford 1880–1885, Dumfries 1886–1905; Solicitor-Gen. 1894, Attorney-Gen. 1894–1895, Ld Chanc. 1905–1912; kt. 1894, cr. Ld Loreburn 1906, Earl 1911.
[37] Thomas Wallace Russell (1841–1920), LU (Lib. from 1904) MP South Tyrone 1886–January 1910, North Tyrone 1911–1918; PS Local Govt Bd 1895–1900, Vice-Pres. Dept of Agriculture for Ireland 1907–1918; Bt 1917.
[38] *Hansard,* 5th series, 1913, LIV, 438–449 for Lloyd George's statement on the Marconi affair, in which he admitted an action which 'lent itself to misconstruction' but severely attacked the Tories for accusing him of corruption.
[39] W.A. Forster Todd, leading Conservative in York; Ld Mayor 1915–1918.

24 June 1913
House of Commons, 7 pm

There are rumours that the House is going to be up shortly,
darling – if so, I shall go and see whether Gerty [Taylor] will come
to a theatre. [...] I don't feel to have accomplished much today. I
had a jolly ride this morning with Seebohm [Rowntree] in the
park – had breakfast with him at the Cavendish Club – read and
worked afterwards at the flat and office – lunched with the Nation
folk and this afternoon spent a long time with Tom King[40] of Bristol
who had come up with a great concern to try and do something
for Mrs Pankhurst[41] and the women in prison before they die but
I don't see what is possible as long as they insist on militant
methods. McKenna is willing to release them all tomorrow if they
will promise to desist from such methods. [...]

25 June 1913
House of Commons

Thank thee, darling, for thy letter. The House rose early last night so
I went off to see the Irish players. Gerty [Taylor] had not arrived back
so I went by myself but as there were 4 MPs in the row in front I did
not feel lonely. I rode again with Seebohm [Rowntree] in the park this
morning but returned early in order to entertain Isaac Sharpless[42] at
breakfast. [...] then for two hours listened to the discussion in committee
upstairs of the enclosed bill of Banbury's which I thought would interest
thee.[43] I am not sure whether I can spare the time to listen to long
arguments between the Vivisectionists and the Antis but it is difficult
to get off this committee. I lunched with G.N.[ewman] at Carol's in
order to talk over the business for tomorrow's Fircroft Council and this
afternoon have been in the precincts of the House most of the time. I
think we may be up again early and I am dining with E.R.C.[ross]
and may possibly go off on a spree with him.

[40] Tom King, Bristol industrialist.
[41] Emmeline Pankhurst (1858–1928), founder of the Women's Social and Political
Union. Sentenced to three years imprisonment on 2 April 1913 for incitement to violence.
[42] Isaac Sharpless (1848–1920), American Quaker; Pres. Haverford College 1887–1917.
[43] The Dogs (Protection) Bill, 1913.

2 July 1913
House of Commons

I have got a pair for tomorrow, darling, so am returning I hope by the
10 train, but I cannot be absolutely certain as if I am up all tonight it
may be best to come by a later train. [...]

I hope the Liberal sale has prospered today. Oscar [Rowntree] is
making great efforts to clear the whole debt. I have had to promise
him £50 or £100. I spent most of this morning over the Dog's
Bill – lunch with Alden and Paish discussing the Railway Enquiry
[...].

I don't feel in much form yet for the spiritual exercises of the week
end but I hope I shall get some opportunity for quiet and thought
when I get to York.

3 July 1913
Chalfonts, York

I was sorry not to get the first train, darling, this morning; but I thought
it best to get 4 hours sleep first and this afternoon I felt quite refreshed
and had a pleasant journey down with Seebohm [Rowntree]. [...] Now
I have had an excellent supper and am expecting Evans[44] shortly. We
did a good stroke of business last night and I now hope the Plural
voters bill will get to the Lords next week. [...]

15 July 1913
House of Commons

[...]
I have been in the House most of the afternoon and put in a plea
for the better treatment of women.[45] It wasn't a large House but
Members were very kind afterwards.

[...]

[44] P.T. Evans, A.S.R.'s accountant.
[45] *Hansard*, 5th series, 1913, LV, 1160–1163 for A.S.R.'s speech on the Second Reading
of the National Insurance (1911) Amendment Bill. He argued that maternity benefit
should be paid directly to women and that married women should be entitled to a benefit
of 30s.

17 July 1913
Swanwick[46]

I didn't see at all clearly until this morning, darling, what was the right thing to do about Swanwick; but after carefully dwelling on the matter I came definitely to the conclusion that it was right to leave Winston and his dreadnoughts (the number of members wanting to speak was so great that it would have been impossible to get called) and to get to Swanwick in time for this evening's meetings. [...] Anyway, I am trying to get pairs for Monday, Tuesday & Wednesday of next week. Now I have definitely decided not to go on the Insurance Committee so our separation won't be so long as thou feared. [...]

18 July 1913
Swanwick

[...]
    This is a wonderful gathering of 800 students most of whom seem very keen on the highest things in life & the meetings interest me greatly. If only Friends were guiding it, there would be fewer things that jar on you. On arrival at Ambergate yesterday when I changed, I was greeted most kindly by the Liverpool University contingent & brought up here with them. I am sleeping in Oxford III tent & the men are all very kind, but I confess to feeling somewhat out of it through not being at college – I don't think I shall have to speak at all but there is much that is suggestive & it is most interesting seeing how strongly they are in favour of peace through their interest in the foreign students. The meeting this morning when the foreign students spoke was most interesting.

6 August 1913
House of Commons

[...] The opium debate is off for tomorrow night – instead several of us are going on a deputation to Grey & Crewe. [...]
    I have been working here this morning – lunched with Barbara [McKenzie] & am now going to plunge into the maternity question in

---

[46] The annual conference of the Student Christian movement at Swanwick, Derbyshire on 14–21 July 1913.

connection with National insurance. 7 pm – Just off to drive with Ted [Harvey] after voting against him in both divisions.[47]

25 August 1913
Tyn-Llwy-dan, Anglesey

After tea yesterday, we walked to Aberffraw (G.N.[ewman], Rufus [Jones], W.C.B.[raithwaite], Wethered and I) to get & send letters – thank thee, darling, for thy P.C. We then went into a chapel for 30 minutes to hear some Welsh singing having previously made it known to the minister that we could only stay a short time. We then returned by the shore & cliff & it was a perfectly glorious evening & were much annoyed twice to be stopped by the agent of Sir George Meyrick who owns all this part of the country. It made us all very angry & provides new reasons for a drastic land bill & the legal minds here are much concerned as to what can be done to alter the law of trespass [...].

28 August 1913
Cocoa Works, York

[...]
We have had a great time in Wales. I wish thou had been with us but we are now going to have a great time in Scotland, darling.

PS I'm pleased to find myself so near Butcher this year in the division list. I thought he would have been 50 ahead.

[...] I am travelling with Joshua [Rowntree] and Maria Ellis (returning from a Peace Board at Leeds) and Edward Grubb.[48] Ernest [Taylor] cannot come till tomorrow [...].

[...]

19 September 1913
7.20, Hermitage Hotel, Le Touquet[49]

I don't know what time the post goes, darling, but I will write at once

[47] At the Committee stage of the National Insurance (1911) Amendment Bill A.S.R. voted against the government twice and in favour of paying maternity benefit directly to wives; *Hansard*, 5th series, 1913, LVI, 1533–1538, 1544–1546.

[48] Edward Grubb (1854–1939), leading liberal theologian within Quakerism; owner and Ed. *British Friend* 1901–1913, Treasurer No-Conscription Fellowship 1915–1919.

[49] A.S.R. was attending a conference organized by the Garton Foundation, an organization set up in 1912 to promote the ideas of Norman Angell.

to let thee know of our safe arrival here. The sea was very kind to us &
we were all happy & I travelled with Uncle Sam[50] to Folkestone & then
on the boat had talks with E.D. Morel[51] of Congo fame, Sarolea[52] the
Editor of Everyman, Sophie Sturge[53] & J.W. Graham.[54] On arrival at
Boulogne after the usual babel at customs we were ushered into
motors & driven at rapid speed to this place. It was dark on arrival so
I have not been able to see much of this place but it is on the coast in
the midst of a great forest & evidently abounds in hotels. Opposite to
us there is a real casino. It boasts the best golf course in Europe. My
room looks very comfortable & on the ground floor & with a bathroom
attached to it so I shall manage to exist! Norman Angell has evidently
secured a cosmopolitan party besides those I have mentioned & several
connected with the Garton foundation. I have already seen or heard
of Raphael[55] (the wealthiest MP), Lord Esher,[56] Lord Weardale,[57]
Colonel Bingham[58] a leading Sheffield Tory who is now writing opposite
to me & Sir Robert Hadfield[59] from Sheffield a great maker of common
plate. So there seems material for plenty of interesting debate.

20 September 1913
7.20 Hotel Hermitage, Le Touquet

[...] This gathering is really very interesting – last night we didn't start
dinner until 8.45 & didn't begin our conference until 10.15 which

[50] Samuel Doncaster (1853–1937), steel manufacturer in Sheffield; brother of A.S.R.'s
stepmother, Helen Doncaster Rowntree.
[51] Edmund Dene Morel (1873–1924), Lab. MP Dundee 1922–1924; Sec. Congo Reform
Association 1904–1912; Ed. *African Mail* 1903–1915; Lib. cand. Birkenhead 1912, but
resigned 1914; leading figure in UDC in World War I.
[52] Charles Sarolea (1870–1953), Lecturer in French Edinburgh University 1894–1931;
Ed. *Everyman* magazine 1912–1917.
[53] Sophia Sturge (1849–1936), Quaker, well known for her work in Ireland.
[54] John William Graham (1859–1932), Quaker historian and philosopher; Principal of
Dalton Hall, Manchester University 1897–1924.
[55] Sir Herbert Henry Raphael (1859–1924), Lib. MP South Derbyshire 1906–1918; Bt
1911.
[56] Reginald Balliol Brett (1852–1930), Lib. MP Penryn & Falmouth 1880–1885; Sec. to
Office of Works 1895–1902, member Cttee of Imperial Defence from 1904; succ. as 2nd
Vt Esher 1899. Royal confidante and inveterate intriguer, especially in military affairs.
At this time a supporter of the Garton Foundation.
[57] Hon. Philip James Stanhope (1847–1923), Lib. MP Wednesbury 1886–1892, Burnley
1893–1900, Market Harborough 1904–1905, when cr. Lord Weardale; anti-armaments
campaigner.
[58] Sir John Edward Bingham (1839–1915), Head of Walker & Hall of Sheffield and
Pres. Hallam Con. Association; Bt 1903.
[59] Sir Robert Abbott Hadfield (1858–1940), Chmn and Managing Dir. Hadfield Ltd;
kt. 1908, Bt 1917; inventor of manganese steel.

continued until midnight. Most of the time was taken up with a ghastly
account of the result of war in the Balkans.

At dinner my side companions were Lady Barlow, Miss Anstruther,[60]
a sister of the Tory member for St Andrews. Opposite was Mrs Whyte[61]
of Edinboro & Sir J.E. Barlow.

Today we conferred until after 1 – after lunch I went with Uncle
Sam [Doncaster], Sir Richard Garton[62] & Colonel Bingham to see
the garden of the man who has really made Le Touquet. Afterwards
we walked back to the shore & saw the sandships propelled by sails
dashing about in the sand. I had a long talk with Sir Richard
Garton who is a curious & somewhat heavy individual about the
work of his foundation. He is a Tory & evidently very much afraid
of the movement going too fast & much scared of the ordinary
peace organization. I have my doubts whether finally this movement
can be directed by a man with so many doubts. Sir John Bingham
who is a bit of a bore seems very busy in promoting a huge
combine of employers to smash Trades Unionism which seems a
curious accompaniment to an international peace movement. On
the other hand, most of the men seem very keen & it is interesting
to find so many keen University men. I have asked Hilton[63] the
Garton lecturer in York on Wednesday night, to stay with us that
night. It was interesting to find a non-Friend Halliday from Newcastle
very anxious for a Friends meeting tomorrow morning so we are
looking to hold one before the conference begins.

18 October 1913
Shaftesbury Hotel, Newport

Thank thee, darling, for thy letter – I hope our efforts here are doing
some good but the movement is in a small way & I am doubtful if
there are leaders here at present who have the power to make it
develop. The two meetings I spoke at last night were both small – I
was billeted with an active Plymouth brother & I had to be careful.

[60] Clementina Caroline Anstruther-Thomson (d. 1921). Her brother was William
Anstruther-Gray (1859–1938), Con. MP St Andrews 1906–January 1910, December 1910–
1918.
[61] Possibly Jane Whyte, wife of Alexander Whyte, Principal New College, Edinburgh
1909–1918.
[62] Sir Richard Charles Garton (1857–1934), Dir. Manbre Garton Ltd and originator of
Garton Foundation; kt. 1908.
[63] John Hilton (1880–1943), journalist; acting sec. Garton Foundation 1914–1918, Asst
Sec. and Dir. of Statistics Min. of Labour 1919–1931, Prof. of Industrial Relations Univ.
of Cambridge 1931–1943.

This morning I have motored with Hobbis our Cardiff traveller up by
Pontypridd to Tony Pandy where the great riots were 18 months ago &
then back by Senghenydd[64] & tonight I am feeling both sad and angry.
The housing conditions are really awful. I am only surprised that for so
long the men have kept as quiet as they have. I was much impressed with
the quiet stern solidity of the crowds at the pit mouth. I didn't see a soul
in tears amongst all the crowds until I was leaving the town when I saw
one young girl weeping, but most of the women folk were evidently inside
the houses. I suppose they know that to wait longer at the pit mouth was
hopeless. Really when one has seen some of the hovels these people live
in one is not without hope that their lot is now better.

[...]

20 October 1913
en route Merthyr

I was sorry, darling, not to get any letter off to thee yesterday but I
was hard at work all day with the exception of two hours in the middle
when I was at dinner with Mordey, the Old Boothamite who now edits
Bootham. We had good meetings on Saturday night with Brace the
miner's MP in the chair & yesterday after attending a large school at
8 am we spent the whole day in conference with 30 of the leaders in
the few schools there are here. It was interesting & one learnt something
of the Welsh character & outlook & it is quite plain that if the Adult
School movement is to grow here it must be given a more Welsh
flavour – but of course how to do this is difficult. Today I spent the
morning going round the new dock at Newport, I believe the largest
in the British Isles and then came on to Cardiff with Mordey who is
giving a lot of time to the Garden City Movement & went with him &
Professor Jevons[65] to their most advanced Garden City at Rhiwbina.
On arrival at Merthyr I go at once to a conference followed by a
public meeting. It is pretty stiff work & I sympathise with the poor
official who has to do this every day of his life!
  I haven't seen much of Barbara [McKenzie] except at the meetings
as we have stayed with different people. She is a good person to go
tiger hunting with & always does well. I am increasingly struck with
her power.
  [...]

[64] Senghenydd; site of a major colliery disaster in which 439 men lost their lives.
[65] Herbert Stanley Jevons (1875–1955), Fulton Prof. of Economics and Political Science
University College, Cardiff 1905–1911; engaged full-time in housing reform in South
Wales 1911–1914; Prof. of Economics, Univ. of Allahabad 1914–1923, Univ. of Rangoon
1923–1930.

26 November 1913
Beccles, Suffolk, 11 am

Thank thee, darling, for thy letter. I think I better get a few lines
written now as I may find it difficult afterwards. I am expecting Barbara
[McKenzie] shortly from Bungay & then we are off in a motor to
Lowestoft & Yarmouth returning for a talk with some of their local
leaders at 4 pm on Village Extension & then afterwards there is a large
evening meeting. We had an excellent meeting last night, Barbara
[McKenzie] in great form – I felt freer than sometimes and chaffed
them vigorously. The presence of a Dr on a platform always enables
me to score & the bit that pleased them best was that under the
insurance act we got 9d for 4d & so did the Drs!

They motored me back here last night. The Dr & his wife are really
splendid & they have four delightful children. The youngest about
Tessa [Rowntree]'s age. The Dr doesn't mind taking an active part in
politics with the consequence that he is boycotted left & right but this
doesn't move him in the slightest & he is adored by his men.

[...]

27 November 1913
4 Victoria St

W.C.B.[raithwaite], Wethered and I are just sitting down here for a
long talk but before we begin I want to send thee a line, darling, to
say that though very busy I think all goes well – an excellent meeting
last night & packed to the doors – a fine feeling.

Today I came up with Barbara [McKenzie], lunched with Will[66] and
then from 3 to 8.30 was in the Fircroft Council Meeting & Officers
Meeting. On the whole both went well. G.N.[ewman] joined us at
dinner but has now run away.

9 December 1913
in train to London

[...] About 20 members turned up at the Armament Conference all
very angry! We didn't do much – they are a cranky set but a deputation

[66] William Fryer Harvey (1885–1937), bro. of M.K.R; doctor, served in FAU 1914,
Surgeon-Lt in Royal Navy 1917; Warden of Fircroft 1920–1925. Author of *We Were Seven*,
a memoir of his family.

to Asquith is to be arranged. I had tea & talk with Ted [Harvey] afterwards. I think five or six of us who think alike with regard to social questions may table a strong amendment to the address & then we talked over the wisdom if these increased armaments are pressed forward of telling the Whip well we are going to leave the House for a month & campaign in the country. If our association agrees, well & good – if not, we are willing to resign. It might be wise to stipulate that we would return for Home Rule divisions. This we are dwelling upon. I have asked Donald Maclean & his wife[67] & Ted & Irene [Harvey] to stay with us over the weekend, January 17–18 so as to attend the Liberal dinner in York. Ted hopes to come, i.e. accept. Donald Maclean will let us know before Christmas but quite hopes to come. I am now travelling to Hitchin.

---

[67] Donald Maclean (1864–1932), Lib. MP Bath 1906–January 1910, Peebles & Selkirk December 1910–1922, North Cornwall 1929–1932; Dep. Chmn Cttee of Ways and Means 1911–1918, Leader in HofC of Asquithian Libs 1919–1920, Pres. Bd of Education 1931–1932; KBE 1917. His wife was Gwendolen Margaret Maclean (nee Devitt).

CHAPTER 5

Letters 1914

8 January 1914
Grims Wood[1]

I came out with G.N.[ewman] last night. Thy friend Janet [Campbell] was at dinner and afterwards G.N.[ewman] talked about his own position at the Board (of Education). I think it is pretty clear now that he will refuse the insurance post as the PM wants him to stay at the B. of E. and he will get a larger salary and a freer hand. [...] I hope thou art having a good time with Barbara, darling. G.N. and Ada [Newman] are very sorry not to have thee here. After tea we shall continue our talk – if we promulgated all we agree to there would be a Quaker Kikuyu![2]

If thou hast seen the D. News today read Gardiner's article on the Crown Prince.[3] I expect the copy next door will not have been destroyed. Thou hast noticed Dinsdale Young's[4] on 'A Chocolate Box' in the British Weekly ?

11 January 1914
Grims Wood

[...]
He [Newman] is very anxious to get Ted [Harvey] into writing and

---

[1] Grims Wood; home of George and Ada Newman in Harrow Weald, Middlesex.

[2] Kikuyu; in June 1913 the evangelical Anglican bishops of Mombasa and Uganda had concluded a concordat at Kikuyu in Kenya with the representatives of several other Protestant denominations. They agreed to federate their missionary societies for future work and the meeting ended with a joint communion service. These actions were denounced by the High Church bishop of Zanzibar, all three bishops returned to London and a huge controversy ensued.

[3] *Daily News*, 7 January 1914 carried a front-page denunciation of Crown Prince Wilhelm of Germany for sending a telegram to Col. von Reuther, congratulating him on upholding the honour of the army by firing on civilians in the Zabern incident in Alsace in 1913.

[4] Revd Dinsdale Thomas Young (1861–1938), leading Methodist minister, who had worked at the Centenary Chapel, York. His article 'A box of chocolates' in *British Weekly*, 8 January 1914 was a humorous piece on the benefits of eating chocolate.

waxes indignant at the thought of his bottle washing for Charlie
Masterman.[5] I believe G.N.[ewman] is right. Perhaps we shall see some
light next Saturday in our walk with J.R.[owntree].
[...]

22 January 1914
Chalfonts

Harry Gilpin[6] has just rung up from the works saying he and J.A.
Baker are coming up to see me so I must scribble thee a few lines
before they arrive, darling. [...]

1 February 1914
Queen's Hotel, Eastbourne – 5.40 pm

Percy [Alden] and I have just come in from a long walk on the downs
past Beach Head.
    [...]
    [...] G.N.[ewman] has let me down a bit – he is an awful man to
make arrangements with & now cannot come to me until Thursday!
so I have arranged with Ron [J.R. Gillett] to come for the day on
Tuesday and Currie Martin that evening for a good walk on Wednesday
so I shall be alright. [...]
    I did two schools in London this morning before coming here and
then directly after lunch we set out on our walk. [...]

2 February 1914
The Esplanade Hotel, Seaford, Sussex

Another glorious day, darling – the sun shining brightly and these high
chalk cliffs looking most beautiful. We have walked over here (12 miles)
and are returning by train as there would not be time to walk back
(even if there was power!) before Percy [Alden] has to return. The larks
have been singing as gaily as that day in June nine years ago. We had

---

    [5] T.E. Harvey had become PPS to C.F.G. Masterman, the Fin. Sec. to the Treasury,
in 1913.
    [6] Edmund Henry Gilpin (1876–1950), Dir. J. Baker & Sons, and creator of Baker,
Perkins Ltd in 1920; resigned from Quakers over his support for First World War; Lib.
cand. Finsbury 1922; kt. 1949.

an interesting talk with one of the coastguard men – a most intelligent mortal – reading Marcus Aurelius, Carlyle and studying theosophy but only receiving 23/- from government. Like so many more feeling this hardly sufficient for the nourishment of the body – this place is growing rapidly but at present very unfinished. It is interesting how schools prosper in these parts – in Eastbourne there are already over 40. Everyone now seems to think of sending children to the seaside not only for play but for work – which shows growing importance attached to *health* in these days.

[...]

The National Council unanimously accepted Peverett[7] on Saturday (as Secretary) so I have got him off my hands now but as we have fixed at once to try to enlarge & improve 'One & All' I have agreed to bear the loss. I don't think I shall be any better off, still I want to make this into an efficient organ before I lay down the work. I think Percy Alden is going to pitch into it with vigour.

[...]

3 February 1914
Queen's Hotel, Eastbourne

Another perfect day, darling, and Ron [J.R. Gillett] and I have had a glorious walk along the downs again. I should think we must have been 14 or 15 miles and I feel much better for these walks. Last night I read for two hours continuously and felt very little trouble with my eyes.

What a charming book 'Folk of the Furrow' is.[8] I think his description of labouring life is excellent.

Currie Martin has arrived and we have just had dinner together. Ron [J.R. Gillett] goes at 9.30.

[...]

Eastbourne is voting today whether it shall purchase the Devonshire Park for £600,000 [...].[9]

[...]

---

[7] George Peverett, Office Sec. NASU 1914–1933, Gen. Sec. 1933–1942.

[8] 'Christopher Holdenby', *Folk of the Furrow* (1913). 'Holdenby' was a pseudonym for the eminent agriculturist Ronald George Hatton (1886–1965); kt. 1949.

[9] Devonshire Parks and Bath Co., set up in 1873 by the Duke of Devonshire, Eastbourne's ground landowner, who owned many of the town's premier recreational facilities, including the eight acres of Devonshire Park. The council was attempting to buy the company – a proposal defeated by the ratepayers in 1913 and again in February 1914 by 3,468 votes to 2,773.

4 February 1914
Eastbourne

Currie Martin has just gone off to Brighton to some meeting there and
I am expecting George Peverett very shortly.
    [...]
I'm very much impressed with what a very fine set of men these
coastguard men are – the navy is really a very good training ground
for handy, all round men and I want to try and work to get them
better supplied with books from the Admiralty.[10] I was wrong yesterday
in saying the Duke wanted £600,000 for the Park at Eastbourne it was
£100,000 – but the citizens defeated the proposal by 600 votes.
    [...]

5 February 1914
Queen's Hotel, Eastbourne

Thanks for thy letter, darling. I am glad that the Sam Bell[11] meeting
passed off well – I don't think it would be wise to leave Ulster entirely
out but I think thou will't see that Asquith is willing to make larger
concessions to them next week – on the lines of Home Rule within
Home Rule.
    The fact that Consols have risen 5 points within the last fortnight
doesn't look as if many people thought there would be civil war! [...]

19 February 1914
242 St James Court

Thank thee, darling, for thy letter. No, I didn't see Helmsley[12] misbehave
as I was with G.N.[ewman] and Ramsay MacDonald – L.G. seemed
amused how angry the Tories get whenever discussing land. Winston

[10] *Hansard,* 5th series, 1914, LIX, 1056 for A.S.R.'s HofC question on reading material
in coastguard libraries.
[11] Samuel Alexander Bell (1863–1936), Ulster Quaker from Lurgan and strong Unionist;
manufacturer of cambric handkerchiefs. He had spoken at the Belfast Friends' Institute
on 3 February 1914 on 'The city's neglected children'.
[12] Charles William Reginald Duncombe, Vt Helmsley (1879–1916), Con. MP Thirsk &
Malton 1906–1915, when succ. as 2nd Earl of Feversham. On 17 February 1914 he had
been one of the Conservative MPs (though not the rudest) who persistently interrupted
Lloyd George during his reply to a Conservative motion condemning the 1909 Budget
and the Land Enquiry; *Hansard,* 5th series, 1914, LVIII, 800–916 for the debate.

[Churchill] that night too was somewhat effusive in the lobby evidently anxious to make friends with small navy men!

I went on a walk with E.R.C.[ross] in the park this morning [...] and this afternoon have been working quietly in the flat on an armament speech I must sometime deliver in the House.

[...]

I enclose invitation to the Asquith reception and first proof of the pamphlet Percy [Alden] and I have been working at.

24 February 1914
House of Commons

Thank thee, darling, for thine − I am glad thou enjoyed the Greek play. Nothing very eventful here. I think I scored nine divisions last night several of which Butcher missed so I have got a little start!

I had Henderson to dinner and a talk with Ted [Harvey] afterwards. He has written his Chairman suggesting he should resign and make way for Masterman but don't expect it will be accepted.[13] I certainly think it would be a dangerous move. [...]

25 February 1914
House of Commons

[...]

The debate last night helped matters I think.[14] The Irish were pleased with Asquith and Bonar Law's wild extravagance was felt to be unworthy of the situation even by Tories. It seems to me that the Tories, by the line they are taking, are ruining their chance of controlling labour in future years if they go to excesses. Ted [Harvey]'s chairman is very adverse to his taking any action towards giving the seat to Masterman. I don't see how he can proceed on those lines in face of his Chairman's view.

After my walk, I worked here this morning & then had G.N.[ewman]

[13] C.F.G. Masterman had been promoted to the Cabinet as Chanc. Duchy of Lancaster, but was defeated in the subsequent by-election in his seat at Bethnal Green, SW on 19 February 1914.
[14] *Hansard*, 5th series, 1914, LVIII, 1691–1728 for the debate on a Conservative motion that the govt should submit its changes to the Home Rule Bill to the HofC. Bonar Law pledged to 'assist Ulster in resisting by force what the Government mean to do'.

and Horne to lunch at the flat and had a very interesting talk
with them about the possibility of Brotherhood[15] and Adult Schools
cooperating for certain pieces of work. I hope Horne will come to the
National Council at Scalby in June for the Saturday at any rate.
Butcher didn't like Dillon's speech.

3 March 1914
House of Commons

[...]

I am glad to find that Dillon is quite happy about the PM's action
over Home Rule[16] & the Irish evidently know what he is going to
suggest and are satisfied.

4 March 1914
House of Commons

The House is up, darling, and after writing this letter I must change
and be off to Lady Barlow's for dinner.

It is extraordinary how directly a compromise is made, discussion
dries up & business is got through with extraordinary rapidity.

I spent the morning after my constitutional through the Park at the
office and then lunched at the flat with Sir George Paish and Percy
[Alden] to discuss the question of evidence before the Railway Commission.

This afternoon I have been to Percy Bigland's[17] to meet Baden
Powell.[18] I induced Percy's brother Alfred[19] to come along with me so
as to pair. There were an interesting group of friends there – F.[rederic]

---

[15] Brotherhood Movement, interdenominational nonconformist organization, founded
1875, aimed at working-class men. Promoted informal Sunday afternoon meetings for
worship, study and discussion.
    [16] Asquith had met the Irish leaders on 2 March 1914 and proposed the exclusion of
Ulster from Home Rule for a limited period.
    [17] Percy Bigland (1856–1926), Quaker and artist; founder member of the Royal Society
of Portrait Painters.
    [18] Sir Robert Stephenson Smyth Baden-Powell (1857–1941), general, famous for his
defence of Mafeking in the Boer War; founded Scout movement 1908; KCB 1909, cr.
Lord Baden-Powell 1929.
    [19] Alfred Bigland (1855–1936), Quaker businessman; Con. MP Birkenhead December
1910–1918, E. Birkenhead 1918–1922; resigned from Quakers autumn 1914.

T.[aylor], A.N.B.,[20] Edminson,[21] J.W. Graham, Arthur Wallis (who I understand is resigning his membership amongst Friends owing to Christian Science), Francis Fox[22] and many more.

B.[aden] P.[owell] is a very simple man and I thought extraordinarily appreciative of the work of Friends. He has I think learnt much in connection with his six years experience of the Scout's movement, has to decide whether to make the movement definitely military or the reverse, is certainly now tending towards the anti-war side though, of course, shooting, etc. for self defence is taught in many corps. Quietly I think Friends may do much to strengthen him on the right side. He is coming to lunch at the flat next Thursday week so thou wilt have an opportunity of seeing him if thou desires so to do. I want to have a good talk with him and G.N.[ewman]. Olive [Rowntree] was at the gathering. I hope she and Ernest[23] will come to breakfast tomorrow.

4 March 1914
House of Commons, 10.45

Lest thou think I was drunk, darling, when I wrote, I think I better explain that when the motion for adjournment came members talked on all sorts of subjects with the object of keeping the House sitting until 8.15 so that the Redistribution motion might come on & succeeded. I along with large numbers of Tories had left thinking the House was up! I have enjoyed my dinner with Lady Barlow but more of that tomorrow. Just returned here but no division.

8 March 1914
House of Commons

[...]
Before I asked Ted [Harvey] to dinner next Tuesday, he asked us so I have accepted. I had lunch with G.N.[ewman] today. L.G. seems

[20] Alfred Neave Brayshaw (1861–1940), old friend of A.S.R.; teacher at Bootham 1892–1903, Woodbrooke 1903–1906, when retd to Scarborough; bro. of Shipley and Russell Brayshaw.

[21] Frederick John Edminson (1860–1922), teacher at Quaker schools, including Leighton Park and Grove House, and convert to Quakerism; Sec. Woodbrooke extension cttee 1912; later Ed. *Police Review* and *The Land Worker*.

[22] Francis William Fox (1841–1918), Quaker businessman; well-known peace advocate and amateur ambassador.

[23] Ernest William Rowntree (1877–1936), senior civil servant at Bd of Trade; bro. of Olive Rowntree.

very keen on children at present and has in mind a children's budget![24]
[...]

13 March 1914
House of Commons

An interesting lunch with L.G., darling – full of life and energy but
taking a serious view of developments here. He thinks that the die-
hards are going to get control of the Conservative party and is expecting
the Army Bill to be thrown out & consequently the hottest election of
modern times.[25]

I have just secured a pair for Monday so I shall be in York for that
night at any rate.

18 March 1914
House of Commons

Thank thee for thine and for telephoning after consultation with
E.R.C.[ross] we decided to encourage Seebohm [Rowntree] to adhere
to his original plan. L.G. is somewhat happier now as he has induced
the PM to let him have a considerable sum out of the party fund for
his campaign. Barnes, the Newcastle man, came to breakfast and we
had a long talk about the Educational Campaign. I am much impressed
by his width of view and great spirit. After spending some time at the
office I speeded off to Golders Green with Barbara [McKenzie] – had
a light lunch with Mr and Mrs J. St G. Heath and then on to the
wedding.[26] The Meeting House is charming and all passed off very
happily. They said their say well and afterwards Mary Snowden
Braithwaite, Barbara [McKenzie] and another lady spoke A.N.B.[ray-
shaw] & Anne Warner Marsh[27] prayed. Barbara's, I thought, much the
most impressive offering on some old mystic's prayers for 'health
strength and sweetness'. After the reception at the Club House

---

[24] This may refer to the fact that on 26 February 1914 Lloyd George had agreed state
funds should be used to provide medical care for school children.

[25] Conservative leaders were considering whether to use the HofL to block the annual
renewal of the Army Bill. This course of action would have theoretically made it
impossible to maintain the Army.

[26] A.S.R. was attending the wedding of: John Percival Davies (1885–1950), Quaker
cotton manufacturer; Lab. cand. Blackburn 1922, 1923, Skipton 1929, 1931, 1933, 1935,
1945; cr. Ld Darwen 1946, Ld-in-Waiting 1949–1950, and Mary Kathleen Brown (d.
1964).

[27] Anne Warner Marsh (1847–1936), American Quaker.

A.N.B.[rayshaw] and I went off to call on Oscar [Rowntree]. He was bright but didn't look to me much better than before the illness. [...]

A.N.B.[rayshaw] is now established in the gallery listening to a very dull debate. I am going to have dinner with him shortly and then he stays the night at the flat.

Others at the wedding or afterwards were: Ted, Irene [Harvey], Lady Ayjah [Ada Newman], Chenda,[28] Henry Harris[29] – several younger Braithwaites, etc.

I thought thou would be interested in Baden Powell's letter.[30] Let me have it back on Thursday. Address letters tomorrow c/o Secretary, Yorkshire Liberal Women's Conference, Dewsbury, as I have to leave London 7.15!

19 March 1914
House of Commons

[...]

It has been an exciting afternoon here.[31] Bonar Law unusually conciliatory, Carson speaking like a man deranged.

Members do not understand what it all means but there is, I fear, real danger of some explosion of feeling in Ulster. A good many members think that a referendum on the lines of Bonar Law's proposal would give a large majority for Home Rule.

[...] [This morning] I went to the office – had a long interview with Mansbridge lunched at the Reform Club with Neil Primrose![32] and this afternoon have listened with great interest to the debate.

[...]

News of the 'mutiny at the Curragh' by army officers who preferred to resign rather than conduct operations against Ulster broke on 21 March 1914. The crisis was compounded on 22 March when Seely, the Secretary of State for War, added two paragraphs to an Army Council note to the officers, promising them that the army would not be used to enforce Home Rule on Ulster. The whole message had then

[28] Richenda Gillett (1873–1953), wife of J. Rowntree Gillett, A.S.R.'s first cousin.

[29] Possibly Henry Vigurs Harris (1850–1944), West-country Quaker.

[30] This letter has not survived. It may have been connected with the fact that A.S.R. joined the Council of the Boy Scouts' Association shortly after this time.

[31] The Cons moved a motion of censure on the govt's Irish policy on 19 March 1914; *Hansard*, 5th series, 1914, LIX, 2256–2380. Bonar Law offered to abide by the result of a referendum of the whole UK on the Libs' Home Rule proposals. Carson referred to the Libs as a 'government of cowards' and 'assassins'.

[32] Hon. Neil James Archibald Primrose (1882–1917), Lib. MP Wisbech January 1910–1917; US Foreign Office 1915, Coalition Lib. whip 1916–1917; youngest s. of ex-PM, Lord Rosebery.

to be repudiated by the Cabinet and Seely resigned on 25 March. Asquith asserted 'in all these matters the real question is whether or not the considered will, judgement, and authority of the people shall prevail'; Hansard, *5th series, 1914, LX, 421.*

25 March 1914
House of Commons

This is an extraordinary place, darling – yesterday the Liberals and Nationalists were in a state of terrible dejection over Seely's[33] mistake but today the PM has done magnificently and taken the war right into the enemy's camp and now the Tories are in the dumps and the Liberals feel that they have weathered splendidly a most difficult position.

Bonar Law's speech was quite the feeblest I have heard from him and the Tories are very anxious about the effects in the country of this new issue of the Army and the people which they have raised.

[...]

G.N.[ewman] had lunch with me today as I wanted to talk over with him the question of the feeding of children which is to come before the House on Friday.[34] I think I better stay for this, darling, as I should like to speak upon it. That means I shall be home at 9.05.

We had an interesting dinner last night in connection with the British Institute of Social Service with the Speaker in the chair. [...]

I am afraid this is a jerky letter but I have been writing in the House whilst Austen [Chamberlain] is speaking.

26 March 1914
The Flat

Thank thee, darling, for thine, & interesting enclosure – I am just going to the House for a few minutes and then to the Officers (Nat. Council) Meeting. Afterwards W.C.B.[raithwaite], G.N.[ewman], Horne, Alden, Henderson and I are going to dine together to talk over the possibility of common work and effort between the Brotherhoods and Adult

[33] John Edward Bernard Seely (1868–1947), Con. MP (Lib. from 1904) Isle of Wight 1900–1906, 1923–1924, Lib. MP Liverpool, Abercromby 1906–January 1910, Ilkeston March 1910–1922; US Colonies 1908–1911, US War Office 1911–1912, Sec. of State for War 1912–1914, PS Ministry of Munitions 1918–1919, US Ministry of Air 1919; cr. Ld Mottistone 1933.

[34] The Education (Provision of Meals) Act, 1914 compelled local authorities to provide school meals, including during holiday periods, and provided a govt subsidy. A.S.R. spoke in favour of the Bill on 27 March 1914; *Hansard*, 5th series, 1914, LX, 767–770.

Schools. I have had Malcolm Spencer[35] to lunch and an interesting talk with him. He is finishing with the Student Volunteers in the summer and seems as if he wished to give most of his time to the Free Church Fellowship but I think he would like to do a certain amount of lecturing for the Fircroft Council.

I believe it is most important for us to get nearer to many of these large men of ideas if we are going to make this educational work really grip the present generation.

I have been putting down a few thoughts for tomorrow's debate. [...]

31 March 1914
House of Commons

The House is very quiet today, darling, after yesterday's extraordinary development.[36] Asquith's great action has somewhat damped the spirits of the Tories and they are unhappy at having raised this great issue. Considering the tragic blunders of the past ten days involving the resignation of one Cabinet minister and two great generals it really is extraordinary that the government is stronger today than a fortnight ago. It would seem they have almost a charmed existence.

We are trying to arrange to present an address to Asquith at York when he travels up to Fife but he hates such things. I don't know whether it will come off.

I have finally decided not to go to Northampton as it is very doubtful if the York resolution will be reached. So I shall hope to come by the 10 o'clock train tomorrow night. I am arranging to go out to Grims Wood. Gerty [Taylor] has been in the House this afternoon and had tea with me. She is much impressed with thy support of Mount institutions [...].

Thy friend Whyte has a daughter. I asked him down to the Liberal meeting they are arranging at York on Saturday night (alas) but he felt bound to see the babe and her mother.

[...]

---

[35] Malcolm Spencer (1877–1950), Congregational minister; helped start the Student Christian Movement in 1905 and the Free Church Fellowship in 1909, as well as organizing numerous postwar interdenominational conferences; 'God's Back-Room Boy'.

[36] Asquith announced on 30 March 1914 that he would take over from Seely as Sec. of State for War. This meant he had to seek re-election in his seat of E. Fife and he left for Scotland on 3 April. The two generals who also resigned were Sir John French (1852–1925), Chief of the Imperial General Staff, and Sir Spencer Ewart (1861–1930), Adjutant-Gen.

6 April 1914
en route to London

I am nearing London after a quiet and uneventful journey, darling. There was little of special interest at the board – the question of constant thieving and dishonesty was again up and we really don't know how to deal with it effectively.

After lunch I went with several of the others to the Victoria Hall to see the film Cadburys are showing in several cinemas 'Cocoa from the Cradle to the Grave'; the West Indian pictures were really very good. [...]

We have the Flounders Trust tomorrow but it will be over in time for me to catch the 5.30 train – if as I hope I shall find that I have got a 'pair'!

15 April 1914
The Cocoa Works, York

I have had an active day here, darling. J.R.[owntree] arrived back yesterday and so we were able to have a meeting with the directors about Elect Cocoa which will shorten proceedings next Monday. [...]

Edith Wilson[37] and Horace Fleming[38] have been over – very full of the Birkenhead experiment. I think there is no doubt our little trust ought to put up the £200 that they want for the three years so that the experiment can be tried.

[...]

18 May 1914
House of Commons

I had a comfortable journey, darling – travelling with Middlebrook[39] from Doncaster – I had tea with Ted [Harvey] just before he left for

[37] Edith Jane Wilson (nee Brayshaw) (1869–1953), leading Quaker; lived in Birkenhead 1902–1915; prominent in peace movements and Asst Clerk of YM 1915–1921; sister of A.N., Shipley, and Russell Brayshaw.

[38] Horace Fleming (1872–1941), Quaker businessman; founder of Birkenhead Educational Settlement (Beechcroft) 1914, and later Chmn Educational Settlements Association 1922–1935. The Joseph Rowntree Charitable Trust provided £200 for three years to pay an assistant warden at Beechcroft.

[39] William Middlebrook (1851–1936), Lib. MP South Leeds 1908–1922; kt. 1916, Bt 1930.

Ipswich. The issue there is very uncertain – Masterman standing at the wish of the PM.[40] Ted [Harvey] is most devoted to Masterman and says he is making an excellent fight. I haven't been much in the House as I wanted to clean up matters at the office. Henderson wants me to speak at the Albert Hall in November at the opening meeting of the Brotherhood Campaign. [...]

19 May 1914
House of Commons

I have little to report, darling. This morning I worked at the office, then lunched with the Nation folk – all very puzzled how the Irish tangle is to be straightened – then to the House and had tea with Ted and Irene [Harvey] and at 7.30 went to the Swarthmore Lecture,[41] able but very dull! and had to stand at the door all the time the crowd was so great.

[...] I am here to vote for the Disestablishment Bill – I hope for the last time. I have just been talking to Henderson and he thinks that it looks as if we were going to have an election in July! but, of course, nothing can be said at present – things seem better every day. There were many enquiries after thee at YM – Holdsworths, Crosfields and Elkintons – I hope to have Joshua [Rowntree] to tea tomorrow.

20 May 1914
House of Commons

An uneventful day, darling. Select Committee until 2.30 then correspondence – and since tea with Frank Pollard[42] & Pounder,[43] a short time in the House listening to the dual between Healy and George. Cousin Joshua [Rowntree] has not been here. I suppose the YM was

[40] C.F.G. Masterman attempted to be re-elected to Parlt in a by-election at Ipswich on 23 May 1914. He lost by 532 votes.
[41] Swarthmore Lecture; annual public lecture on Quakerism inaugurated by the Woodbrooke Extension Cttee in 1908. In 1914 it was delivered by Edward Grubb on 'The historic and inward Christ'.
[42] Francis Edward Pollard (1872–1951), Quaker and teacher at Bootham School 1890–1920; Lib. representative for Bootham ward on York council 1910–1913; m. Mary (nee Spence Watson) (1875–1962), daughter of Robert Spence Watson, and hence J.B. Morrell's brother-in-law.
[43] Pounders; a family closely connected with Leeman Road Adult School in York, where A.S.R. taught for many years.

too interesting. Frank Pollard said a good discussion on Kikuyu was proceeding.[44] I am not quite sure what I shall do tonight. I think possibly after an important division at 8.15 I shall go off to the theatre as I feel in need of a change. [...]

9 June 1914
House of Commons

Just a line, darling, to let thee know that I had a comfortable journey travelling with Bowes and Bertha [Morrell] most of the way discussing newspapers. I then had an hour with Peverett preparing for Scalby and dined with Ted [Harvey] and other members here. I have just had an interesting talk with Redmond about Nationalist volunteers. I have a very full day tomorrow beginning with Currie Martin to breakfast and Ernest Taylor sleeps at the flat tonight. [...]

10 June 1914
House of Commons

[...] I have had a busy day. Currie Martin to breakfast – office – Select Committee lunch with Barbara [McKenzie] and then to House when I spoke on the Postal question[45] evidently with some acceptance by the kind things that were said afterwards and it ended in my being called into consultation with Ramsay MacDonald and I hope we have fixed up a plan which the government will accept. Dinner with Ramsay Mac[Donald] and Henderson and a heart-to-heart talk with the latter about Brotherhoods and Adult Schools – then Evans and Headleys[46] and now I return to the House to hear the government answer Ramsay's speech.

I thought your account of Miss Feldwick's funeral showed it to be a very honourable one.

[44] The report of the Friends' Foreign Mission Association provoked a long debate on whether Quakers could join an interdenominational missionary organization, like that set up in Kikuyu in 1913.

[45] *Hansard*, 5th series, 1914, LXIII, 343–347. In the debate on Post Office supply day, A.S.R. argued for a higher minimum wage for Post Office employees and arbitration of industrial disputes.

[46] Headley Bros; Quaker printing and publishing firm set up in Canterbury in 1881 by Herbert Dimsdale Headley (1862–1937) and Burgess Henry Headley (1866–1943).

11 June 1914
House of Commons

A somewhat dismal day, darling! The morning over Headley's difficulties
with Ernest Taylor and lunch in connection with the Sunday Closing
Bill Assoc., this afternoon in the House listening for some time to the
Women's debate[47] – then with Mr Slade over Backhouse's difficulties![48]
and now I am expecting a telegram saying that the Brayshaws are
coming! [...]

23 June 1914
House of Commons

Just a line, darling, to let thee know that I had a comfortable journey
up with Sebastian [Meyer] and a long interesting talk. Then lunch with
the Nation people whom I found very apprehensive about the Irish
situation. A very short tea with Mr and Mrs Noel Buxton[49] – very
enthusiastic about their honeymoon at Assissi – then an interview with
the Board of Trade regarding light railways with Sebastian [Meyer] –
then our little group who were all very angry about the government's
collapse yesterday and we are urging the abolition of the sugar duties
instead of dropping the Income Tax.[50] Now I am going across to have
dinner with Gerty [Taylor] and Richard [Cross], then I will go to hear
Mrs Besant.[51]

30 June 1914
House of Commons

There is little to record, darling, except a scorchingly hot journey and
sojourn in London. [...] attended the Nation lunch spent most of the
afternoon here and a few minutes in the Westminster bath – saw [Dr

[47] *Hansard,* 5th series, 1914, LXIII, 508–560; a debate on suffragette violence and the
treatment of suffragette prisoners inaugurated by Lord Robert Cecil.

[48] James Backhouse (1861–1945), Quaker nurseryman at Acomb, near York.

[49] Noel Buxton m. Lucy Edith Pelham (nee Burn) (1888–1960) on 30 April 1914. She
succeeded him as Lab. MP North Norfolk 1930–1931, and was then Lab. MP Norwich
1945–1950.

[50] Lloyd George's 1914 Budget ran into procedural difficulties in the HofC. On 22 June
1914 Herbert Samuel announced that as increased grants to local authorities could not
be paid that year, the top rate of income tax would only be increased by 1d, rather than
2d.

[51] Annie Besant (1847–1933), activist in numerous causes, including at various times
atheism, birth control, Fabianism, theosophy, and Indian Home Rule.

Peter] Mac[donald] and his wife – dined with Leif Jones and tried hard to get him to arrange with Lady Carlisle[52] to attend to her property on the Castle Howard Estate. He evidently has tried hard to do this but so far has failed. I listened to the Railway debate and said a few words.[53] Now we are off 30 minutes earlier than expected.

1 July 1914
House of Commons

[...]
    Sir George Paish and Ernest (Rowntree) came to breakfast to discuss a difficulty connected with the Railway Commission. [...]
    Then I lunched with Malcolm Spencer to talk over his future, then a few minutes chat with William Cadbury and Harrison Barrow[54] who were up in a private bill. Harrison is very pressed to take the Lord Mayoralty and will, I think, accept. His chief fear is lest the King should descend on Birmingham and knight him!
    Then a long talk with Peverett on the Autumn Conference – tea with Richard [Cross] and Slade over Backhouse's affairs and I hope to have Richard [Cross], Dillon and Ponsonby to dine and talk over Ireland – such is our little program on a baking day. [...] I am going to Sheffield on Friday to the Wilson memorial service[55] which means that I shall not reach York until 4.35 [...].

2 July 1914
House of Commons

It has been a relief, darling, to have it cooler today. I spent the morning at the office and lunched at the Reform and had an interesting talk with Hamar Greenwood afterwards – he's expecting another youngster in October. Then I had long talk with Barbara [McKenzie] [...].

---

[52] Rosalind Frances Howard, Countess of Carlisle (1845–1921), widow of 9th Earl of Carlisle; acted as his estate agent from 1888, inherited Castle Howard after his death 1911; temperance fanatic, leading suffrage activist and President Womens' Liberal Federation 1891–1901, 1906–1914. Leif Jones had been her secretary.

[53] *Hansard*, 5th series, 1914, LXIV, 326–328 for A.S.R.'s brief intervention on the Great Northern Railway Bill.

[54] Harrison Barrow (1868–1953), cousin of George Cadbury; Managing Dir. Barrows Stores in Birmingham; Birmingham councillor as a Lib. 1898, 1899–1902, 1904–1918, Lab. 1922–1925, 1926–1930, Alderman 1930–1949; accepted Ld Mayoralty in 1914, but withdrew on outbreak of war. As Chmn FSC in 1918, accepted responsibility for publishing *A Challenge to Militarism* and served six months in prison.

[55] Henry Joseph Wilson died 29 June 1914.

8 July 1914
House of Commons

I have little of interest, darling, to report. I was most of the morning
at the Select Committee. Lunched with Carol and G.N.[ewman] at the
abode of the former – had a long talk this afternoon with Ramsay
MacDonald and Ward[56] (of the Brotherhood) about Adult Education
and in between whiles have been working at the office. Tonight Fleming
is coming to see me from Birkenhead about their settlement. [...] I
hope to stay Friday night with G.N.[ewman] and Theodora[57] says it is
alright for me to go to Selly Wood on Saturday.

9 July 1914
House of Commons

I had a satisfactory interview last night, darling, with Fleming and hope
I was able to get the Birkenhead Settlement going – today I was at the
office during the morning – lunched with G.N.[ewman] at the Reform
Club and then entertained these 30 German students on the terrace
with the assistance of Ethel Johnson[58] and Elsie Chittick and several
MPs.

Then attended a committee to hear members on Foreign relations &
tonight dine with the Baker family.

[...]

10 July 1914
House of Commons

[...]

[...] I have been to the office this morning, went with Cross to the
flat to lunch and Gerty [Taylor] came in shortly afterwards so I got a
good talk with her. I am going off shortly with G.N.[ewman] and hope
to get some tennis tonight, shall attend the WEA Council at Toynbee
tomorrow and then go off to Selly Wood. [...]

---

[56] William Ward, leading figure in Brotherhood movement and author *Brotherhood and
Democracy* (1910).

[57] Theodora Lloyd Wilson (nee Harris) (1865–1947), wife of Henry Lloyd Wilson.

[58] Ethel Sturge Johnson, schoolteacher in USA, cousin of M.K.R.; Elsie Chittick, her
close friend.

14 July 1914
House of Commons

A line, darling, to let thee know of a comfortable journey, of lunch
with the Nation people and entertaining the Elkintons[59] on the terrace.
They were very pleased to be able to hear debates both in the House
of Commons and Lords. Their only grief was that thou wast not here
to share. Tonight I have a little dinner party consisting of E.R.C.[ross],
Heath, Winifred [Sturge], Alden, W.C.B.[raithwaite], Margaret Harris[60]
and Lynn to discuss education to rural villages. [...]

15 July 1914
House of Commons

There is little to report, darling. The dinner last night passed off very
well. Margaret Harris, the Secretary of the AOS, was particularly cordial
and helpful. W.C.B.[raithwaite] came home with me afterwards – he
is anxious to spend a few days with us in September at the Huts or
elsewhere! Today, I was at the School Committee this morning – we
finished our report – and this afternoon have spent most of the time
here having tea with the Toulmins[61] & Lady Toulmin says she met us
at Warwick in 1905! [...]

21 July 1914
House of Commons

There is little to report, darling, but I hope thou hast had a comfortable
day and art feeling really stronger. I had a quiet journey up including
a short talk with Sydney Leetham on the usual. Home and lunch with
the Nation folk. Then went to the Liberal meeting of members greatly
concerned at the King's interference about Home Rule[62] [...].

It is thought that present tendencies point somewhat strongly to an
early general election, but I don't think it is any use speculating as
things alter so quickly. We must first live in the belief that there is an

[59] Joseph Elkinton (1859–1920), Philadelphia Quaker, widely-travelled and well-known
as a minister and author. His wife was Sarah West Passmore.

[60] Margaret Harris, Sec. Ackworth Old Scholars' Association.

[61] Sir George Toulmin (1857–1923), Lib. MP Bury 1902–1918; kt. 1911; m. 1882 Mary
Elizabeth (nee Edelston).

[62] On 21 July 1914 a conference of the Liberal, Conservative, Irish Nationalist, and
Unionist leaders met at Buckingham Palace to attempt to settle the Ulster crisis.

overruling providence and that we shall be guided aright and therefore are at peace.

[...]

22 July 1914
House of Commons

[...]
[...] I had lunch with Merrttens[63] and have been at the House this afternoon having tea with Ted and Irene [Harvey].

Members are incensed at the King's speech – thou willst see that Asquith accepts responsibility though it is clear from the way he answered the question that it was the King's wording or rather Lord Stamfordham's,[64] I expect.

Dillon told me this afternoon that Stamfordham said to him at the Palace this morning, 'It is clear now that the old view the King can do no wrong doesn't hold now – in fact, the reverse seems the case. He can never do anything right'! an interesting remark from the man who probably more than anyone else is advising the King in the risky course. However, Dillon takes a hopeful view and thinks the resentment the King's speech will excite will have the effect of making the King very careful not to put himself further against the people in refusing to sign the Home Rule Bill – or signing it under conditions.

I hope thou will't get back safely to Chalfonts tomorrow, darling. I forgot to tell thee thou was invited to Asquith's garden party which takes place tomorrow afternoon. So I shall have to go alone.

23 July 1914
242 St James Court

I have just come from the PM's garden party darling – a somewhat dull affair. I thought perhaps that was because I was without thee. However, I only stayed a very few minutes. Mrs Asquith was much concerned with the state of the weather, said she wouldn't have gone to a garden party today for a £1000! I spent most of the morning at a

---

[63] Frederick Merrttens (1849–1935), German-born industrialist. Active in Adult School movement in Rugby and in furthering international links. Joined Quakers 1914.

[64] Arthur John Bigge (1849–1931), Private Sec. Queen Victoria 1895–1901, extra equerry Edward VII 1901–1910, Private Sec. George V 1910–1931; cr. Lord Stamfordham 1911. A.S.R. is referring to George V's message to the Buckingham Palace conference. In reply to Arthur Ponsonby's question, Asquith stated, rather ambiguously, 'I take the whole responsibility for it'; *Hansard*, 5th series, 1914, LXV, 454.

hard committee with Seebohm [Rowntree] and Cross and two or three Liberal agents discussing the wisdom of the government declaring for a general minimum wage policy for the Towns.[65] [...]

I think probably the Conference will fail and now I believe the government are considering the policy I have tried greatly to urge upon them – the policy of the 'clean cut' and then allowing each county to vote itself into the Irish parliament. If they agreed to this we should, of course, have to pass the Amending Bill[66] through the House of Commons on these lines and throw the responsibility of rejecting it upon the Lords.

[...]

28 July 1914
House of Commons

[...]
[...] Richard [Cross] joined me and had a comfortable journey and sojourn at Doncaster. This morning we managed to get the Bill giving power to feed school children during the holidays. I am writing this whilst our little 'Social Reform' committee is sitting.

[...]
Everything here is very uncertain but I think there is no doubt that the chances of keeping European peace is distinctly better than yesterday though I fear Austria will fight Servia.

The Amending Bill is now down for Thursday. I hope we shall be able to pass it thru the House but Sunday's proceedings[67] have, of course, angered the Nationalists and they would much prefer that we dropped it.

[...]

29 July 1914
House of Commons

[...] I was at the office most of this morning. Lunched with G.N.[ewman] at Carol's and have had tea with Ted and Irene [Harvey]. Tonight our little group is entertaining Mr and Mrs Noel Buxton. I am going now

[65] Asquith had approved a national minimum wage for towns as part of the Liberals' Land Campaign on 11 June 1914.
[66] Amending bill; the govt bill to amend the Home Rule Bill, allowing concessions to Ulster.
[67] Irish Volunteers landed a consignment of guns at Howth on 26 July 1914; troops opened fire in Dublin, killing three people.

to see Slade about James Backhouse and then we have an important
meeting to discuss the European situation which as thou will't see is
very grave.[68]

[...]

30 July 1914
The Reform Club

I think I better take the present opportunity, darling, of sending thee a
few lines as it may be difficult afterwards. We had a very happy dinner
party last night which I think the Buxtons enjoyed. Afterwards Richard
[Cross] and I had a considerable talk with Redmond in his room. Prior
to the dinner the Liberal Foreign Affairs group[69] met to discuss the
European situation. There is, of course, amongst the group very strong
feeling that whatever happens amongst the other European powers
England must keep herself out of the quarrel and whilst it is hoped
and believed that the government and Grey are absolutely agreed upon
this at present, there are very strong influences being brought to bear
on the other side. Both the Tories and the Pall Mall [Gazette] today
are urging the government to state publicly at once that if Russia and
France are brought into the conflict this country will be behind them.
It is because of this that several believe that liberal MPs must speak
out strongly on the other side and that is why I have felt it was right
to speak to the Executive in York on Friday night if they wish.
    One cannot do much and whatever happens in the future one wants
to feel that we did what we could. I shall write to Barmoor when I
hear from York if the meeting has been arranged.
    This European crisis has for the moment put a general election out
of mind but I cannot feel sure yet that this will be for long because if
things get worse and this country seems being pressed into war I feel
very strongly the government should resign rather than be forced to
direct a movement they wholly disapproved of.
    This afternoon the Amending Bill comes on – then we have another
Foreign Affairs Meeting – then I have the Nat. Council Officers
Meeting followed by dinner to the group who are interviewing the
Brotherhood group tomorrow morning. So thou sees I am very busy.
    This morning I have paid a very interesting visit to Mrs Humphrey

[68] About twelve Liberal MPs discussed the outbreak of war between Serbia and Austria
and sent a letter to Grey demanding British neutrality.
[69] Liberal Foreign Affairs group; group of Liberal MPs critical of Grey's foreign policy,
set up in 1911. At their meeting on 30 July 1914 about twenty-five MPs demanded Britain
remain neutral in any war.

Ward's[70] vacation school at the Passmore Edward's Settlement and was greatly pleased with it but I will tell thee about it when we meet.

I won't close as I may be able to add a few lines later, dearest.

Foreign Affairs Meeting – 6 pm. Matters are terribly grave. I have agreed to speak at York tomorrow and wired thee to that effect. I hope I shall get to thee early Saturday.

31 July 1914
Chalfonts

This will hardly reach thee, darling, before I am with thee but I thought I would just send a line to say that I believe it was right to have the meeting – it was really a very solemn time and they were absolutely unanimous in favour of non-intervention.

Thou will't see how very serious matters are; both Russia and Germany mobilising but there is even yet time for peaceful intreaty.

We were very busy all yesterday over 'A Call to the Nation' but eventually this morning on Lord Bryce's[71] suggestion decided to confine it to a manifesto to Adult Schools and Brotherhoods (as another is going out this week).[72] But I will tell thee all about it when we meet and about my visit to the Archbishop of Canterbury[73] late last night.

3 August 1914
House of Commons (in the chamber in pencil)

No time to write, darling, except to say that things are as grave as they can be and that the country will be at war in, I fear, very few hours.

Grey's speech has of course made a great effect but it is really a

[70] Mary Augusta Ward (1851–1920), grand-daughter of Thomas Arnold and famous novelist; opposed women's suffrage, but active in many philanthropic causes, including founding play centres and schools for handicapped children.

[71] James Bryce (1838–1922), Lib. MP Tower Hamlets 1880–1885, S. Aberdeen 1885–1907; US Foreign Office 1886, Chanc. Duchy of Lancaster 1892–1894, Pres. Bd of Trade 1894–1895, Chief Sec. for Ireland 1906–1907, Amb. to USA 1907–1913; cr. Vt Bryce 1914.

[72] The officers of the National Council of Adult Schools issued a message on 30 July 1914, urging prayer for peace. A few days later a further message called on all members to aid those of foreign birth, work for relief of suffering, and be ready to help forward a speedy end to the war.

[73] Randall Thomas Davidson (1848–1930), Dean of Windsor 1883–1891, Bishop of Rochester 1891–1895, Bishop of Winchester 1895–1903, Archbishop of Canterbury 1903–1928, when cr. Ld Davidson of Lambeth. J.A. Baker saw Davidson on the night of 30 July to represent the views of the Lib. MPs opposed to war, so presumably he was accompanied by A.S.R.

damning indictment of the Balance of Power – Grey's pet policy.

Germany's action in connection with Belgium and now I hear in taking Basle makes our path more difficult.[74] I will try and write later but I must now just try and put down a few thoughts if it seems best to speak.

3 August 1914
House of Commons

Only a line, darling, to let thee know that Ted [Harvey] spoke magnificently tonight – quite the best speech made against the government and excellently received. I said a few words but never was able to strike the great note he did.[75] However, friends and opponents were very kind to us both afterwards. Tonight a few of us have had a long talk with Ramsay MacDonald and tomorrow are going to have a joint meeting with the Labour group. It looks as if some coalition with them was possible but I will write more of this tomorrow.

Germany, of course, is making it all very difficult for us. I am refusing at the moment meetings as I believe I must stay here whilst the House is sitting. One can do something by consultation.

4 August 1914
House of Commons, 5.15 pm

The House is up, darling, but I have two more committees to attend so I must get a few lines off to thee now. I forgot to mention that Henry Scattergood[76] arrived yesterday. He is with a cricket team and hopes to be able to come and see us at Barmoor (if that is convenient) on August 22nd. He came this morning to breakfast. I have been spending practically all day in connection with war matters. This morning at the Neutrality Committee[77] (Graham Wallas,[78] Cross,

[74] There were persistent false rumours on 3 August 1914 that Germany had already invaded Belgium and had also invaded the Netherlands and Switzerland.

[75] *Hansard*, 5th series, 1914, LXV, 1838–1839 for T.E. Harvey's speech and 1845–1847 for A.S.R.'s.

[76] Joseph Henry Scattergood (1877–1953), Quaker businessman from Philadelphia; best man at A.S.R.'s wedding.

[77] British Neutrality Cttee; a cttee organized by Graham Wallas and financed by C.P. Trevelyan. Mainly consisted of Lib. intellectuals and journalists. This was its first meeting; it was wound up the next day.

[78] Graham Wallas (1858–1932), Lib. educationalist and social theorist; teacher and lecturer, latterly at London School of Economics 1895–1923.

Macaulay Trevelyan,[79] Hobson, etc.) then at the Nation lunch and since in the House. But one feels almost powerless against the tremendous influence against one or one is so unutterably sad about the whole matter that it is difficult to work and as thou will't see the action of Germany makes it much more difficult to keep even men of goodwill straight. Ted [Harvey]'s speech last night was quite the happiest interlude I have had.

I am not sure of future action it looks as if the House would be up at the end of the week. I am pressed to go to Manchester for Sunday but if war is declared I am not sure that there is any good in holding meetings. However, I shall not reply until tomorrow.[80]

5 August 1914
House of Commons

Thank thee, darling, for thine – what an awful time it is we are living through. I have never felt before so unutterably sad but I am trying not to let it conquer me and am working as hard as ever I can – it is the only way to keep one's equilibrium. Last night Ted [Harvey], Cross and I dined at the Victoria Restaurant so as to be able to meet Baker and Dickinson on their return from Constance[81] but somehow missed them and it wasn't until 11.30 that we managed to get together but of course it was too late for them to do anything then. Then Harry Gilpin wanted to talk about Friends *service* which has taken much thought and I think we are going to make a call on 500 young Friends to give themselves to the Prince of Wales National Relief Committee.[82] This morning Norman Angell breakfasted with us and we talked over future policy. Then to a meeting of the Neutrality Committee which was wound up – lunch with G.N.[ewman] and talk over Friends service, advice to Adult scholars, then a talk with Jack Pease – he is not going to resign but definitely going to stay in the Cabinet with the object being there to urge settlement at the earliest opportunity and to help to

[79] George Macaulay Trevelyan (1876–1962), Lib. historian, already well-known for his trilogy on Garibaldi; Regius Prof. of Modern History Cambridge Univ. 1927–1940, Master of Trinity College, Cambridge 1940–1951; bro. of C.P. Trevelyan.

[80] A.S.R. did not speak at this meeting.

[81] Baker and Dickinson had been instrumental in setting up the Associated Councils of Churches in the British and German Empires in 1911. They had been attending an international church conference on peace at Constance when war was declared.

[82] The Prince of Wales was Pres. of the National Relief Fund, an organization set up to distribute charitable donations to those in distress. It collected over £1 million in a week.

feed, along with G.N.[ewman], 9 million children if this is necessary. Then an hour in the House – tea with John[83] and Henry [Scattergood] (John looked tired but very interested in all his experiences) then to a meeting of Liberal members re cooperation with Labour and now I am off to the office and then home. Henry Hodgkin,[84] Ted [Harvey], Cross, Phil Baker[85] and G.N.[ewman] to dinner at the flat to consider what we are to say to Friends and Adult Scholars etc., afterwards Gilpin comes in to discuss Relief etc., so thou sees we are having a very active time.

Excuse more now, darling, as I must be off to my other letters.

6 August 1914
House of Commons, 11.30 pm

These are terrific days, darling, but hard work is the best solace for getting through these difficult sad days. Last night Henry Hodgkin, Cross, Ted [Harvey], Phil Baker and I had a very useful time here at dinner and afterwards talking over a manifesto to Adult Schools for Saturday and the action Friends should take. The result is we have I think produced a helpful document that is going to the schools and Henry [Hodgkin] has today written a really great letter which we hope the Meeting for Sufferings will adopt tomorrow and send out for next Sunday and put in the papers for general consumption.[86] Then at 10.30 Gilpin came for public discussion of the call to Friends for personal service and we are going tomorrow to try and get this endorsed by the Meeting for Sufferings. This morning Henry Scattergood came to breakfast and all the cricket matches nearby are being cancelled so he will, I think, come to us on Sunday week – August 15–16 which would

[83] John Wilfred Harvey (1889–1967), younger bro. of M.K.R.; lecturer in philosophy Birmingham Univ., prof. of philosophy Leeds Univ. 1932–1954. Active in FAU.

[84] Dr Henry Theodore Hodgkin (1877–1933), leading Quaker, particularly concerned with missions to China; Sec. Friends' Foreign Mission Association 1910–1920, Chmn Fellowship of Reconciliation 1915–1920; nephew of Thomas Hodgkin.

[85] Philip John Baker (Noel-Baker from 1923) (1889–1982), s. of J.A. Baker and leading young Quaker; Officer Commanding FAU 1914–1915; Lab. MP Coventry 1929–1931, Derby 1936–1950, S. Derby 1950–1970; PS Ministry of War Transport 1942–1925, Min. of State 1945–1946, Sec. of State for Air 1946–1947, Sec. of State Commonwealth Relations 1947–1950, Min. Fuel and Power 1950–1951; cr. Ld Noel-Baker 1977. Variously a silver medallist at 1920 Olympics, Cassell Prof. of International Relations at LSE 1924–1929, and winner of Nobel Peace Prize 1959.

[86] The Society of Friends issued a general statement on 8 August 1914. It described the conditions which caused the war as 'unChristian', urged consideration of the situation that would arise after the war and hoped the war would not be conducted in a vindictive spirit. Nine newspapers carried it as an advert and 475,000 copies were distributed.

enable thee to go to Margaret[87] on the 17th & 18th. At 9 Heath and Allen Baker arrived and then all the morning we discussed at Masterman's request ways of stimulating employment – we want to give steady employment rather than relief if we can. We wired to Seebohm [Rowntree] to come up and now he and Reiss[88] are hard at work at the same problem. One of the points Cross and I have been busy at is trying to arrange a compromise with the Tories to let the Housing Bill[89] go through which would enable 100,000 houses to be built. I am very hopeful we have been successful but I don't want to be too sure less disappointment follows. I spoke this afternoon for a few minutes[90] then saw Henry Hodgkin about his letter and then dined with John Burns and Ted [Harvey]. There is a very strong spirit of comradeship growing up amongst those of us opposed to the war which cheers one. Burns had just come from the King whom he had been frightening but I will tell thee about this when we meet. About this I cannot tell until after tomorrow it depends upon whether Masterman or Samuel want us any more immediately. I know thou wants me to stay as long as I can effectively help. I am sending thee some letters which came today which are a sample of those arriving at present.

Farewell, darling one – I feel thou art near me constantly helping.

7 August 1914
Chalfonts, 10.15

[...]

A satisfactory Meeting for Sufferings which heartily adopted our little committee's suggestion and tomorrow thou will't see in the papers the really wonderful message which Henry Hodgkin has written.

What an awful slaughter of Germans this is. I didn't like wiring the account to thee but I gathered thou really wanted to know news.

[...]

---

[87] Margaret Ford (nee Harvey) (1881–1917), sister of M.K.R.; m. Rawlinson Charles Ford (1879–1964), Quaker silk manufacturer.

[88] Richard Leopold Reiss (1883–1959), barrister and univ. lecturer; Lib. cand. Chichester January, December 1910, St Pancras SE 1918, Lab. cand. Colchester 1922, 1923, 1924, 1929, Preston 1935; head organizer rural section of Land Enquiry 1912–1914, Chmn Executive Cttee Town and Country Planning Association 1918–1929.

[89] The Housing (No. 2) Bill, 1914 provided state subsidies for local authorities to construct housing. It was introduced on 8 August 1914 and passed on 10 August.

[90] *Hansard*, 5th series, 1914, LXV, 2096–2097 for A.S.R.'s speech on the vote of credit for the war.

10 August 1914
House of Commons

The post is just going, darling, but I want to let thee know that I had a comfortable journey – attending two meetings of our group (one the committee) and we decided to lie low at present.[91] Was in the House whilst the Housing Bill was going through and had to defend our compromise against Hogge's onslaught.[92] In a few minutes I am going to dinner at Morrell's[93] to meet Trevelyan,[94] Angell, MacDonald and several others to discuss the kind of question Cross and I were talking over last night. [...]

11 August 1914
House of Commons, 1.30

I am not sure whether I shall have an opportunity of writing thee later, darling, so whilst waiting for lunch I want just to let thee know that I fear I shall not get up to thee until the end of the week. Seebohm [Rowntree] has been asked to undertake the enquiry work for the whole country except London in connection with the Prince of Wales Fund and after enquiring to advise the Executive week by week as to where the money shall be spent and how, and he is agreeing to do this on the understanding that four or five of us shall unite with him and so I must stay here and help all I can. It will probably be helpful to the Friends organisations. Harry Gilpin and Allen Baker who came to see me this morning have over 600 applications already. We are very anxious to get some of them placed *quickly* and we have another conference this evening.

The dinner last night at Morrell's was very interesting. MacDonald, E.D. Morel, Angell, Ponsonby, Trevelyan – we talked until late last

[91] When co-operation with the Lab. Party was stymied by its prowar stance, Libs with doubts about the war formed a new group on 6 August. A.S.R. was included on its cttee, which was authorized on 7 August to draw up a statement on Grey's foreign policy. A.S.R. fully concurred with the agreement on 10 August not to make public any such statement.

[92] *Hansard,* 5th series, 1914, LXV, 2283 and 2285 for Hogge's objections and A.S.R.'s speech defending the compromise arrangements with the Cons to pass the Housing (No. 2) Bill.

[93] The decision to form the UDC was taken at a series of meetings, of which this was one, at Philip Morrell's house at 44 Bedford Square.

[94] Charles Philips Trevelyan (1870–1958), Lib. MP Elland 1899–1918, Lab. MP Newcastle-upon-Tyne Central 1922–1931; PS Bd of Education 1908–1914, when resigned in protest at decision to declare war, Pres. Bd of Education 1924, 1929–1931; succ. as 3rd Bt 1928.

night about the organisation that will be required in future to advocate a safe foreign policy and the way in which this will probably effect parties in the future. Its early days to speak yet but it looks to me as if this war will probably result in the creation of a new party composed of men from both the Radical and Labour parties.

[...]

The requests for the Meeting for Sufferings appeals is very large – Isaac Sharp[95] tells me 100,000 are having to be printed.

11 August 1914
Chalfonts, York

[...] There is an appalling amount of muddle, confusion and overlapping in connection with the organisation of the various schemes in London for the stimulation of employment and relief of distress. Seebohm [Rowntree] and I spent a good deal of time yesterday trying to systematise this work and suggest lines for future action but now little Benn[96] who asked Seebohm to do this has been superseded and the jealousies of departments prevent a really effective scheme on the lines we discussed being carried through, so greatly to our personal inclinations and relief we have felt free to retire from the fray. This will give us time to look after the business where many of the problems are very difficult, and the consideration of what to do with all the folks who we are largely responsible for financing engaged in social, political and educational work will all require great care. We made out there were nearly 80 of such! I fear we must be prepared for considerably reduced dividends and this will, of course, seriously effect this work we have been trying to carry on because all our money and all the Trust money comes from the same source.

[...]

Farewell, darling one. I am living in fear of an awful slaughter at the first great battle – however, we cannot help it and must try to keep calm and confident.

PS The Territorials have now commandeered our large dining room!

[95] Isaac Sharp (1847–1917), Recording Clerk of London YM 1890–1917.

[96] William Wedgwood Benn (1877–1960), Lib. MP Tower Hamlets, St George's 1906–1918, Leith 1918–1927, Lab. MP N. Aberdeen 1928–1931, Manchester, Gorton 1937–1942, when cr. Vt Stansgate; junior Lib. whip 1910–1915, Sec. of State India 1929–1931, Sec. of State for Air 1945–1946. In 1914 was Chmn and chief organizer of National Relief Fund.

17 August 1914
The Cocoa Works, York

Just a line, darling, to let thee know that I have had an interesting but active day here and in the city with many new problems to discuss.

The committee this afternoon was quite satisfactory.[97] I think one was able to help. Butcher was very agreeable and backed me up alright.
[...]

19 August 1914
The Cocoa Works, York

[...]
[...] This was written before the schools committee. Now 6.40 I have only a few minutes before going to the Mansion House to the Distress Committee. Father, Ted [Harvey], Miss Harrison and Julia were there in addition to most members of the sub. Tomorrow I will send thee a copy of the minutes I have just drafted summing up our decisions which were as follows:

1. On the whole strongly in favour having the Mount elsewhere. The most likely place mentioned was St Winifred's Boarding House in Colwyn Bay (Miss Woods!). The name thought very suitable! but further inquiry is to be made. There seems nothing very suitable at Harrogate.

2. Junior School to be continued at York.

3. Nothing definitely fixed about Bootham but on the whole Committee in favour of housing practically the whole school in St Mary's as far as possible working in the – 'Master's House' – but again further enquiry is to be made at Swanwick and other places. [...]

20 August 1914
The Cocoa Works, York

[...]
There was little of interest in the Relief Committee except the presentation of the different sub-committee reports. [...]
[...] I don't think thou need worry about York relief – that organisation is getting on well and there are hosts of workers. I don't think thou will be needed at the Mount at present. [...]

[97] The Relief Cttee set up to deal with distress arising from the war in York.

[...] I don't altogether agree with Frank and Edie [Sturge] about the Ambulance Corps[98] as long as it is unofficial.

24 August 1914
en route York from Scarbro, 10.15

A busy day, darling, and not quite finished yet as I still have Waller[99] and Appleton to see before leaving York at 1.32 am. It is a great relief to have the school question settled and notices I hope will go out to parents tomorrow summoning the pupils for September 29th (12 days late). Sir Thomas Pilkington,[100] the military authority I had dealings with, was very pleasant. [...]

I had several matters to see J.R.[owntree] about chiefly the 'Nation' policy which is bothering several people. Richard [Cross] joined us and is coming up to town tomorrow to further confer with Massingham.

[...]

Thou will't see there is bad news today from the front. Richard [Cross] says the ministers take a gloomy view of the immediate situation owing to the superior German force and (Private) the feeling is growing that it will be a long war. Paish thinks it will cost us 1000 millions!

Now I must write one or two other letters so farewell, darling one. Keep up thy spirits and let us be thankful that we have a triple alliance who can live through the present with a joyous unconcern at all the horror that is passing through Europe.

25 August 1914
House of Commons, 3.15

[...] The House is now up and it seems probable that it may continue sitting beyond this week as it is clear that further serious reverses are expected. I was at two committees this morning of our anti-war group

---

[98] Friends' Ambulance Unit; Philip Baker published his appeal for volunteers in the *Friend* on 21 August 1914, but A.S.R. had been closely involved in preliminary discussions to create the unit. The FAU was not, however, an official Quaker body, as some Friends objected to its close links with the military.

[99] William James Waller (1877–1929), York Quaker and Rowntree & Co. employee; later Company Sec.

[100] Colonel Sir Thomas Edward Milborne-Swinnerton-Pilkington (1857–1944), Yorkshire soldier and landowner; Commander 14th Battalion Kings Royal Rifles 1914–1916; succ. as 12th Bt 1901.

but of course at present very little can be done.[101] I then went to the Nation lunch where again people were all very gloomy.

While it probably does not alter the final result the first effect of the war would seem to point to the success of the Germans over the French and the English and then the successes will be gained by the Russians which will not assist in securing the final satisfactory settlement that we desire, still we musn't lose hope.

[...]

I had visits from Stephen Hobhouse and Rachel Braithwaite[102] this morning about housing German aliens. They want Adult Scholars to undertake this but I'm not quite sure whether this is very practicable.

26 August 1914
House of Commons

What extraordinary times these are darling – one seems asked to face hour by hour problems one never expected. At breakfast Gibbon,[103] the LGB statistician, was in discussing with Seebohm [Rowntree] the best way of obtaining weekly statistics for the cabinet re unemployment relief etc. – at 9.30 Malcolm Spencer to talk over the feeling of the Free church fellowship people with regard to future peace propaganda etc. at 11.00 Philip Benson[104] to ask advice about the future of the advertising business [...] at 1.30 lunch with Phil Baker to talk over the ambulance scheme and so on.

6.45 – I had hoped to be able to write more but have been so busy must post this now and perhaps can write later. Just off to Ramsay MacDonald, Trevelyan and Angell meeting.

[101] This was the last meeting of the group of Lib MPs founded on 6 August that A.S.R. attended. No decisions were taken about the group's future actions and it was wound up in February 1915.

[102] Rachel Barclay Braithwaite (1859–1946), sister of W.C. Braithwaite and leading Quaker active in the anti-opium movement. She and Hobhouse were seeing A.S.R. about the business of the emergency cttee set up on 7 August 1914 on Hobhouse's initiative to look after the interests of enemy aliens in Britain.

[103] Ioan Gwilym Gibbon (1874–1948), civil servant with the Post Office and then the Local Govt Bd, rising to be Dir. of Local Government in the postwar Ministry of Health; kt. 1936.

[104] Philip de Gylpyn Benson (1883–1931), s. of S.H. Benson; succ. his father as Chmn of his advertising firm in 1914.

26 August 1914
The Flat, 11.40

Just got in, darling, from a very interesting gathering at Morrell's –
with Ramsay, Ponsonby, E.D. Morel and Trevelyan – laying our plans
for future organisation. We are going to have two important gatherings
next Thursday week to somewhat enlarge the group. I am going to
invite representative religious folk to lunch and Morrell the same day
political folk to dinner but more of this when we meet. I told thee of
my morning. This afternoon Frank, Edie [Sturge], Henry Scattergood,
Christie Morris,[105] Percy Whitlock,[106] Phil Baker and E.R.C.[ross] all
turned up to tea at the House. So I had an active time with them.
     [...]
One of the difficulties yesterday which I didn't tell thee because I
knew it would blow over was that Richard [Cross] felt he might have
to resign the chairmanship of the Nation because he was afraid that
he didn't go as far as J.R.[owntree] and I would, but happily this is
alright now. He went down to see Massingham at Brighton yesterday
and today returned having he hoped straightened matters out [...].

27 August 1914
House of Commons

The rush here continues, darling, and like everyone else I suppose one
has one's moods and today I felt have felt low and discouraged. This
morning Stephen Hobhouse and Robert Mennell came to talk over
the right course to take about housing German aliens.
     Then Merrttens came to lunch – poor man he is dreadfully cut up –
is very doubtful whether his business will be able to weather the storm
and has of course had to stand a large amount of abuse in Rugby.
     This afternoon I have been trying to face the position in the Adult
School office. We shall have to half our expenditure and yet how can
you turn off men like Gilbert, Boyd, Fullwood and others? and yet if
money is not going to come in what can you do.
     Henderson too for tea talking to me – the government are seriously
concerned at the way things are going and feel that a tremendous effort
will have to be made to obtain recruits and they are going to try and
get all political organisations to unite in a great campaign meeting,
canvass etc. for that purpose and now that the actual safety of the

[105] Christie Morris, American Quaker and enthusiastic cricketer.
[106] Percy Whitlock, Master at Bootham School; left for India in December 1914 to take
up a post as Prof. of English at Ravenshaw College, Cuttack.

country is held up as in risk he and the Labour party are greatly in doubt as to what course to take.

[...]

9 September 1914
House of Commons

I had a comfortable journey, darling, part of the way with Hamilton[107] [...] I was in the House for an hour the Indian message is really very remarkable.[108] The attitude of India and the colonies is a wonderful testimony to the value of liberal ideas of colonisation. I hope it means a great advance in democratic development in India. I had tea with Ted [Harvey] and good talk. I think he will shortly be going to Holland to assist in a work that Friends may help in – in dealing with non-combatant refugees there who have crossed the border and are greatly in need of succour.[109] He is enjoying Jordans[110] but it is hard work. I am now (7 pm) on my way to Hitchin to see Fred and Gerty [Taylor] but shall return tonight as I have Norman Angell to breakfast.

16 September 1914
House of Commons

Thank thee, darling, for thine. We can talk about the Belgians when we meet. Thy proposals seem to me right. I expect the Committee will be acquiring more information shortly. I should think thou ought to go on the Central Committee. I have been working at the office and reading in my room most of the day. Henry Hodgkin and Seebohm [Rowntree] are coming to dinner tonight to discuss the Friends document and the attitude they (Friends) should take. I rather hope I may get to Jordans tomorrow but shall return to the flat for the night.

[107] James Hamilton (1857–1935), Dir. Yorkshire Insurance Co.; kt. 1929.
[108] *Hansard*, 5th series, 1914, LXVI, 574–577 for the message from the Indian Viceroy to the HofC, detailing pledges of loyalty and aid from India.
[109] On 4 September 1914 Meeting for Sufferings had established the Friends' War Victims' Relief Ctte, with T.E. Harvey as one of its Hon. Secs. See *Friend*, 2 October 1914 for his account of his visit to Holland.
[110] Jordans, Buckinghamshire, Quaker centre, including a seventeeth-century meeting house and the grave of William Penn. In early September 1914, a training camp for about sixty Quakers was set up there to prepare them to serve in the embryonic FAU.

17 September 1914
House of Commons

Thank thee, darling, for thy letter which however was late in arriving.
I had an interesting time last night with Henry [Hodgkin] and Seebohm
[Rowntree] discussing the Friends position. It is very difficult to draw
up anything that satisfies one and I am not yet very happy about the
draft Henry had prepared. However, I hope it may act as a basis for
discussion amongst a few during the next few days. I trust that at
Llandudno we may see more light.[111]

I forgot to mention to thee that when I applied for Llandudno I said
I hope thou would be able to come with me so I trust thou will't turn
it over favourably in thy mind.

I went to camp today at Jordans for lunch and had a good talk with
Will and John [Harvey]. Both are in good spirits and generally enjoying
the experience. Laurie[112] too looked in good form. He and Colin[113] are
victualing – unfortunately Phil Baker was away so I didn't hear if he
had any definite news as to when the corps will go but Will evidently
expects that they will come to some arrangements with the French
army. Some of them hope to go to Belgium with Hilda Clark[114] and
assist with non-combatants but of course all this is vague until Ted
[Harvey] returns. I am going tomorrow night to stay with William
Charles [Braithwaite] at Banbury and shall go on to Birmingham on
Saturday morning in the hope of seeing Tom Bryan and Harrison
Barrow and then meet thee at 1.35. I am telling Gillman that he can
send any letters by thee on Saturday.

[...]

6 October 1914
National Liberal Club, 9 pm

I have just had dinner, darling, with Seebohm [Rowntree] and Walter
Rea and an interesting talk with Masterman and Whitehouse who were

[111] In April 1914 four Quaker organizations had called for a conference at Llandudno
on 25–30 September 1914 on the 'needs of the world'. It became a meeting of Christian
pacifists of various shades of opinion.
[112] Laurence Edmund Rowntree (1895–1917), s. of John Wilhelm Rowntree; medical
student at Cambridge; early member of the FAU, but volunteered to join the Army in
1916 and was killed at Passchendaele.
[113] Colin Rowntree (1891–1966), architect, s. of Frederick Rowntree, a cousin of A.S.R.
from the Scarborough branch of the family.
[114] Dr Hilda Clark (1881–1955), younger sister of Roger Clark; joint Hon. Sec. of the
Friends' War Victims' Relief Cttee.

at the adjoining table. Masterman is very anxious that the Jordans brigade should go out to Servia where he says the need is appalling – plaintive appeals come to the government for help and they can do nothing – he says Winston [Churchill] would gladly give them a ship to take them from Brindisi.

Whitehouse too gave an awful account of the desolation in Belgium and said that at the beginning of the war they had no chloroform so that they were frightfully ill prepared to relieve suffering.

I have just phoned Ted [Harvey] again who was out on my arrival in London and have arranged to go and stay there tonight so I will be off at once.

Masterman takes a serious view of things in France and believes this battle will go on for a long time yet.

7 October 1914
Land Enquiry Office

I have been at work, darling, all day and am keen to get back to Ted [Harvey]'s but send thee a line first. We had a very weighty committee this AM with Phil Baker and Will [Harvey] but came to no decision and meet again on Friday. It is an extraordinarily difficult position and we all feel very hard to advise upon there is so much at stake and all the responsibility of advising this fine body of young men to face tremendous dangers is very serious.

[...] Then went to a Llandudno subcommittee and then to the Literary War Paper Group[115] where we talked *very* frankly and on the whole I feel relieved.

Dinner with Richard and Mary Cross and then two hours with Graham Wallas & Lowes Dickinson[116] and others over the Peace Settlement.

I have invited Whitehouse for Sunday. He is full of interesting matter about Belgium and wants to see Bootham.

[115] 'Papers for War-Time' was a series of forty-eight pamphlets issued to counteract the war's 'degradation of ideals'. The Ed.-in-chief was William Temple and the pamphlets represented a range of Christian opinion on the war.

[116] Goldsworthy Lowes Dickinson (1862–1932), historian and Fellow of King's College, Cambridge; originator of the 'Bryce Group', which privately discussed the shape of the postwar settlement; may have invented the term 'League of Nations'.

8 October 1914
Rowntree & Co., London Office, 16 Eastcheap

[...] I stayed with Ted and Irene [Harvey] last night again and am probably going there again tonight as G.N.[ewman] is very busy and I think it is better not to trouble him. I have been working at the office this morning and lunched at the Reform Club and this afternoon have come on here to see about a few matters.

Ted [Harvey] seems to me tired – the difficulties connected with coming to any definite plans in France seem manifold and he is feeling the Servian enterprise very responsible to decide upon. I hope we shall see some light tomorrow when we meet.

The war news makes one low. I believe the fall of Antwerp is feared at any time. London presents a most unusual appearance at night time now. There are very few street lights and the shops are darkened so that great care is needed in crossing streets. The people seem very quiet and I have seen no horseplay – folks are really chastened I think by all that is going on.
[...]

28 October 1914
The Office

I had a comfortable journey, darling, and came direct here. Cross, Alden and Whitehouse came in soon after arrival and we talked over the Belgium refugee problem and came fairly clearly to the conclusion that the first course to take was to get a few well concerned friends to visit Havre to consult with the Belgian government and then proceed to Holland to investigate and report. With the knowledge at present available it seems clear no one knows whether it would be possible to encourage the refugees to return to Belgium or to make arrangements for their being housed in Holland or whether a large number should be brought here.

If it seems the best after further conversation tonight, I think possibly Cross, Seebohm [Rowntree], Alden and I might offer to do this investigation. I know that thou will't not object if it seems clearly the right thing to do. I shouldn't be much use in conversation with the individuals on the spot because of my ignorance of the language but I probably should be more useful afterwards in this country if I had seen conditions on the spot and in consultation with the others I might be of service in helping to get out a scheme.

I have had an interesting talk to Barbara [McKenzie] this afternoon and a conversation with G.N.[ewman] on the telephone, he is pleased with the new scheme for Phil Baker's corps[117] – says he has secured some good surgeons today. There is a committee tomorrow at 3 about the matter.

(Private) Whitehouse has just been in and says that the government have offered Holland a ¼ of a million towards the expenses of refugees which has been refused! So that any commission would have to be unofficial at first. It looks as if Holland was piqued – we are now going to try and see the Dutch minister.

2 November 1914
National Liberal Club

Through Percy Alden not getting his letter this morning no appointment with Vandervelde[118] had been made for us but with some difficulty we have tracked him to his host; E. Speyer[119] at Elstree and now Seebohm [Rowntree], Cross and I are going down to have dinner with him at this somewhat suspicious house. This means that we shall certainly not get off tomorrow (as no passports have transpired) but evidently from what Percy [Alden] says Samuel and Grey do want us to go to Holland so it may be Wednesday.

Harry Gilpin was here on arrival and I had tea with him. [...]
[...]

2 November 1914
National Liberal Club, 11.30 pm

Just a line, darling, to let thee know we have had an interesting dinner at Mr. Speyer's at Elstree. He certainly is a German but his wife is a Belgian, the mother of Vandervelde's wife. He has a great mansion and was *very* glad to see us and we had an interesting talk to Vandervelde. The upshot is that we meet V. along with two other Belgian Ministers tomorrow morning so it seems clear the Havre journey is saved.

V. also said that the Liberal leader and another Minister were in

[117] The FAU had finally received leave to depart for Belgium on 26 October 1914.

[118] Emile Vandervelde (1866–1938), Belgian socialist leader; accepted office as Min. without Portfolio, 4 August 1914, Min. of War 1916–1917, Min. of Home Affairs 1917–1918, Min. of Justice 1918–1921, Min. of Foreign Affairs 1925–1927.

[119] Sir Edgar Speyer (1862–1932), German Jewish financier, naturalized as a British citizen 1892; friend of the Asquiths and donor to Liberal funds; Bt 1906. Widely suspected of pro-German sympathies; left for USA May 1915 and naturalization revoked 1921. His wife, Leonora, daughter of Ferdinand, Count von Stosch, was well-known in London as a patroness of music.

Holland at the present time and were expected back in a few days. So it may turn out best at any rate to wait until their return before going across to Holland.

Hymans,[120] the Liberal minister, Speyer considered the best man of all to advise. If as seems possible we postpone our visit I fear I shall have to stay in town until Friday evening as I have committees each day till then I ought to attend if in England.

3 November 1914
Reform Club

Things have turned out, darling, as I expected. After interviewing the Belgian Minister this morning it was clear that the next thing to do was to await the arrival of the two who at present are visiting Holland and this we decided to do. Consequently Seebohm [Rowntree] and Richard [Cross] have returned to York tonight. I was sorely tempted to do the same but I should have had to return first thing on Thursday and as I want to see W.C.B.[raithwaite] tomorrow I thought probably it was best to stay here especially as I wanted to get some reading done.

I wonder if thou art busy with Belgian refugees tonight. If so, I hope all goes well & that thou won't get overtired. The municipal elections are as satisfactory as one could expect.[121] I don't think the Tories will feel much satisfaction in having as a result of their contests succeeded in defeating by a few votes the one man who couldn't take part in the contest because he was healing the wounds of the French, wrought by the allies.

[...]

4 November 1914
Reform Club

Thank thee, darling, for thy letter. I think it was right for me to stay here (even though I had great longings to get home) as I have had a good talk with Merrttens – an important conclave with G.N.[ewman]

[120] Paul Hymans (1865–1941), Belgian Lib. politician; Amb. to Court of St James's 1915–1917, Min. of Foreign Affairs 1918–1920, 1924–1925, 1927–1935, Min. of Justice 1926–1927.
[121] There was no electoral truce in the municipal elections in York in November 1914 and three wards were contested. The only seat to change hands was in Castlegate, where the Quaker solicitor, George Henry Mennell (1873–1944), bro. of R.O. Mennell, lost to a Con. by seventy votes. For much of the campaign Mennell was in France on a private mission to give medical assistance to the wounded and refugees.

and W.C.B.[raithwaite] about the future of the Friend and a good talk also with W.C.B.[raithwaite] on general matters. In a few moments I am going to Charing Cross to see Laurie [Rowntree] and a few more of the Baker party off and then I go up to Winchmore Hill to see Henry Hodgkin who is kept to the house with lumbago, to see whether I can settle this Friend difficulty. It arises through 13 good friends signing a letter criticising G.N.[ewman]'s article in the Friend of the 16th all relative to the Inner Light.[122] What G.N.[ewman] feels is that whilst such a letter if signed by one person would have been thoroughly suitable for insertion when signed by 13 it became a manifesto practically calling for the resignation of the Editor and so he didn't insert it. I hope I shall be able to smooth matters over because notwithstanding all his faults G.N.[ewman] has really done the 'Friend' very well and it would be a great pity to have him resign now. Henry [Hodgkin] ought to have gone and had a talk with G.N.[ewman] and written a signed article.

Merrttens has seen Anna Thomas[123] and enlisted for service with the Aliens Emergency Committee beginning next Monday. He is much happier at having secured a definite job. Poor man, he is being sadly bullied at Rugby.

We meet Hymans, the Belgian Liberal Minister, tomorow at 11 and afterwards there is the Flounders Trust and Ambulance Corps Committee.

5 November 1914
National Liberal Club

I have little to report, darling. Mr Hymans had not returned so our committee came to naught this morning. I then walked to Devonshire House and had a talk with Father and lunch with Roger Clark. Then attended the Flounders Meeting and then the committee about the Ambulance Corps. The reports are all good about the boys and a message has come from the Admiralty hoping that more may be sent out but as we had no definite report from Phil Baker or the surgeon we thought we had better wait a few days before absolutely deciding, but I think it looks as though John [Harvey] would not have very long to wait.

[...]

[122] Newman was presumably the author of the leading article, 'For general consideration', *Friend*, 16 October 1914, pp. 755–757. Only one critical letter, by A. Wadham, appeared in the *Friend*, 6 November 1914.

[123] Anna Lloyd Thomas (1854–1947), sister of W.C. Braithwaite; sec. emergency cttee to help enemy aliens in Britain.

9 November 1914
en route Folkestone

[...] One cannot speak definitely about return but if we divide up as I think seems likely I should suppose we should finish this week. The Belgian Minister has given Percy [Alden] £10,000 to disburse as seems best. I don't expect this will go far!
   [...]

9 November 1914
from SS Prinses Juliana[124]

Dear Friends,
   We have so far had a most comfortable journey. We left Folkestone about 10.30 am in glorious sunshine on this boat belonging to a Dutch company, and with the sea as calm as one could desire.
   For the first ninety minutes, we hugged the coast, passing Dover, St Margarets, Deal & Ramsgate. There are not many passengers on board & the majority are Belgians so the stewardess tells us with a sprinkling of Dutch, English, Americans and Germans. The journey so far has been uneventful but it has been interesting watching all the shipping and flags and names have much greater interest than usually.
   We passed a handsome Hospital Ship painted we thought with the colours of the WSPU making for one of the French ports. Shortly afterwards we were stopped by a mine sweeper – evidently to receive instructions given by a naval officer on board with the assistance of a megaphone and then we sighted four masts peering above the water evidently all that was left of a ship wrecked in the Shallows – the stewards and stewardesses have had a busy time in tackling all the refugees and the three English stewardesses with whom we had quite a long talk before lunch weren't at all keen at the thought of having to tackle 50,000 more.
   4.30 pm. We have just seen the Dutch coast and the Purser tells us we shall be at Flushing in 1½ hours – 45 minutes before time which speaks well of the favouring wind & sea.
   PS. No white bread has been offered to us on this journey and in Holland we can't procure any without the assistance of a medical certificate to say it is necessary for our physical condition!

[124] A.S.R., Seebohm Rowntree, E.R. Cross, and Percy Alden visited the Netherlands at the request of both the British and Belgian goverments to assess how Quakers could help the 750,000 Belgian refugees who had fled the new German offensive in October 1914.

9 November 1914
Middelburg Grand Hotel

Dear Friends,
We arrived at Flushing before 5.30 and found Mr and Mrs Enke[125] waiting to greet us. They had made arrangements for us to stay at this place in this comfortable hotel – four miles from Flushing – we waited at Flushing until 7.45 so as to catch the train (the trams do not carry luggage) and had dinner in the crowded waiting room. Later Monsieur van Couwelaert, one of the Antwerp deputies, joined us as he is going round with us to the various camps and Seebohm [Rowntree] stays behind with him to make arrangements for our journey tomorrow. The Enkes came with us here, and will I think stay with us and help in the enquiry. They are most kind, full of information, excellent linguists and their knowledge and sound judgement will be of great value. It is delightful to find oneself under the Mount School influence at such a time.

Curiously enough Professor Battin[126] of America who accompanied Mrs Crosfield[127] and party walked into the waiting room whilst we were having dinner and recognised me from having seen me at the Bournville meeting a few weeks ago. He had just been to Berlin and seen several interesting people both in the East and West! Practically no news adverse to Germany is allowed to be known. With the exception of Bernstein[128] & Liebknecht[129] (the socialists) everyone there is expecting the Germans to be victorious and the Pastors are quite the most bellicose men he found.

[...]

---

[125] H.B. Enke, Belgian manufacturer married to an Englishwoman.

[126] Benjamin Franklin Battin, Prof. of German at Swarthmore, a Quaker College in Pennsylvania, USA; in Europe as part of American Quaker Peace Mission. Had visited Netherlands with G. Crosfield to investigate reports of stranded orphan refugees. Returned to Europe 1915 as organizer for World Alliance of Churches for Promoting International Fellowship.

[127] Gulielma Crosfield (1851–1945), prominent Quaker from Cambridge.

[128] Eduard Bernstein (1850–1932), leading 'revisionist' German Social Democrat; opposed his party's support for the war and later helped found breakaway Independent German Social Democratic Party 1917.

[129] Karl Liebknecht (1871–1919), first Social Democrat member of *Reichstag* to oppose war credits in December 1914. In prison 1916–1918; helped found German Communist Party and murdered 1919.

11 November 1914
en route Terneuzen from Flushing

[...] This morning we have divided again & Seebohm [Rowntree],
Alden and the Belgian deputy making further enquiries in the Mid-
delburg district whilst Richard [Cross], the Enkes and I are off to
Terneuzen – Axel and a great government camp at Hontenisse – we
join the others again later tonight and shall then go probably to
Amsterdam by the evening train – be there tomorrow and return to
Flushing by the Hague – the Enkes will leave us tonight [...].

We have not come to any very definite conclusion yet but I think it
is clear that the Dutch have more refugees on their hands than they
can tackle and that we shall advise bringing more to England. It is
fairly clear that many who had money and who had securities are
getting through their money and that some kind of loan bank will want
establishing.

By far the worst conditions we have seen so far have been at Flushing
where the destitute refugees are really housed worse than many pigs.
We have not yet found out why the treatment is so different to other
places, but it is clear that the arrangements are considerably influenced
by the sympathies of the Burgomaster and Flushing seems pro-German
in sympathy.

I was interested this morning seeing one of the Dutch submarines.
The weather is dull but warmer today than yesterday. Thy maternal
sympathies would be touched by the sight of the kiddies especially in
a place like Flushing where it seems impossible to obtain any milk. In
Sluis where the government or the Queen[130] had established a special
hospital for mothers and children and put a nurse in charge things
were entirely different even though the nurse had 150 to look after.

17 November 1914

[...]
We are nearing London. I had a pleasant journey – travelling with
Mr Hamilton and having a long talk with him – on arrival at London
I go straight to the office to try to get our Belgian report into shape
with Alden and then I go to preside for Temple at the Collegium[131]
unless I find that George has proposed some new taxation which will

---

[130] Wilhelmina (1880–1962), Queen of the Netherlands 1890–1948.
[131] Collegium, Christian group for study of social problems that grew out of Student
Christian Movement meeting at Matlock 1909. Its headquarters were at St George's
Square and William Temple was its first Chairman.

affect our business and upon which it will be necessary to take immediate action.[132]

I expect W.A. Albright[133] to breakfast tomorrow to talk over the Belgians in Holland then Mr Preston[134] the ex-Canadian Commissioner on the same quest, then I shall go to the office expecting to see Grubb about the circulation of the Llandudno report and later there is the committee about the Anglo-Belgian corps and on the evening Reigate where I stay with J.B. Crosfield.[135] [...]

1 December 1914
138 Bishopsgate, Friends' Institute

I had a comfortable journey, darling, along with Richard [Cross] and have spent most of the afternoon in connection with the Relief Committee[136] first with W.A. Albright then in a long committee. It is not a very strong body. I fear there have been many difficulties. However they took kindly to my little scheme of a model village and have appointed a measurably tame subcommittee!

[...]

[132] Lloyd George presented his first war budget 17 November 1914.

[133] William Arthur Albright (1853–1942), Quaker businessman; Dir. Albright & Wilson, phosphorus manufacturers from 1877, Chmn 1903–1915, resigning when firm agreed to undertake war contracts. First Chmn Friends' War Victims' Relief Cttee 1914–1916.

[134] William Rochester Preston (1851–1942), Canadian journalist and Lib. politician. Appointed commissioner of emigration for Canada in London 1902.

[135] James Backhouse Crosfield, tea dealer and s. of Joseph Crosfield, leading mid-nineteenth-century Quaker.

[136] Friends' War Victims' Relief Cttee; one of its most valuable roles was to reconstruct French civilian housing damaged during the war and to build temporary accommodation for refugees and the homeless.

CHAPTER 6

Letters 1915

14 January 1915
National Liberal Club

I am quite hoping, darling, to reach York tomorrow evening at 6.30. We have had an interesting Ambulance Committee and decided to go ahead with a hospital for Typhoid cases of which there are at present in Dunkirk over 4000, receiving hardly any medical attendance.

All the reports of the work being done are excellent and the PM amongst others is anxious the Friends should undertake the work.

[...]

10 February 1915
House of Commons, 7.45

I have not received thy letter yet, darling, but expect it is waiting for me at Cowley Street.

I have had a busy day – spending most of the morning over the Educational Scheme,[1] lunching with Mansbridge and the afternoon at a long Ambulance Committee. Phil Baker is trying to rush us into a 400 bed Typhoid scheme at Dunkirk but we resist as we think 150 is quite sufficient to begin with. I am writing this at the office where I have been with Peverett since the committee. I see dear Cousin Joshua [Rowntree] has passed away. I suppose the funeral will be on Saturday. I fear that it will be impossible for me to be present unless it is in the morning which is improbable. I think I shall try to return to York on Friday as I should like to get something done there before going on to Manchester.

---

[1] Council for the Study of International Relations, series of local study groups set up in 1915, based on the Adult Schools, to discuss the origins of the war and principles for a future peace.

16 February 1915
12 Cowley Street, Westminster, SW 10.15 pm

A comfortable journey, darling, and dinner at the House with
E.R.C.[ross], B.S.R.[owntree] and Hobson to talk over the possibility
of getting a rise in wages to help to cover the cost of the increase in
living.[2]

The chief item of news at the House was that Bonar Law's brother
is charged with trading with the enemy[3] – a particularly bad case –
shipping iron ore for Krupps! He is at present out on bail. I doubt
whether Bonar Law will be able to continue as leader if his brother is
convicted – but the trial is not for some time yet. Richard [Cross] says
there is also a struggle going on in the cabinet over Winston [Churchill]'s
retaliatory proposals to the new German menace.[4]

18 February 1915
Vailima, 1 Ravens Croft Ave, Golders Green, NW

I have just arrived here, darling, after a fairly full day – work at the
office this morning, lunch with Sir George Paish at the Reform Club –
poor man he has been somewhat bullied at the Treasury by one or
two of the leading civil servants – then off to the Peace Committee[5]
where I found I was in a minority of two who doubted the wisdom of
approaching the Cabinet at the present time to ask for a cessation
of hostilities, then back to the meeting of National Council
Officers afterwards dining with W.C.B.[raithwaite], G.N.[ewman] and
Wethered. Poor Wethered is much distressed at what he thinks to be
the wrong attitude Friends are taking over this war and fears he will
have to resign. I have agreed with him to come over to Street on
Sunday afternoon in his car and motor me back to Bristol so that I
can stay with him that night and catch the 9.45 express to York on
Monday which reaches York at 3 o'clock. [...]

Now I must go down and make myself pleasant to the Currie
Martins.

  [2] *Hansard*, 5th series, 1915, LXIX, 1221–1224, 1236–1238 for A.S.R.'s speeches in the
HofC debate on rising prices. He called for an extension of the wage board system.

  [3] Bonar Law had been a partner in the merchants William Jacks & Co., and his bro.,
John Law, was still a partner. In August 1914 the firm had supplied about 7,500 tons of
iron ore to Krupps and two other German firms, at least six days after the first
proclamation against trading with the enemy. John Law was not prosecuted but two
other partners were imprisoned in June 1915.

  [4] Zeppelin raids on British towns had begun in January 1915.

  [5] Peace Cttee, a cttee of YM set up in 1888; A.S.R. and T.E. Harvey had joined the
cttee 7 August 1914.

5 March 1915
Grims Wood

I have enjoyed a quiet day here, darling, preparing the business for tomorrow, getting my speech ready for Monday, and reading Mill's 'Liberty'.[6] G.N.[ewman]'s library is an excellent room to live in. [...] The letters in the papers have already brought many enquiries and offers of help towards the promotion of the study scheme including Miss Jones[7] the head of Girton! Alden and Peverett are very busy with it all.

I wonder if thou hast seen the Times today.[8] There is an interesting article on the Russian army, speaking once more of the extraordinary effect of the Vodka prohibition – and also a striking account of the Battle of Ypres when it seems that 120,000 English were faced by 600,000 Germans and that English casualties are supposed to have been about 50,000 and the German 375,000.

21 March 1915
Rowan Tree, Rose Mount, Birkenhead

Just a line, darling, to let thee know I had a comfortable journey yesterday – alone all the way. I had tea at the station and then made my way to Beechcroft – the Settlement where Horace Fleming rules – it is a delightful place and doing excellent work – a great triumph I think to have started it during the war when places like Ruskin College are closing down! Ransome[9] was in the chair. Currie Martin, Boyd, Mr and Mrs Alec Wilson,[10] Russell Brayshaw[11] were all there too.

I spoke on the lines of my address at Old Priory last week.[12]

---

[6] John Stuart Mill (1806–1873), philosopher and economist; Lib. MP Westminster 1865–1868; author of *On Liberty* (1859).

[7] Constance Jones (d. 1922), philosopher; Mistress of Girton College, Cambridge 1903–1916.

[8] *The Times*, 5 March 1915 carried an article by Stanley Washburn, its special correspondent in Russia. He claimed that due to the ban on the sale of vodka he had not seen a drunk soldier for six months.

[9] John Alfred Ransome (1873–1920), Quaker gas stove manufacturer from Warrington; active in the Adult School movement.

[10] Edith J. Wilson and her husband, Alexander Cowan Wilson (1866–1955), son of H.J. Wilson; retd civil engineer; converted to Quakerism 1899.

[11] Edmund Russell Brayshaw (1879–1965), bro. of Edith Wilson and A.N. and Shipley Brayshaw, and partner in the engineering firm Shipley set up in Stockport; leading Liberal in Wilmslow.

[12] *Yorkshire Gazette*, 20 March 1915 reported A.S.R.'s speech at Old Priory Adult School, York on 14 March 1915. Its subject was 'The tasks of democracy', most prominent of which was the need to institute popular control of foreign policy.

Incidentally I had left my notes in the library! so had to reconstruct en
route from the Gazette account. J.B. Braithwaite[13] who is staying the
weekend with the Emmotts[14] appeared during the evening also! I came
here afterwards with George Thompson[15] and found 'Fanny'[16] very
much better than when she was in York and after supper went up to
G.T.[hompson]'s room and smoked.

[...]

Miss Dismore[17] is coming to supper tonight as F.T.[hompson] thought
I should be interested in seeing her communicate with the spirit world!

25 March 1915
House of Commons

I have been feeling distinctly better, darling, today and am looking
forward greatly to our visit to Dunkirk. I lunched with Wilson, was
glad to find that he was perfectly willing to start on Saturday which
suits me much better and will enable us to attend the meeting on
Sunday night which I was anxious to do.

If tomorrow any suitable poem or extract suitable for the meeting
occurs to thee do help me by sending it. I feel it is a responsible and
difficult thing speaking to those young fellows and shall want thy help.
At present my mind goes towards dwelling on *expression in acts* such as
they are performing as possibly a truer expression of religion than
words.

Have just come from an interesting Ambulance Committee – probably we are going to move our headquarters from Dunkirk to Poperinge
as the British Red Cross wants us to put up a hospital there for the
British soldiers.

William Charles [Braithwaite] will arrive in York at 9.5 on Saturday
and find his way up to thee. I have told him thou will't be asking

[13] Joseph Bevan Braithwaite, Jr (1855–1934), Quaker stockbroker and businessman;
Hon. Treasurer NASU 1899–1907; bro. of W.C. Braithwaite.
[14] George Henry Emmott (1855–1916), Quaker. Prof. of law Univ. of Liverpool 1896–
1916; m. Elizabeth (nee Braithwaite) (1858–1946), sister of J.B. Braithwaite, Jr and W.C.
Braithwaite.
[15] George Edward Thompson (1845–1924), Quaker from Birkenhead and noted amateur
photographer.
[16] Frances Thompson (1840–1926), sister of George Thompson, with whom she lived;
prominent Quaker, active in peace and temperance movements and Pres. Mount School
Old Scholars' Association 1891–1918.
[17] Miss Dismore, presumably a local medium. Frances Thompson was a friend of the
physicist Sir Oliver Lodge, a leading figure in the Society for Psychical Research. Joseph
Rowntree also shared an interest in spritualism.

Richard [Cross] and Kenneth[18] up to dinner on Sunday and he would like to go to Bootham School to tea – will't thou arrange with Dr Hodgson.[19] If thou has arranged with Frank Sturge it will of course be alright. He will have to leave before breakfast on Monday but I have said that will not disturb thee.

I have wired asking thee to send by Gillman my riding breeches and leggings as Dr Maxwell[20] says it is so very muddy.

We shall reach London on Monday night and have a conference with G.N.[ewman] on Tuesday morning. I shall hope to reach York at 6.3 (let Watson[21] meet me).

I don't expect I shall come to Barmoor until Thursday as Dr Maxwell is going to meet me in York on Wednesday afternoon. I have invited him to stay with me in bachelor fashion at Chalfonts that night.

Farewell, darling one. I must be off directly to the Friend Trustee gathering.

26 March 1915
House of Commons

I am sorry, darling, at our being parted on the 29th – I must really try hard to reform next year so that we can spend our 'copper' together. [...]
        [...]
We had quite an interesting Friend Trustee dinner last night followed by a very frank talk.

I have to preside at the dinner tonight and about 100 folk coming. [...]
        6 pm. I have had an interesting talk with Professor Adams[22] of Oxford who is very keen on the study schemes. He is speaking tonight.

[18] Kenneth Edward Towler Wilkinson (1871–1955), A.S.R.'s solicitor; prominent Lib. on York council, where he represented Walmgate from 1906; m. Marion (nee Rowntree) (1881–1966) from the Scarborough branch of the family.

[19] Charles Edward Hodgson (1877–1938), Quaker; Master at Bootham 1907–1920, Warden of Swarthmore settlement, Leeds 1920–1927, Bursar at Bootham and the Mount 1927–1938.

[20] Leslie B. Maxwell, Adjutant FAU 1914–1915, Officer Commanding 1915–1917, when he resumed his medical studies.

[21] Watson, A.S.R.'s chauffeur.

[22] William George Stewart Adams (1874–1966), Gladstone Prof. of Political Theory and Institutions at Oxford Univ. 1912–1933, Warden of All Souls 1933–1945; member of Lloyd George's wartime Secretariat.

27 March 1915
House of Commons 10.45 am

Thank thee, darling, for thine. I am glad to have such a good account
of Theodore [Rowntree]. I am sending him a few lines this morning.

I hope the dinner last night went off well. I was in the chair and
confess myself that it wasn't quite what I wanted but the others all
seemed pleased and therefore suppose I was nervy myself and biased
accordingly.

I sat between Angell and Adams of Oxford both of whom made
good speeches. Angell says he understands that probably Holland will
come in on our side. I shudder to think of that country suffering the
same treatment as Belgium and cannot understand why it is necessary
for her to intervene.

[...]

27 March 1915
Royal Pavilion Hotel, Folkestone

We have had our first delay, darling – owing to some new regulation
with regard to Passports the French officials refused to let us go to
Calais and we are therefore waiting two hours here for the Boulogne
boat. I hope we shall get to Dunkirk tonight but we cannot be sure,
but a Red Cross official took a message to Baker who was to meet us
at Calais to come on with the motor to Boulogne. This however *may*
mean another day at Dunkirk if we fail to get on tonight so I just send
this warning.

We are very happy and the sea looks calm.

29 March 1915
12 Cowley St, Westminster

Just a line, darling, to say that all has gone well – good crossings both
ways and a really wonderful day yesterday driving early from Boulogne
(where we stayed Saturday night) to Dunkirk then to Poperinge for
lunch then to Ypres, back by Woesten home to Dunkirk. At Ypres just
as we were leaving a Taube[23] flew over the Sacre Coeur[24] and dropped
a bomb within 200 yards of us. After which there was most vigorous

---

[23] Taube, German monoplane.
[24] Sacre Coeur Hospital at Ypres, hospital run by the FAU until its evacuation on 23
April 1915 after continuous shelling.

firing to bring it down but to no avail. We are greatly impressed with the work, far more is being accomplished of really absolutely first order than we are aware of! I feel it to have been a very wonderful experience and am very proud of what all the boys are doing but more of this when we meet. [...]

Philip Baker had taken a central role in setting up the FAU but strains over his leadership were becoming apparent in early 1915. Arnold Rowntree and J.W. Wilson reported to the FAU Committee on 15 April 1915 that 'further co-ordination and delegation of responsibility had now become necessary'. Baker resigned as Officer Commanding at the end of June 1915, citing, among other reasons, 'lack of confidence' in him from the Committee, his unwillingness to accept its suggestions to reorganize the FAU, and his declining influence in the Unit.

30 March 1915
The Cocoa Works, York

I have had a busy day here, darling, but it is a great relief to find that Maxwell entirely takes our view about the Baker difficulty and we have come to complete agreement as to the course to take. [...]

From February 1915 there had been increasing concern in government circles at the adverse impact of drinking on munitions production and Lloyd George was interested in the idea of a state-controlled liquor trade. The Daily Express *for 12 April 1915 carried the headline 'Beer! Beer! Glorious Government Beer!' and claimed the Cabinet planned a government buy-out of all public houses and breweries. The details were allegedly being planned by a committee headed by Herbert Samuel and including Arnold Rowntree and T.P. Whittaker. The* Express *leader condemned 'the triumph of the killjoy and the fanatic' and adverse public reaction to this kite was part of the reason the Cabinet decided on 19 April 1915 only to look into restrictions on opening hours.*

12 April 1915
Mansion House, York[25]

I had a comfortable journey, darling. A reporter met me at Malton to know my views on the subject of the State Monopoly of the liquor trade!

[25] Mansion House, York, official residence of York's Ld Mayor; in 1914–1915 this office was held by J.B. Morrell.

A wild article in the Express says the government are going to take over the manufacture and distribution of liquor and that I am on the committee! Another reporter met me at York! I have told Gillman to send thee a copy of the paper.

Bertha [Morrell] was just off to the Council Meeting when I reached here so I have had a solo supper and am now hoping to get a quiet time writing and working at my two addresses. [...]

13 April 1915
Bannisdale, Malton, 6.40 pm

I have just finished a very cosy tea with Ernest and K. [Taylor] – darling, and am off shortly for my lecture. I wish I had had time to prepare some fresh matter I don't feel very happy serving up cold pork.

I enjoyed staying at the Mansion House though I doubt whether it is really a very healthy place. The spare room smelt I thought rather fusty still I fared very well in it. Bertha [Morrell] looks to me very thin. She says she has lost lbs – I wish Bowes [Morrell] would get her away for a change. She's a very charming unconventional hostess – the little boy is a perfect dear.

We had a long board spending most of the time over the girls' wage question – eventually deciding to refuse the application. Later in the day when Seebohm [Rowntree] saw Miss Sloan, the girl's negotiator, she privately admitted she felt the girls had a weak case. So I hope that there will not be much further difficulty. Miss Sloan was meeting the girls tonight.
[...]

14 April 1915
Darlington

I am just getting some tea before going to the meeting, darling. I didn't feel very happy about my meeting last night. I fear I was too heavy and perhaps tried to cover too much ground – still they were kind about it and I enjoyed staying with Ernest and K. [Taylor]. This morning at the Works we had Cudworth[26] giving his report and an interesting Russian who wants to begin selling our goods in Russia. [...]

[26] Alfred James Cudworth (1857–1926), Birmingham Quaker; accountant and auditor to Rowntree & Co.

15 April 1915
House of Commons

I think I got comfortably through the Darlington meeting, darling, then went up to supper with Edward Backhouse[27] (along with Dennis[28] of Ayton and E. Dodgshun) and about 11.30 set out to walk to the station. The night was very dark and once I walked into a great heap of leaves but got down alright to the station where there was considerable excitement of the Zeppelin raid at Newcastle. Still the train was not very late. I fared as comfortably as one can on a night journey. The breakfast this morning with the officers responsible for training leaders was quite interesting and afterwards I had a long talk with Alden and Peverett about the organisation of the CSIR. Lunch with G.N.[ewman] and Addison at Carols and this afternoon a long committee about the Ambulance Unit. [...]

22 April 1915
House of Commons

[...] Today I have been interviewing different people here and lunching with Mansbridge.

Tonight I am going to Grims Wood along with Wilson to discuss Ambulance matters. George [Newman] has been poorly this week and staying indoors.

The committee with the Victims[29] has not come off as W.A. Albright seems to see some difficulties.

I forgot to mention yesterday that I saw Hugh[30] in the restaurant where Ron [J.R. Gillett] and I were lunching – he gave a good account of Nell. Did I tell thee that Miss Noel[31] and Phil are now engaged! It is private however until Miss Noel's father consents and he is in Greece! J.A.B.[aker] whom I got today to admit the truth of the statement seems pleased about it.

[...]

[27] Edward Backhouse (1876–1922), Darlington Quaker and banker; retd 1916 and devoted himself to peace causes; 'Peace by Negotiation' cand. Stockton-on-Tees 1917, and prospective Lab. cand. Bedford 1922; killed climbing in the Alps.

[28] Herbert Dennis (1881–1966), Headmaster Ayton School, Yorkshire (a Quaker school) 1913–1940.

[29] Friends' War Victims' Relief Cttee.

[30] Hugh Theodore Crosfield (1883–1944), Quaker tea merchant; m. 1911 M.K.R.'s sister Helen Grace Harvey (Nell) (1882–1944).

[31] Irene Noel (d. 1956), daughter of Frank Noel, large landowner on the Greek island of Euboea; worked for the FAU; m. June 1915 Philip Baker.

28 April 1915
House of Commons

I had a comfortable journey, darling, lunch with G.N.[ewman] at the
House and then we met W.A. Albright, Wright Brooks[32] and Ruth
Fry[33] at J.W. Wilson's flat and had a lengthy but useful talk. I think we
shall get nearer together – receive more help from them for civilian
work and eventually be able to help one another in developing work
in Belgium.

Both Will and John [Harvey] are thought to be at Pop, they are
certainly not at Ypres according to the list I saw. Information has come
through today that the Sacre Coeur has been burnt to the ground –
so it is well the evacuation took place last week. You will have seen
that Pop is being shelled and the temporary hospital established last
week for wounded soldiers has had to be moved – but I hope that with
the more decisive offensive the allies have taken, Pop may soon be
safer.

The boys evidently are doing splendidly – carrying 1000 wounded a
day and altogether must be feeling thankful that they are able to render
such wonderful service.

Goodbye, darling. I will send a line to Mother.

PS Donald Allen was driving a car when a shell descended upon it
and smashed it up completely. He is wounded in the rear and wrist
but is progressing well. Dr Mallabar has also got splintered with
shrapnel in the face but not seriously.

14 May 1915
House of Commons

I had a comfortable journey up here, darling, and went straight to
Cowley Street to talk over the business to come before the Committee
with G.N.[ewman]. Then a long committee – we feel that after Baker's
wedding we must invest in a long honeymoon so that we can try to
get things straight in his absence. Dr Thomson gave a good account
of John [Harvey] who is at Hazebrouck. Afterwards I went to the
House for a few minutes and then to Grims Wood with G.N.[ewman]
to finish the report which is to be issued next week.

The bluebells there are wonderful. Today I have been busy at the

---

[32] Edmund Wright Brooks (1834–1928), prominent Quaker and cement manufacturer;
Lib. cand. Essex SE 1892; member of Friends' War Victims' Relief Cttee.
[33] Anna Ruth Fry (1878–1962), Sec. Friends' War Victims' Relief Cttee; daughter of
Sir Edward Fry and sister of Roger and Joan Fry.

office and with interviews with Paish and Bell[34] (the general manager
of Lloyds) about the possibility of a bank [loan] in connection with the
Sheffield Independent.

Now I am off to Oxford with Alden and Peverett to prepare for
Sunday's Meeting. I hope we shall get a good walk tomorrow.

Folks are gloomy about the outlook. Poor Merrttens with whom I
lunched gave harrowing accounts of the work that is now falling on
the Alien's Committee.[35]

16 May 1915
Balliol College, Oxford

I am sorry, darling, I was too late for the post last night. We have had
an interesting time here. Percy [Alden], Peverett and I came down on
Friday evening and yesterday walked about in the morning. I had
lunch with Arthur [Gillett], W.C.B.[raithwaite] and then A.L. Smith
took us for a delightful walk. We came back for tea at his house and
then had a committee with Adams and himself preparing for the larger
committee later. An excellent dinner at Balliol followed and then we
talked for two hours Smith, Grant,[36] Ramsay Muir,[37] Clay,[38] Lowes
Dickinson, E.R.C.[ross] and I think we made some real progress – I
feel *very* ignorant amongst such learned men but possibly one's great
ignorance is sometimes helpful!

If Parliament meets tomorrow I fear I must go to London in order
to vote for Carson's prohibition amendment[39] but if as I think it doesn't
meet until Tuesday then I shall reach York at 3.5 tomorrow. [...]

[34] Henry Bell (d. 1935), Dir. Lloyds Bank; later prominent on many government
financial cttees.
[35] Emergency Cttee for the Assistance of Germans, Austrians, Hungarians and Turks
in Distress.
[36] Arthur James Grant (1862–1948), Prof. of History Univ. of Leeds 1897–1927.
[37] John Ramsay Bryce Muir (1872–1941), Prof. of Modern History at Univs of Liverpool
1906–1913 and Manchester 1913–1921; Lib. MP Rochdale 1923–1924; Chmn Nat. Lib.
Federation 1931–1933, Pres. 1933–1936.
[38] Henry Clay (1883–1954), economist; WEA tutor 1907–1917; worked with A.S.R. on
establishing Whitley Council in the pottery industry; Prof. Manchester Univ. 1921–1930,
Economic Advisor to Bank of England 1930–1944, Warden of Nuffield College, Oxford
1944–1949; kt. 1946.
[39] On 20 April 1915 Lloyd George had introduced a 3rd amending bill to the Defence
of the Realm Act, giving the govt greater powers to regulate the drink trade.

1 June 1915
Chalfonts

I fared as well as I expected last night, darling, getting snatches of sleep at intervals. At Newcastle when I was getting some hot milk in the refreshment room (the hours for procuring brandy had passed!) Taff[40] turned up on the same quest. He was travelling to Oban to recruit there for a week after an attack of influenza. There was a through carriage to Stranraer from Newcastle and as I managed to find an empty one I was quite comfortable. Will [Harvey] was waiting for me on the boat – and clad in our special waistcoats we faced the crossing with equanimity. Happily it was calm though windy.

Linton, our Irish traveller, met us in Belfast and after breakfast we spent some time in seeing the city – looking at confectioner's shops, calling on one customer & taking a tram ride into the country. We are now travelling to Dublin [...].

I enclose a modest account of Phil and Irene [Baker] which appears in the Sketch today![41] Farewell, dearest love to the kiddies. Will seems better.

2 June 1915
William's Hotel, Macroom, Co. Cork (Thursday aft.)

We had an active day yesterday, darling, setting out from Waterford in a car about 9 am and reaching Mallow at 10.30 pm. We visited several Creameries, the most interesting one being at Portlaw in part of the old Malcolmson cotton factory which forty years ago would employ 2000 hands but which collapsed in the nineties and since then has been unoccupied except for the small portion required for the Dairy.

I think probably the most likely district for us to begin in would be round about there. The Mr Anderson who manages for Malcolmson was very anxious that we should buy the whole derelict mill and village! It is very depressing to see such a derelict factory surrounded by such extraordinary beauty and hundreds of the houses where the people lived all closed.

We suffered yesterday by being 'teetotalers'! All the people we visited were so hospitable that when we refused whisky it meant accepting tea

---

[40] Alfred Rowntree (1869–1956), cousin of A.S.R.'s from the Scarborough branch of the family; dairy farmer in Wensleydale.

[41] *Daily Sketch*, 1 June 1915 announced the wedding of Philip Baker and Irene Noel and claimed 'It is entirely due to her and to Mr P.J. Baker with the help of efficient officers, that the unit has been able to accomplish such excellent work as a voluntary unit'.

with a considerable spread – three such meals we had to consume.
This morning we have been continuing our search in beautiful weather.
Tomorrow evening we hope to reach Dublin and if all's well return to
England on Saturday morning by the morning boat which should land
me into York by six o'clock at night.

I do hope you will have a happy time with Uncle Joel[42] and Aunt
Maria – please tell them how very sorry I am to miss taking them a
good excursion on Saturday but I know thou will't give them a good
time.

[...]

23 June 1915
House of Commons, 9.30 pm

I had a comfortable journey up, darling – lunched at Cowley Street
with G.N.[ewman] and have been here since. George's speech[43] seemed
to me an awful condemnation of the late government and members
are much discouraged at the outlook. I had dinner with Harmsworth[44]
the late Under Sec. at the Home Office – a sincere man who always
attracts me.

2 July 1915
Reform Club

Thank thee, darling, for thine. I had a long evening with G.N.[ewman]
over Ambulance matters and this morning spent practically the whole
of my time at Vere Street interviewing Little, Nockolds and Young[45]
and have lunched here with Nockolds.

[42] Joel Cadbury (1838–1916), button manufacturer in Birmingham and cousin of George
Cadbury. Maria Cadbury (nee Hotham) (1841–1928), sister of A.S.R.'s mother. A.S.R.
lived with his uncle and aunt in 1875–1878 after the early death of his mother.
[43] Lloyd George's speech in the debate on the Munitions of War Supply Bill, defining
the powers of the new Min. of Munitions. He argued subcontracting had failed and the
Min. intended to deal directly with businesses. See *Hansard*, 5th series, 1915, LXXII,
1183–1206.
[44] Cecil Bisshopp Harmsworth (1869–1948), Lib. MP Droitwich 1906–January 1910,
Luton 1911–1922; US Home Office February–May 1915, US Foreign Office 1919–1922;
cr. Ld Harmsworth 1939; one of Ld Northcliffe's younger brothers.
[45] J. Raymond Little, Hon. Sec. FAU 1914–1919. Dr Humphrey Nockolds (d. 1964),
Principal Medical Officer FAU 1914–1919. Geoffrey Winthrop Young (1876–1958),
member FAU Cttee and Officer in Charge of Field Stations 1914–1915, Anglo-Italian
Ambulance Unit 1915–1919; s. of Sir George Young Bt.; poet and mountaineer who
joined the FAU after working as a war correspondent.

I hope all will go well now, but I don't at present see how to heal the sore in the Baker family.[46]

I have just had a talk with Gulland about the registration bill[47] – it is a quiet way of letting down Curzon and Long but evidently it is going to meet with very strong opposition. I think I have decided to return to York on Sunday whether I go to town for the second reading on Monday or not.

I am going very shortly to the Young Friends Service Committee.[48] I think perhaps I better do my best to help them this afternoon even if I retire afterwards.

[...]

3 July 1915
Selly Wood

I am writing here, darling, just before setting off to Uffculme where the half yearly meeting takes place at which I have to speak.[49] I think I told thee last night that in order to attend the Friends Service Committee I had given up Swanwick[50] and so that enabled me to get to Birmingham this morning in good time and I lunched at Woodbrooke with Herbert Wood and have been able to get a good talk with him about Woodbrooke, Fircroft, and the general question of training.

I came in here for tea but found them expecting a large company of 'Reconciliation' folk[51] so have only had a few minutes talk with them.

Mrs Herbert Wood was invisible as she is expecting a baby at any time. [...] I am still hoping to reach home tomorrow but I shall probably have to go to London for the National Registration Bill next day probably returning through the night – so letters to York will be right.

---

[46] P.J. Baker's resignation as Officer Commanding the FAU was announced at the cttee meeting of 1 July 1915. His brother, Allan R. Baker, also resigned from the FAU in protest at P.J. Baker's treatment.

[47] National Registration Bill was introduced on 29 June 1915. It set up a register of all British citizens aged 15–65 and could either be seen as a prelude to, or a substitute for, conscription.

[48] The Friends' Service Cttee was set up by YM in May 1915 to 'strengthen the Peace testimony among Friends of military age'.

[49] A.S.R. was speaking at the Council meeting of the Midland Adult School Union.

[50] The fourth United Summer School of the Social Service Unions of various churches was being held at Swanwick, Derbyshire.

[51] Fellowship of Reconciliation, interdenominational Christian body set up in December 1914 to promote pacifism. Its first conference was at Swanwick on 5–12 July 1915.

4 July 1915
Chalfonts

[...]
I fear I shall have to go to London tomorrow as the Meeting for Sufferings seems a little fussy and it may be necessary to meet some Friends about one or two amendments they wish to introduce.[52] After I wrote thee yesterday afternoon I set off to walk through Bournville to Uffculme and alighted on George Cadbury and Henry [Cadbury] – the former insisted on motoring me to Uffculme. There were about 800 folks there but not many Friends. Wilfred Southall,[53] the Gilberts, Twyman, Edward Smith, Walter Priestman[54] however graced the scene. They seemed satisfied with my deliverance which was a relief. Two men there whirled me off to Walsall where I stayed with a nice conservative solicitor, Mr Evans. This morning the rain was pouring down and so instead of 600 they had 100. However we got on nicely and then after an early lunch Mr Evans' son motored me in to Birmingham and I caught the train which landed me here at 6.20.
[...]

6 July 1915
at Grantham

We had Board this morning, darling, and nothing very exciting and now I am journeying up to town by the 2.30 from York. [...] I shall try hard to get back on Thursday night. It depends somewhat on Little's return from France. I want to see him as soon as possible as I have promised to relieve G.N.[ewman] as far as I can by selecting men along with Little. [...]
[...]

7 July 1915
House of Commons

I have little to report, darling, today. I went this morning for half an hour to Holland House to see the flower show, then to Vere Street[55] to

[52] Meeting for Sufferings on 2 July 1915 had urged Quakers to put themselves on the national register of manpower proposed in the Registration Bill, but to state they would not accept military service.

[53] Wilfred Francis Southall (1864–1953), Birmingham Quaker; chemist.

[54] Walter Priestman (1855–1920), Quaker worsted spinner from Horton, Lancashire.

[55] Vere Street, London headquarters of the FAU 1915–1916.

do some work in connection with the Unit and then to the office lunching with Carol [Eddington] and Cousin Janet [Campbell] at Cowley Street.

This afternoon I have spent all the time in the House and now there is a debate proceeding on the question of withdrawing women from the scope of this stupid register.[56]

I fear events are not going on very well for us at present – the Dardanelles enterprise is proving frightfully difficult and very little confidence is expressed as to a favourable result. I fear I shall not be back until Friday evening as I must see Little and he does not return until late tomorrow night. I am sorry but I think I must help him all I can now that G.N.[ewman] cannot do so much.

26 July 1915
Chalfonts, 7.20 pm

[...]

I had a letter from Ruth Fry saying she would much prefer this week to next so if the passports are procurable it would seem as if I should have to miss Street altogether. If so thou will't tell Roger and Sarah[57] how very, very much I regret being unable to join you.

[...]

27 July 1915
Chalfonts

[...]

I have had a busy day at the Works but feel to be clearing up things nicely. I hope the way is opening for a few days holiday. I engaged one more man for the unit and now we have 40 and Fox[58] thinks things are going well. [...]

---

[56] The debate was on the National Registration Bill. See *Hansard*, 5th series, 1915, LXXIII, 433–443 for J.H. Whitehouse's amendment to remove women from the bill.

[57] Sarah Clark (1877–1973), American Quaker; wife of Roger Clark of Street.

[58] Edward Bonvile Fox (1886–1944), Quaker merchant from the West Country; Commandant of the FAU unit in York. In 1915 Rowntree & Co. offered the War Office the use of part of their Haxby Rd works in York as a war hospital. In June 1915 the War Office asked the FAU to staff the new hospital and some forty volunteers started training at St Mary's Educational Settlement (also a Rowntree foundation).

29 July 1915
House of Commons

We had a somewhat uncomfortable committee this afternoon as Philip [Baker] has been getting men for the Italian Unit[59] in a way which G.N.[ewman] takes great exception to. However I hope matters smoothed over eventually. I think it looks now as if the visit to France would be postponed. So I am hoping to get down to Street on *Friday*. I fear the executive of the International Relations Council won't be over in time to let me catch the 5.50 from here tomorrow. [...]

I spent this morning at Vere Street and this evening I shall stay here for dinner as a division is expected.

30 July 1915
House of Commons

Thank thee, darling, for thy letter. I have had another busy day – breakfast with Little and Maxwell – work at Vere Street all the morning – lunch with G.N.[ewman] at Carol's – Advisory Council and Executive of CSIR this afternoon and now have just had a visit from Harold Wright[60] about Angell's affairs.

Bryce, Clifford[61] and Acworth, the Railway expert, were the only 3 members of the Advisory Council present other than the members of the Executive, still we had a good meeting – it seems to me the Council is getting into its stride.

There is a great deal of work to be done tomorrow at Vere Street and I certainly shall not get off before the 10 o'clock train and probably the 3.30 is more likely. [...]

23 August 1915
Chalfonts

[...]

Little has been here today. We went together to the opening of the training corps at the Settlement. The enclosed from J.R.[owntree] has

[59] Italian Unit, the Anglo-Italian Ambulance Unit, a new volunteer ambulance body, headed by G.M. Trevelyan, which intended to serve on the Italian Front. Baker was its second in command and sixteen of the sixty-six initial members were Quakers.

[60] Harold Wright (1883–1934), Lib. journalist and one of Norman Angell's chief lieutenants; Asst Ed. *Nation* 1923–1930, Ed. 1930–1931.

[61] John Clifford (1836–1923), leading Baptist preacher.

194 CHAPTER 6

come tonight which would seem to confirm my feeling that probably the present was not quite the opportune time to visit the States.

I've just cancelled my visit to London this week so as to get more time with Ted [Harvey] and thee. It was very nice having Ted yesterday. What a useful thing a telephone is!

30 August 1915
Chalfonts

[...]

I had a comfortable journey travelling with Canon Bell[62] from Gilling with whom I had a very open talk about the war – religion etc. When I got to the Works I found Muir[63] wanting to see me and his mission was to tell me that he must have 30 more men at once and a further 30 in six weeks time! Which means that the 30 we have in training here tomorrow go to the Works. However I arranged with Muir that Walker should still help to train them after 6 pm each night – and I hope this may answer – Walker and Hodgson have done very well this week but I had quite an active time fixing these new arrangements up and interviewing 5 or 6 new men who appeared. [...]

[...]

1 September 1915
National Liberal Club

[...]

I spent this morning at the office on Ambulance work, lunched with J.W. Wilson here and then met Ruth Fry for a tete a tete before the joint committee at 2 o'clock. The Victims are going to give £200 a month to the 'Aide Civile Belge'[64] for the present and I think we made real progress towards efficient joint administration. We had a long and interesting Unit Committee afterwards. Countess d'Ursel[65] and Dr Mallabar were both present for part of the time. G.N.[ewman] was not present. I think perhaps for once it was well to be free from the feeling of strain we have felt at recent committees.

There are several matters needing attention abroad and if I can get

[62] Revd Charles Carlyle Bell (1868–1954), Canon Residentiary of York Minster 1914–1953.
[63] Dr G. Muir, Medical Officer in charge of the Haxby Rd hospital.
[64] Aide Civile Belge, a joint cttee of the FAU and Belgian relief organizations.
[65] Countess Louise d'Ursel, Lady-in-Waiting to the Queen of the Belgians and cttee member of Aide Civile Belge.

leave from the Red Cross I think I shall go to Dunkirk next Friday week. I hope J.W.W.[ilson] will come with me again.

[...]

7 September 1915
The Cocoa Works, York

I have had a very active day here, darling. Board until lunch, Wilfred C.[rosland][66] to lunch to arrange about his going into the Ambulance, and details of training at St Mary's. Newspaper Board this afternoon and in between several interviews. I am expecting Muir any moment now then I go to A.[rthur] R.[owntree] for a talk and tea – and then return to the hospital to talk to the men after supper about several points that have arisen. [...]

13 September 1915
Chalfonts

I have had an active day at the Works, darling – chiefly over Unit work. Three men are going to France from the York hospital – new men have had to be interviewed and I went down to talk to the new trainees who have entered the Settlement.

[...]

14 September 1915
Chalfonts, York, 6.20 pm

Another full day at the Works, darling [...]. The enclosed has come from Mrs Soltau, the wife of the Professor[67] who has been hounded out of Bristol for a FOR speech and is training at St Mary's. If thou approves I should like to ask her to come and stay with us for a few days when she comes to York. She is very nice and simple. I think thou would like her and I want if possible to get Winifred [Sturge] to take her on as a supernumary (without payment) at the Mount. Will't thou

[66] Robert Wilfred Crosland (1876–1961), relation of A.S.R.'s through his stepmother. Long career in adult education and social work; Sub-warden St Mary's Educational Settlement, York 1909–1925.
[67] Roger Henry Soltau (1887–1953), historian and political scientist; Lecturer Bristol Univ., 1911–1915; converted to Quakerism 1915 and served with FAU 1915–1919, then returned to lecturing, holding posts at Univ. of Leeds, London School of Economics, Univ. of Wales and American Univ. of Beirut; m. 1912 Irene Constance (nee Whelpton).

write her saying thou will't be at home after Friday and glad to see
her if she will come, not expecting to be entertained etc. I feel very
much for them and feel this is a small bit of national service we can
perhaps perform! but if thou doesn't feel up to it it will be alright (I
have not acknowledged the letter).

[...]

The car went down to the Works this AM to be sold if a good offer
came along. It didn't remain long there as the FAU car has collapsed
and so I offered to lend ours in emergency.

[...]

15 September 1915
House of Commons

I came up by the early train, darling, and after an hour's work at Vere
Street came on here and have heard Asquith and Kitchener[68] – the
chief topic of discussion at present is the danger of conscription – I
had a talk with Runciman who says that L.G. is almost fanatical on
the question and threatens to force an election on the point if Asquith
doesn't give way.

The general view amongst Liberal members is that if the government
attempt it, a most serious industrial crisis will at once develop – but I
cannot believe with all the evidence they have on this side that they
will be so mad.

Birrell is back and spoke most warmly of his visit and how much he
enjoyed being with Ted [Harvey].

Later. Wilson and I have decided to proceed to Boulogne tomorrow
despite the fact there is a little doubt as to whether we get further but
it seems as if it would be easier to get a further pass at Boulogne than
here.

[...]

15 September 1915
Westminster Palace Hotel, 9.30 pm

[...]

I shall expect to be back in London on Monday night at the latest

[68] Horatio Herbert Kitchener (1850–1916), Sirdar of Egyptian Army 1892–1899, Chief
of Staff in South Africa 1899–1900, Commander-in-Chief 1900–1902, Commander-in-
Chief in India 1902–1909, Agent and Consul-Gen. in Egypt 1911–1914, Sec. of State for
War 1914–1916; cr. Ld Kitchener 1898, Vt 1902, Earl 1914.

ready for the Budget next day[69] but of course if we cannot get to Dunkirk we shall return earlier.

[...]

The situation about conscription is grave – because it looks as if whichever way it was settled there might be serious internal division.

[...]

16 September 1915
Folkestone

Safely on the Boulogne boat with every prospect of the calmest passage. There are a large number of Belgian soldiers returning and Whitley,[70] the Chairman of Committees, is also on board. So far I have seen no one else I know.

The number of officials to pass increases every journey but so far no serious difficulty though J.W.W.[ilson] had to give up all his gold and accept notes instead.

26 October 1915
House of Commons

Just a line, darling, to let thee know that I had a comfortable journey and am feeling nicely. I had a talk with Gulland and fear our little scheme of resignation may not come off as Gulland says that several have wanted to resign and that it is difficult to get the other whips to agree that the truce should apply to voluntary resignation.[71] However I will tell thee further about this when we meet.

27 October 1915
House of Commons

Thank thee, darling, for thine. I have been busy all day interviewing conscientious objectors – over 20 and whilst very interesting

---

[69] The Budget of 21 September 1915 – the first presented by Reginald McKenna, who had succeeded Lloyd George as Chanc. of the Exchequer on 25 May 1915.

[70] John Henry Whitley (1866–1935), Lib. MP Halifax 1900–1928; Lib. whip 1907–1910; Dep. Chmn Ways and Means 1910–1911, Dep. Speaker and Chmn Ways and Means 1911–1921; Speaker 1921–1928.

[71] The whips of the three major parties had agreed in August 1914 that the candidate of the party holding a seat would not be opposed in any by-election.

somewhat tiring – to be quite honest after interviewing 6 I long for the breeze of a good military man! I had lunch with Maxwell and J.W. Wilson, on the whole unit matters progress well – [...]. Folks are very depressed here about the outlook and everything is very uncertain.

[...]

2 November 1915
House of Commons

[...] had lunch with the wild writers of the 'Nation' who as usual were at sixes and sevens and then came on here and most unusual we have been in the House for four hours! Asquith's speech[72] was an able defence and his closing sentences really very touching, but he strikes me as a tired almost broken man and I have my doubts whether he is really strong enough in nerve and will power to go through. Sir Edward Grey too looked *very* sad and weary. The general view here is that conscription is dead but perhaps it is too early to talk definitely. Carson's speech[73] was extraordinary.

24 November 1915
House of Commons, 6.30 pm

I have just returned, darling, from Rochester where I spoke for 50 minutes to the delegates of the Kent Union and then slipped away in time to catch the express back. They were all very kind [...]. I had a comfortable journey up yesterday and after a short time spent in the House had dinner with J.W.W.[ilson], Maxwell and Little. This morning I had an active time at the FAU office with applications – E. Dodgshun acting as Sec. to the Selection Board (Little and myself). We begin a camp of 80 next week at Jordans. [...]

---

[72] *Hansard*, 5th series, 1915, LXXV, 503–529 for Asquith's speech on conscription. While defending the voluntary system he did not completely rule out conscription, though he called it 'a contingency which I do not think is ever likely to arise'.
[73] Carson had resigned office on 12 October to protest at the government's failure to aid Serbia against German attack. His resignation speech severely criticized the government and called for the creation of a War Cabinet; *Hansard*, 5th series, 1915, LXXV, 529–537.

1 December 1915
House of Commons

I was at the FAU office this morning, darling, interviewing and then had lunch with G.N.[ewman] and Wilson to discuss this letter of Lord Derby's[74] re Red Cross men enlisting. G.N.[ewman] is seeing Lord Derby this afternoon and we have a Committee at 5 to hear his report.[75] I expect thou will have heard the terribly sad news of Walter Messer's[76] death – a bomb landed just in front of the car and killed him instantly. Poor Messer has taken it splendidly and written out to Andrew to stick at his job. It will be a sad weekend but I am glad I am going. I am off to R. Roberts[77] to sleep tonight but am writing early as I may not have an opportunity later.

8 December 1915
House of Commons

[...]
   Ted [Harvey] is just off to Bournemouth – he brings a good account of Irene. Tonight I have dinner with Dillon and Thomas and the no-conscriptionists – I shall ask J.W.W.[ilson] to take Ted's place.
   I have been at the office most of this morning and had a lunch with Sir George Paish at the Reform Club and a very discouraging talk with Burns here since.
   I shall try hard so as to be with thee in decent time.
   Farewell, darling one, and keep thy courage and faith – [...].

14 December 1915
National Liberal Club

[...]
   I have little to report – Board until lunch time then a moderately

---

[74] Edward George Villiers Stanley (1865–1948), Con. MP Westhoughton 1892–1906; Junior Ld of Treasury 1895–1900, Fin. Sec. to War Office 1900–1903, Postmaster-Gen. 1903–1905, Dir.-Gen. of Recruiting 1915–1916, US War Office 1916, Sec. of State for War 1916–1918, 1922–1924, Amb. to France 1918–1920; succ. as 17th Earl of Derby 1908.
   [75] Sir George Newman saw Derby at the War Office. He indicated he would exempt the whole FAU from conscription.
   [76] Walter Messer (d. 1915), s. of Dr Andrew Messer; Walter's brother, A.I. Messer, was also in the FAU.
   [77] Revd Richard Roberts (1874–1945), Presbyterian minister and Gen. Sec. FOR 1914–1915.

comfortable journey to town somewhat disturbed by the presence in
the dining car where I was by a naval officer whose mind had evidently
given way.

I went straight to the House heard a few of the speeches and since
have had a long talk with Thomas about the conscription question. It
is acute again notwithstanding the great success of the Derby recruiting
scheme[78] owing to Derby not knowing what to do with the married
men who have attested on account of the PM's pledge that they should
not be called up until all the young men had first been summoned and
of course there are a considerable number of these who have refused
to come 'until they are fetched'. We are going to have a deputation to
the PM on Thursday to try to stiffen his back.

15 December 1915
House of Commons

[...] I spent the morning at Vere Street. Maxwell was there bringing
the news that our 3rd train was to be laid up for a few months so we
are in some difficulty as to what to do with our last 40 men who are
now training at Jordans not to speak of those whom we had partially
promised should join a January camp.

Maxwell is seeing Lawley[79] this afternoon and will I hope be able to
fix up other work.

I have just seen Thomas who has been having 90 minutes with
Derby this morning. This pledge to married men is very difficult to get
over and Thomas's last suggestion to Derby is that before anything
further is done the single men should have the opportunity of stating
before the local tribunals why they have not attested. If this was done
he thinks that the actual numbers of those who could not give a
satisfactory reason would be so small that the government would see
that it was useless dividing the country over that negligible quantity.

[...]

[78] Derby Recruiting Scheme. Lord Derby had announced on 19 October 1915 that all
men aged 19–41 would be asked to 'attest' their willingness to serve in the Army if called.
In his speech to the Commons on 2 November 1915 Asquith had promised that married
men would not be conscripted until all unmarried men had been called on to enlist.

[79] Sir Arthur Lawley (1860–1932), aristocratic soldier; Administrator Matabeleland
1897–1901, Gov. W. Australia 1901–1902, Lt-Gov. Transvaal 1902–1905, Gov. Madras
1906–1911. At this time Commissioner of the Joint War Cttee of the British Red Cross
and the Order of St John of Jerusalem; KCMG 1901; succ. his brother as 6th and last
Ld Wenlock 1931.

16 December 1915
House of Commons

[...]

This morning I was at the office and then a little committee with
G.N.[ewman] about Unit matters.

This afternoon I have been with the deputation to the PM. On the
whole we were encouraged with his reply. He evidently is against any
compulsion Bill and sees no need for it, on the other hand he thinks
the general arguments against it are all strengthened by recent events.

The outstanding difficulty is this rash pledge to the married men
and a suggestion was made by Thomas that possibly it might be the
right thing to appoint some tribunal before which in writing or in some
other way the unmarried men who have not attested might state their
reason why. It is thought that when all the valid reasons have been
given (conscientious and other) it would be found that the quantity that
remained would be *negligible* and therefore no action need be taken.

[...]

17 December 1915
Mount Villas, York

[...]

I returned last night by the eight o'clock train travelling with
Seebohm [Rowntree] with whom I had a good long talk. It seems
amusing to think of his joining the Ministry of Munitions[80] but I think
it is right and if as seems likely he obtains an absolutely free hand I
think he will do most excellent work among the thousands of women
in the Munition factories. L.G. is very anxious that conditions should
be really satisfactory so there would seem to be unlimited scope for
'welfare work'.

21 December 1915
House of Commons

I hope thou had a comfortable journey darling and found all well at
home. I have been in Vere Street – sat in the House for several hours
and been across to see G.N.[ewman] having a talk with Lord Derby

[80] Seebohm Rowntree was appointed Dir. of the Welfare Dept of the Ministry of
Munitions 3 January 1916.

en route. He was interested in hearing that in Germany conscientious objectors were shot! I was very sorry to be out of the House with G.N.[ewman] when Ted [Harvey] spoke[81] – several members have spoken to me in warm appreciation of what he said.

    [...] I expect to go to Jordans in the afternoon.

[81] T.E. Harvey called for any scheme of conscription to provide COs with the opportunity to serve in a non-combatant role; *Hansard*, 5th series, 1915, LXXVII, 268–270.

CHAPTER 7

Letters 1916

On the 'fateful day', 5 January 1916, Asquith introduced the first National Service Bill or 'Bachelors Bill'. It conscripted all single men (and widowers without dependent children) aged 18 to 41, apart from those that local tribunals exempted on grounds of 'work of national importance', hardship to their families or businesses, ill health, or conscientious objection to war. Sir John Simon resigned as Home Secretary rather than accept the bill and it was condemned by a special Labour Conference on 6 January. On the First Reading the same day, the Bill was opposed by 105 MPs. For Asquith and Simon's speeches see Hansard, *5th series, 1916, LXXVII, 949–962 and 962–978. But despite this opposition, the bill had overwhelming political support and it was law by the end of the month.*

5 January 1916
House of Commons

The fateful day is nearly over, darling, and my own impression is that there will be an election before the month is over! Poor Asquith was evidently very unhappy and Simon tore to pieces the necessity of the Bill. *If* the Bill was necessary it has been framed on generous lines to the conscientious objector but we are of course going to divide in the first reading tomorrow and shall I think muster well over 100 votes. Thomas tells me he thinks the Trade Congress will reject the Bill too tomorrow. I made up my mind to speak this morning but I believe I was right in keeping silence the men who have been recruiting are really the men who are influencing votes *inside*.

Unit matters are a difficulty – the last train and the Abbeville hospital[1] are both 'off' so we have numbers of men without work. However we discuss this tomorrow.

Farewell, darling.

[1] The FAU had run the British Red Cross's hospital at Abbeville 23 July 1915–8 January 1916, when it was closed. They also operated two hospital trains and acquired a third in January 1916. A fourth was not obtained until August 1916.

6 January 1916
House of Commons

I have been feeling headachy today, darling, and discouraged. These
are heartracking times and it is difficult to get one's feet firm – I have
had Richard Roberts here tonight and he says all the Fellowship of
Reconciliation men are dead against alternative service and I think are
out to break the machine. I dread the Meeting for Sufferings tomorrow
but think I must stay at any rate for the morning session.[2] I shall hope
to be back for supper.

10 January 1916
House of Commons

I feel distinctly happier tonight, darling – we had a very good meeting
with a large deputation of anti-conscriptionists and there is going to be
a great fight put up. I spoke a few sentences and got warmly thanked
by Robert Mennell. Then had tea with Henry Hodgkin and Ted
[Harvey] and found Henry very reasonable and helpful. I shall try to
speak tomorrow or Wednesday. Just going to have dinner with Ted
[Harvey] and Dillon.

11 January 1916
House of Commons

I have tried hard to get in,[3] darling, today but there were so many that
I have failed to catch the speaker's eye and am thus returning to the
Club with my tail between my legs.

I had lunch with G.N.[ewman] – otherwise have been largely
wrapped up with this matter. The division will be very bad – the Irish
do not feel that they can continue their opposition and this will have
a bad effect on the others.[4]

In time of war like this the opponents of such a measure seem simply
crushed.

---

[2] Meeting for Sufferings on 7 January 1916 reaffirmed Quakers' total opposition to
conscription and informed the PM that the Cabinet's Bill did not meet the needs of
COs.

[3] A.S.R. had tried to speak in the Second Reading debate on the Nat. Service Bill,
but without success.

[4] The Irish Nats' opposition to the Nat. Service Bill was largely symbolic as Ireland
was excluded from its provisions. They voted against the First Reading on 6 January but
abstained thereafter.

12 January 1916
House of Commons

Our numbers, darling, are vanishing and I fear we shall have a very
bad division. I got in for a ¼ of an hour but was under promise to the
Speaker not to speak for more than that so couldn't do more than say
a little about the Conscientious Objector.[5] People were very kind
afterwards but I believe it would have been better to leave it to Ted
[Harvey].
    I fear we are in for a very bad period of slanging!

17 January 1916
House of Commons

I had a comfortable journey,[6] darling, despite the crowding and have
been diligently attending the House since arrival. The last two hours
the Conscriptionists have shown their hand by trying to get in an
amendment by which all boys on reaching 18 would automatically
become conscripts.[7] Happily the government have resisted, much to
the indignation of the Tories.

18 January 1916
House of Commons – midnight

We have had a long day here, darling, and so far have not been able
to get much from the government but the main discussion on the
conscientious objectors has still to come on. Ted [Harvey] has always
done well when he has intervened. I only spoke once and then only
for two minutes.[8]
    I had lunch with the Nation group, all in very bad spirits – and this
evening have had a long talk with Henderson when he has poured out

    [5] *Hansard*, 5th series, 1916, LXXVII, pp. 1684–1687 for A.S.R.'s speech on the Second
Reading of the Nat. Service Bill. He pointed out that many COs wished to serve their
country in a non-combatant role, but those who could not do this should not be
persecuted and that local tribunals were not ideally constituted.
    [6] A.S.R. was returning from York, where he had attended two very divided meetings
with York Libs on his attitude to the Nat. Service Bill; see *Yorkshire Herald*, 15 January
1916.
    [7] *Hansard*, 5th series, 1916, LXXVIII, 83–106 and 141–155 for amendments to this effect
from William Du Pré and Sir Ivor Herbert.
    [8] *Hansard*, 5th series, 1916, LXXVIII, 261. A.S.R. supported an amendment moved by
T.E. Harvey, allowing a CO's case to be considered by a tribunal even if he had not
applied for exemption within the allotted time.

his woes to me. Poor man, I think he feels his career is almost at an end.

I had dinner with Byles[9] who told me he was 77 and was expecting to die within the year with all his hopes shattered and with his old belief in immortality gone. I did my best to quicken the fading flame. I hope the conscientious objection will be left over until tomorrow, but we are preparing to sit late.

19 January 1916
House of Commons

Ted [Harvey] has scored, darling, a magnificent success this afternoon in his speech, it was wonderfully done and made a very great impression. I thought it best to put my notes in my pocket after such an utterance.[10] We have got a slight concession but I greatly fear difficulty owing to the government failing to meet us further, but their difficulty is that the House is in the temper to ask for much more drastic treatment. We went to bed at 2 o'clock this morning, but I am feeling nicely.

20 January 1916
House of Commons

I have to go down to Jordans, darling, tomorrow morning but I hope to catch the 2.30 home. [...] On the whole I feel we have not done badly this week – the Tories are wild at the concessions made so our policy now is to keep quiet and get others to make the points for us. J.W.W.[ilson] and I are looking to France the week after next and I am ordering clothes this afternoon.

Arnold Rowntree, J.W. Wilson and Sir George Newman met Lord Derby on 24 January 1916. He agreed that the FAU would be recognized by the War Office as performing 'approved' work. This meant that Quakers and other COs could be referred to the FAU by local tribunals and the War Office agreed to find work for the Unit to occupy its new recruits. The modest outcome was the General Service Section of the FAU which mainly employed COs on agricultural work. But this co-

---

9 Sir William Pollard Byles (1839–1917), Lib. MP Shipley 1892–1895, N. Salford 1906–1917; kt. 1911.

10 A.S.R. and T.E. Harvey tabled an amendment that allowed tribunals to exempt COs from all military service if they performed work of 'national importance'. Bonar Law accepted this amendment on behalf of the Cabinet and this concession was followed by Harvey's speech; *Hansard*, 5th series, 1916, LXXVIII, 430–431, 431–436.

operation with the military was heavily criticized by some Quakers for compromising the FAU's independence.

24 January 1916
House of Commons

Just a line, darling, to let thee know we had a very satisfactory talk with Lord Derby, of 1¼ hours duration. I think we are going to get a fairly satisfactory arrangement for conscientious objection, but I fear it is going to mean a heavy load of work. But more of this when we meet. I reach York tomorrow at 1.42.

28 January 1916
National Liberal Club

Just a line, darling, before I go to bed though I fear it will not reach thee until night. I was at the office this morning until noon, then presided at an FAU meeting when the committee were much pleased with arrangements entered with Lord Derby.

Then lunch with Ted [Harvey] and Richard [Cross] and on to Devonshire House.[11] I sat with Gerty [Taylor] through the afternoon sitting and when Mennell and Barry Brown[12] and Ted [Harvey] held forth, the latter splendidly, the others moderately and in a good spirit. Tea with Taff [Alfred Rowntree] and Arthur [Rowntree] and then the evening sitting when Harold Morland, Graham and others held forth on the State and the individual, quite a good meeting – very large – great numbers of young men. We come to grips tomorrow and I hope all will go well. [...]

3 February 1916
National Liberal Club

I had a comfortable journey, darling, having talks with E.R.C.[ross]

---

[11] An adjourned YM on 28–30 January 1916 again considered the issue of conscription. YM confirmed it would support all Quaker COs, including those who refused any form of alternative service.

[12] Alfred Barratt Brown (1887–1947), leading member FSC and No-Conscription Fellowship, later imprisoned as an 'absolutist' CO; Lecturer Woodbrooke 1912–1921, Vice-Principal Ruskin College 1921–1926, Principal 1926–1944.

with whom I travelled, the Weighalls, Edward Hodgkin,[13] Arthur
R.[owntree], Hudson MP,[14] Barnes and Shackleton,[15] the dilution of
labour commissioners so there was plenty of variety! After trying on
my khaki (which we are not going to take) I went to the office, consulted
with J.W.W.[ilson], decided to go, notwithstanding certain difficulties
and then went and got our passports signed, etc. John [Harvey] was at
the office to say goodbye, he hopes to set sail for Corsica on Saturday.
I had tea here with the Catchpool brothers[16] and am now going to
dine with J.W.W.[ilson]. Corder Catchpool hopes to come with us. [...]

16 February 1916
House of Commons

[...] I went out to Grims Wood last night and had a long talk with
G.N.[ewman] over Unit matters. Spent all this morning at the new
Unit office[17] – lunched with that nice Norwegian barrister (I made
friends with some weeks ago) at the Savoy Hotel – there wasn't much
sign of economy there! Then on to a long Unit committee where the
question of our attitude towards the government, etc., had to be very
carefully considered, and then came here in time to hear Balfour's very
feeble defence of the government aircraft policy.[18] [...]

[13] Jonathan Edward Hodgkin (1875–1953), Quaker businessman from Darlington,
mainly involved in the electrical engineering industry.
[14] Walter Hudson (1852–1935), Pres. Amalgamated Society of Railway Servants 1891–
1899, Irish Sec. 1898–1906; Lab. MP Newcastle 1906–1918.
[15] David James Shackleton (1863–1938), Lab. MP Clitheroe 1902–November 1910;
Senior Labour Advisor to Home Office 1910–1911, National Insurance Commissioner
1912–1916, PUS Ministry of Labour 1916–1921, Chief Labour Adviser 1921–1925; KCB
1917.
[16] Corder Pettifor Catchpool (1883–1952) and Egerton St John Pettifor 'Jack' Catchpool
(1890–1971), two Quaker brothers serving in the FAU. Corder was later welfare supervisor
at J.P. Davies's mills 1921–1931 and worked at the Quaker Centre in Berlin 1931–1937.
Jack was Sub-Warden Toynbee Hall 1920–1929 and First Sec. Youth Hostels Association
1930–1950. Neither accepted the FAU's new relationship with the War Office and Corder
was imprisoned 1917–1919 while Jack transferred to the Friends' War Victims' Relief
Cttee.
[17] The FAU Headquarters moved from Vere Street to 8 Weymouth Street in early
1916 and remained there for the rest of the war.
[18] *Hansard*, 5th series, 1916, LXXX, 117–125 for Balfour's statement in his capacity as
First Lord of the Admiralty.

22 February 1916
House of Commons

A busy day, darling, with Peverett and Boyd to begin with – then a long conference with G.N.[ewman], Henry Hodgkin and the FOR people over a National Service Scheme – lunch with the Nation folk – a conference with McKenna with J.B.M.[orrell] and Starmer over [...] paper and then some Adult School matters at the Office. Ted [Harvey] is about today and seems very well – [...].

1 March 1916
House of Commons

I had a comfortable journey, darling, having lunch en route with William Temple who had been leading a devotional hour at the SPG[19] meetings. I unburdened my soul to him freely. He told me that the Bishop of Oxford had recently said that the only moral good that could come to a country through war was if it was defeated, and he added, 'shall we go to Grosvenor Square and pray for defeat?!' After going to the Office I have been sitting in the House for a short time listening to a discussion on the National Stud.[20] I have seen Butcher and thanked him. Tonight we have the Junior Dinner which I hope to thoroughly enjoy.

2 March 1916
House of Commons

I do not feel very happy about my day's work, darling, but I suppose this feeling is inevitable nowadays.

   Interviews at the Club first, then preparation for Saturday's meeting – lunch at the Reform and have been here this afternoon. The Tribunals are really acting monstrously, and a large number of hard cases keep coming in to us. Ted [Harvey] and I are hoping to get a private interview with Long about several cases shortly [...].

[19] Society for the Propagation of the Gospel in Foreign Parts, Anglican missionary organization founded in 1701.
[20] *Hansard,* 5th series, 1916, LXXX, 1101–1139. The debate was on a motion to devote £50,100 to buying the stud and two estates of Col. William Hall Walker, Con. MP for Widnes, for use in breeding horses for the Army.

3 March 1916
Board of Education, Whitehall, London

After I wrote last night, darling, there was quite an interesting discussion on the closing of the British Museum upon which Ted [Harvey] and Butcher spoke well.[21] I then had dinner with Ted [Harvey] and Edward Hodgkin and afterwards Simon asked Ted and me to go home with him to talk over matters. Every post Simon receives hundreds of letters from men who are being badly treated by the military authorities. It is wonderful how he seems to stand as the representative of thousands [of] browbeaten men at the present time and that they look on him as the one man who can secure them justice, a great position.

Today I have been to the Meeting for Sufferings and listened to a long discussion on the excesses of the Friends Service Committee and the lack of control of the Meeting for Sufferings[22] – 2 hours!

Then a hurried discussion on the work of the Tribunals, lunch with Henry Hodgkin and with J.W.G.[raham], a satisfactory talk at the LGB with Ted [Harvey] and with Long about the incredible folly of the Tribunals, who was genuinely sympathetic. A talk with G.N.[ewman] about the new committee to be set up to find work for conscientious [objectors] [...].

Now (5.15) I am expecting Little and then in an hour's time W.C.B.[raithwaite] and Barrow Cadbury, then the Executive – so one is having a fairly full day.

7 March 1916
House of Commons

I had a comfortable journey, darling, first to York where I was glad to have 2½ hours to finish work that I left over yesterday, and then on to London with Whyte. I reached the House in time to hear the close of Balfour's speech and stayed in to hear Churchill's somewhat dramatic reappearance.[23] The inner meaning of his warnings and his demand for the recall of Fisher[24] is not yet understood by the members I have spoken to.

---

[21] *Hansard*, 5th series, 1916, LXXX, 1291–1308 for the debate and 1291–1297 and 1299–1301 for the contributions by Butcher and Harvey, who both opposed the closure.

[22] Meeting for Sufferings decided it had no control over the FSC because both were only responsible to YM.

[23] *Hansard*, 5th series, 1916, LXXX, 1401–1420 for Balfour's statement and 1420–1430 for Churchill's speech. The latter had resigned as Chanc. of the Duchy of Lancaster in November 1915 and had been commanding a battalion in France.

[24] John Arbuthnot Fisher (1841–1920), First Sea Ld 1904–1910, 1914–1915; cr. Ld Fisher 1909.

I gather that the chief damage done by the Zepp raid was in Hull, but that Goole was also visited. [...]

Hogge tells me that three German raiders that had escaped have been captured – one in the North Sea which I told thee about because 100 German prisoners had been landed at Leith and two more in St George's channel – so there is a good deal of uneasiness as to whether there are many who have eluded our fleet.

[...]

9 March 1916
en route York

[...] This morning I spent at the Office interviewing folk, etc., lunched with Davies[25] at the NLC, the assistant secretary of the Fellowship of Reconciliation and then went off to a long committee of the Unit largely taken up with a discussion of the extension of the work of the Unit owing to the Military Service Act. I fear the government are going to act unwisely with regard to the majority of COs as they have now retired the committee that was proposed to arrange Nat. Service for them. I think it is Walter Long who is stubborn.

13 March 1916
Mount Villas, York

[...]
There was nothing very special at the Board except the serious position owing to the expected early withdrawal of the married men.
[...]
Herbert Waller[26] and seven other COs come up before the tribunal tomorrow.
[...]

[25] George Maitland Lloyd Davies (1880–1949), Asst Sec. FOR; imprisoned 1917–1919; later a Presbyterian minister and Christian Pacifist MP Univ. of Wales 1923–1924.
[26] Herbert Ingle Waller (1879–1956), York Quaker, bro. of W.J. Waller of Rowntree & Co.

14 March 1916
10 Grosvenor Terrace, York

[...]

Bowes [Morrell] was at the Tribunal this morning and succeeded in getting off most of the men whom we considered indispensable, including W.J. Waller! Edie [Sturge] has been there this afternoon and says Percy Fletcher[27] secured total exemption.

I am going to Bowes [Morrell] this evening to meet some officers of the Liberal Association. I shall tell them plainly that I think the right thing for me to do is to retire at the next election so that they shall take the initiative if they want anything different.

[...]

15 March 1916
House of Commons

Thank thee, darling, for thy letters. We had a pleasant meeting at Bowes [Morrell]'s last night with the officials of the various wards. They were all very cordial and absolutely refused to accept my resignation so I fear it looks as if the only way to get out of the impasse was to fight and be defeated, but of course we must just wait and see how events turn out. [...]

I travelled up this morning alone and this afternoon have heard Derby and Kitchener in the Lords.[28]

The muddle following the passage of the National Service Act is appalling and feeling is I fear becoming very bitter in the country. [...]

22 March 1916
House of Commons

I have spent today, darling, at the B of E and here. All the morning we were at the FAU sub committee where the question of dealing with Friends and others referred to us by the Tribunal was discussed. The position is very difficult but I hope will be eased in a few days time by

---

[27] John Percy Frederic Fletcher (1884–1961), already had long record of opposing compulsory military training in Australia 1912–1915; leading light of the FSC and No-Conscription Fellowship. His exemption was overturned on appeal and he was imprisoned 1917–1919.

[28] *Hansard*, 5th series, 1916, XXI, 397–407 and 407–409 for the speeches by Derby and Kitchener. Derby defended his record in charge of recruiting and Kitchener called on all married men to enlist voluntarily.

the appointment of a small civilian committee by the Board of Trade to deal with non-Friends upon which Ted [Harvey] would sit.[29]

This afternoon I have seen several callers here.

The position of the COs gets steadily worse and the cases of gross injustice increase. It seems impossible in wartime to get judicial decisions.

28 March 1916
in Corby near Grantham – 5.40 pm

We have had a extraordinary journey, darling, so far, and when we shall reach London seems most uncertain. I started by the 12.15 as arranged and all went well until nearing Retford when we entered into the zone of blizzard and snow and mile by mile the position has grown steadily worse. Grantham, which we should have passed through about 2.15 we reached at 4.00, since we have taken about 1.40 minutes running 10 miles! The telegraph wires are broken in many places so signalling by wire is impossible. Drifts 3 or 4 feet one sees continually and the sides and windows of some of the houses are absolutely covered with snow. The wind keeps these heavy coaches continually rocking.

I bought eggs at the station before starting and have just been to the Dining Car to get some cutlets, not knowing whether the food will last out long and am storing a little bread and cheese for eventualities! The stewards say that they will not be able to provide dinner as the gas has run out.

Of course after Peterborough we may get into smooth running and if so we shall be alright. I think the effect of the hardships entailed by others during the war has really made its mark on the people here. Despite all the inconveniences of so late an arrival in London and the monotony of stops every mile I have not heard anyone grumble!

[...]

4 April 1916
House of Commons

I had a comfortable journey, darling, by myself – a great contrast in temperature to the one we had last week. We had to come round by

[29] This was the Cttee on Work of National Importance, or Pelham Cttee as it was chaired by Hon. Thomas Henry William Pelham (1847–1916), Asst Sec. Bd of Trade 1895–1913; T.E. Harvey was a member. Its purpose was to find work for COs who had been exempted from military duties by their tribunal.

Ackworth to Doncaster as trucks were off the line at Selby, still we
were only 30 minutes late altogether.

I went to the Nation lunch and have been at the House since.
McKenna's budget statement and on the whole his new taxes, except
the increase on Railway travelling, are I think good.[30] But to raise
cocoa from 1½ to 6 is very serious and I fear may have grave
consequences for us.

[...]

17 April 1916
House of Commons

The post goes almost directly, darling, but I just wanted to send thee
a line to say that I have been at Ambulance Work all the day with the
exception of two committees here on the present deplorable state of
the COs. Work arising out of this and pressure owing to the Budget
prevents me getting off tonight but I shall strive hard to manage
tomorrow either by the 5.30 or 8.

Matters are serious too with regard to the Government generally –
and it is not at all unlikely that it may fall shortly. The work at present
is very discouraging but one must persevere and do one's best and it is
especially hard when I feel I want to be at home with thee. [...]

18 April 1916
House of Commons

I had an uneventful quiet journey by myself, darling, and after going
with the very hard case of one of our traveller's sons, came on here.
The whole place is in a whirl of excitement and the future all very
uncertain.

The military staff are declaring for compulsion[31] – Jellicoe[32] most
anxious about the condition of merchant shipping and dead against
compulsion. George backing up the staff, wanting compulsion for the
sake of munitions works, the King backing Asquith strongly – such is
the gossip I hear. I am going to the Club to dine with Ted [Harvey]

---

[30] McKenna imposed a tax on all railway tickets costing over 9d and raised the duty
on cocoa from 1½d to 6d per lb; *Hansard*, 5th series, 1916, LXXXI, 1058–1059.

[31] Compulsion; the extension of conscription to married men.

[32] Admiral Sir John Rushworth Jellicoe (1859–1935), Commander-in-Chief Grand Fleet
1914–1916, First Sea Ld 1916–1917, Gov.-Gen. New Zealand 1920–1924; GCB 1915, cr.
Vt Jellicoe 1917, Earl 1925.

and discuss various matters. As things have turned out I might have stayed in York until this evening.

Several members have enquired after thee – Gulland, Rea, Whyte and others. I was very glad to be able to give them a good account. [...]
    [...]

25 April 1916
nearing London

It is a perfect spring day, darling, and the country is looking most beautiful. The train is *very* full and we shall be 40 minutes late into town, but I have fared comfortably. There are several MPs from the ILP conference at Newcastle and I have had talks with Anderson[33] and Snowden[34] who have their wives with them.

Also a long talk with Trevelyan who seemed to me in an unusually tender mood. Poor man, he has just lost one of his twin boys with meningitis. He tells me he and his wife want to see Bootham and so I had to tell him that when thee was well we should be glad to have them for a Sunday!

Asquith and Carson have now spoken – Asquith for two hours.[35] They evidently feel after reviewing the whole situation that they cannot expect to get more than 200,000 men more from the unattested married men and as they must have these immediately they are going to bring in a measure of compulsion in one month's time unless 50,000 men are obtained in the next four weeks and if demands of 15,000 per week until the 200,000 are obtained. But what is exercising members much more is the Siege of Dublin by the Sinn Feinners.[36] They are in possession of the Post Office, Dublin Castle, and they think the Vice Regal Lodge.

Carson very severe at this great delay in bringing in general compulsion.

[33] William Crawford Anderson (1877–1919), Lab. MP Sheffield, Attercliffe 1914–1918; Chmn ILP 1911–1913; m. 1911 Mary Reid Macarthur (1880–1921), Sec. Womens' Trade Union League.
[34] Philip Snowden (1864–1937), Lab. MP Blackburn 1906–1918, Colne Valley 1922–1931, when cr. Vt Snowden; Chanc. of Exchequer 1924, 1929–1931, Ld Privy Seal 1931–1932. Chmn ILP 1904–1907, 1917–1920; m. 1905 Ethel Snowden (nee Annakin) (1881–1951), suffragist; Gov. BBC 1927–1933.
[35] At a secret session of the Commons, Asquith announced a compromise to avoid the immediate extension of conscription to all married men; *Hansard*, 5th series, 1916, LXXXI, 2463–2466. The plan was savagely attacked and dropped by the Cabinet on 29 April 1916.
[36] The Easter Rising by a section of the Irish Volunteers had begun on 23 April 1916.

26 April 1916
House of Commons

[...] Things here are most discouraging. Many of those who seem to know most are taking a very gloomy view as to the final result of the war and consequently I fear this increased dose of compulsion proposed to the government will go through with comparatively little opposition.

The first reading of the first bill comes tomorrow, but as we are not going to divide on the first reading (waiting for the second next week) owing to so many of our men being away I don't think I shall stay late but come back by the 5.30 train if not earlier. I shall have to attend the continuation of the Ambulance Committee in the morning, there were so many cases today that we couldn't possibly get through. I fear from what Maxwell says that many of the men are getting very restless at Dunkirk and we may have several resignations owing to the men feeling that their duty is in England to suffer[37] [...]. [*2nd page of letter missing*]

2 May 1916
House of Commons

[...] Here alas the gloom remains. Asquith has capitulated to the compulsionists[38] and tomorrow the Bill is introduced that will compel *all* and on Thursday it will receive a 2nd reading! I fear this will probably mean I shall have to stay part of Friday to consider amendments as it is to be rushed through next week.

I am going to see Henderson for a few minutes about the conscientious objectors to see if he can do anything. I have not seen Ted [Harvey] yet. I think he must have been at the War Victims Committee.
[...]

3 May 1916
House of Commons

We are in the midst of the Ambulance Committee, darling. A deputation has come over from Dunkirk and have been somewhat stirred up by

---

[37] About a dozen members resigned from the FAU in protest at what they saw as its co-operation with the imposition of conscription.
[38] Asquith announced the withdrawal of his compromise measure on 2 May 1916; *Hansard,* 5th series, 1916, LXXXI, 2611–2616. The next day he introduced the Military Service Bill (1916) which conscripted all men aged 18–41.

the Service Committee and I fear we shall have a few resignations. This morning we sit to deal with the new cases.

I had an hour last night with Henderson about the Military Service Act but fear didn't get very far – the conversation proved how frightfully prejudiced the position of the CO is by the extreme attitude of the men who will not serve. I am having to miss the PM this afternoon but felt I must come to the committee owing to this difficulty. I hope Ted [Harvey] will speak sometime this evening.

Just post time so must send now. Have had a serious talk with Massingham who is very gloomy.

9 May 1916
House of Commons

A somewhat clashing day, darling. Breakfast with Richard [Cross], a short time at the Unit Office and then at my own, [...] then at the House in this wretched committee and with interviews.

Ted [Harvey] and I are much concerned by the news that came last night that Wyatt[39] and the other conscientious objectors had been sent to France – it seems to us as if they were going to be shot, or might be. Thou willst see I called the PM's attention to their case by private question.[40]

We are putting great pressure on the PM to see that these men are removed to a civilian prison. Until we get these men out of the clutches of the military, we shall not feel safe.

23 May 1916
House of Commons

I had a comfortable and quiet journey up here, darling. Went straight on arrival to the NLC and to the Nation lunch where Massingham was talking interestingly on his visit to Ireland. He was giving an awful account of military despotism there. Then on here, where I had two questions to the PM but on arrival I found a note from his secretary asking me to withdraw them and to see McKenna as to the reason.[41]

[39] The first batch of COs arrived in France on 8 May 1916. Rendel Wyatt, a Quaker schoolteacher, was one of five court-martialled at Boulogne on 15 June 1916; four of them were condemned to death, but had the sentences commuted to ten years penal servitude. In all, thirty-four COs underwent this procedure in France.

[40] *Hansard,* 5th series, 1916, LXXXII, 440.

[41] Kitchener had already stated in the Lords on 22 May 1916 that the govt intended to place all 'genuine' COs under civilian authority; *Hansard,* 5th series, 1916, XXII, 14.

This I found to be that they have decided on the principle of treating all genuine COs under civilian control but don't like to say so too specifically for fear of promoting an awful crop of shams! But of course we cannot keep quiet unless they agree to stop all arrests and to stop all bullying in military garrisons, so we shall try to come to terms tomorrow.

Edward Backhouse's tea party of the FAU and Social Service Committees went off very well and an excellent spirit prevailed. Now I am off to the Kingsley Hotel to hear Henry [Hodgkin].

30 May 1916
House of Commons

I hope thou hast fared well, darling, since I left thee. I travelled up with Richard [Cross] talking en route for a short time with Mr Yapp[42] the man responsible for all this YMCA activity. This morning after a short time at the office I went to the YM to the adjourned sitting on Peace – all interesting but it was clear that there was not sufficient unanimity on any one suggestion to decide anything, so it was adjourned again until the afternoon. One of the great difficulties is to get any time for quiet, united prayer – two efforts were made but failed!

[...] then on here where I met Mother and Irene [Harvey] and got them into the gallery. McKenna has been doing his best to stop the 16 from Richmond[43] going to France, and at last this morning got Macready,[44] the Adjutant General, contrary to all regulations, to wire stopping them. So Ted [Harvey] withdrew his question. McKenna is the *one* member who really has done his level best to stop the scandals. Five or six of us had a further interview with him at question time.

[...]

12 August 1916
Buttermere Hotel in Cockermouth

There is just time, darling, before the post goes, to send thee a few lines. Thou would hear of this terrible blow before me. I knew nothing

[42] Arthur Keysall Yapp (1869–1936), Nat. Sec. Young Mens' Christian Association 1912–1929; KBE 1917.

[43] A number of COs were being held in military detention for disobeying orders at Richmond Castle, Yorkshire.

[44] Sir Cecil Frederick Nevil Macready (1862–1946), Adjutant British Expeditionary Force 1914–1916, Adjutant to the Forces 1916–1918, Commissioner Metropolitan Police 1918–1920, Gen. Officer to Commander-in-Chief in Ireland 1920–1922; KCB 1912, Bt 1923.

until C[45] and I got to the top of Honister where Bedford[46] was waiting for us. He at once told C. that Mary[47] was a few yards lower down and that he wanted to speak to me and then he told me all the sad tragic history. Richard [Cross] had returned about 12 after rowing Ken and Marion [Wilkinson] to the other end of the lake as they were leaving for home. He was hot and came in for his bathing dress and told Sally[48] and the others he was just going to bathe before he took the maids over the lake to a picnic that they were arranging.

Perhaps 10 or 15 minutes after Richard went, Sally and Margery Pierce[49] went down to the lake and couldn't find Richard and then suddenly Margery saw him lying at the bottom of the water – the lake deepens very quickly. [...]

[...]

Thou can imagine how I feel – since John Wilhelm[50] died I feel to have relied on three people, first is thee, then Richard [Cross] and J.R.[owntree] and naturally Richard being more my age I have been more intimate with him than I could be with J.R.[owntree]. He has been simply wonderful in counsel and advice. I think just among my letters I had on me when I reached here I wanted his help with three! But one mustn't think of one's own loss that is small and as long as thou and the kiddies are left I shall not despair of life and its problems! The funeral is arranged for Pardshaw at 3.30 on Monday and as I said in my wire I think as I am an executor I better go home with Sally as she meets with Mr Black,[51] Richard's partner, and to York on Tuesday. [...]

13 August 1916
The Buttermere Hotel in Cockermouth

[...] After dinner I had a very pleasant stroll with J.A. Hobson who is very much cut up, and we talked about the article for next week's Nation – Richard [Cross] will be sorely missed there amongst that clever but somewhat erratic coterie of writers. Each one however

[45] Christopher Rowntree, eldest child of A.S.R., born 1907.
[46] Dr Bedford Pierce (1861–1932), Superintendent of Quaker asylum in York, The Retreat 1892–1922, and distinguished psychiatrist.
[47] Mary Halliday Cross, eldest daughter of Richard Cross.
[48] Sarah Cross (nee Halliday) (1869–1943), wife of E.R. Cross.
[49] Margery Pierce (1894–1980), daughter of Dr Bedford Pierce; psychiatrist; worked at Tavistock Clinic 1925–1950, Gov. of The Retreat 1936–1969.
[50] John Wilhelm Rowntree (1868–1905), eldest s. of Joseph Rowntree; partner in H.I. Rowntree & Co. 1889–1897, Dir. Rowntree & Co. 1897–1899 until ill health forced his retirement; leading figure in English Quaker Renaissance, and close friend of A.S.R.
[51] George Barnard Black, Scarborough solicitor and partner of E.R. Cross.

respected his opinion and his judgement and balance backed by his great knowledge and wonderful memory was invaluable in keeping them altogether and helping them to turn out a paper with at any rate some degree of balance. I don't know how we shall supply this now he has gone. Poor Uncle [Joseph Rowntree] too will I fear be feeling his sudden departure terribly. He was constantly consulting Richard [Cross] about his wishes for the future and I should think Uncle must have altered his will or rather added to it twice a year at least for years past. Richard had always done this and knew all the arrangements that he wanted carrying out.

[...]

15 August 1916
York

[...]
[...] I went off with Bedford [Pierce] to help in the removal from Gatesgarth. Bedford agreed to go with Sally [Cross] to Pardshaw so I went later in a motor from the hotel with Mrs Pierce and the Hobsons. It was a beautiful drive as the sun shone brightly after the storm and Meldrake especially was brilliantly purple with the glistening purple heather.

The burial ground at Pardshaw was as peaceful as ever and the view glorious. Arthur [Rowntree] and Ellie[52] and Ailie[53] had lined the grave with heather and club moss, the long grass had just been cut and with the fine bank of lake mountains to gaze upon it would have been impossible to have chosen a more peaceful spot in which to rest.

Josiah Hall,[54] the Grahams, Irwins,[55] Walkers, Coopers[56] (including W.A. who has just been released 'on furlough'), Horace Alexander[57] etc. were all there. About 3.30 Aunt Anna Mary,[58] Uncle W.S.R.,[59]

---

[52] Ellen Hurndall Rowntree (1859–1950), wife of Arthur Rowntree.
[53] Alysonn Hurndall Rowntree (1897–1980), daughter of Arthur Rowntree; later became a doctor.
[54] Josiah Hall (1850–1921), Quaker merchant from Cockermouth.
[55] Wilfred Irwin (1858–1928), Quaker industrialist, living in Cockermouth; owned chemical plants at Flimby and Maryport; m. Mary Louisa (nee Grest) (1880–1926).
[56] William Arthur Cooper (1883–1943), Quaker CO; later mathematics master at Bootham and Headmaster of Ackworth School.
[57] Horace Gundry Alexander (1889–1989), Quaker CO; appointed Merrttens Lecturer in International Relations at Woodbrooke 1919.
[58] Anna Mary Rowntree (nee Doncaster) (1849–1938), sister of A.S.R.'s stepmother; m. 1876 W.S. Rowntree.
[59] William Stickney Rowntree (1848–1939), cousin of A.S.R.'s from the Scarborough branch of the family; in business as a draper and father of Ernest and Olive Rowntree.

Philip Burtt drove up and said that Connie [Rowntree], Margaret,[60] Ken [Wilkinson] and Bowes [Morrell] and Mrs Daniel were all behind, hoping to be able to reach the graveyard but unable to get a motor or vehicle at Cockermouth. One was immediately sent back and Sally [Cross] of course wished the funeral delayed until Con [Rowntree] and others arrived. I think perhaps we waited 15 minutes for them but there was no sense of uneasiness because we told the few friends there why it was and folks were glad to quietly wait under such beautiful surroundings.

At the graveside Josiah Hall read the 121 Psalm and after a pause Bedford [Pierce] read the Deserted House. We then went into the Meeting House – W.S.R.[owntree], George Prior[61] (I think), J.W.G.[raham], Arthur [Rowntree] and John Cross[62] all ministered to us most helpfully. I think it was a Meeting that Richard [Cross] would have approved of.

Afterwards we had tea at the Globe Hotel in Cockermouth and left at 6 arriving York at 11.30. Sally, Kate and Mary [Cross] bore the journey with wonderful calm and courage, though naturally *very* tired when they reached the journey's end. Most of those who came from a distance returned with us. W.S.R.[owntree] and P.B.[urtt] very enthusiastic over the success of the Woodbrooke meetings (under Marvin's[63] auspices). [...]

16 August 1916
House of Commons – 6.30

I have been round to the Nation Office to see Massingham. He is very much cut up over Richard [Cross]'s death. [...]

22 August 1916
en route Scarborough

[...]

I hope to meet Bowes [Morrell] in Scarbro for a few minutes about Nation matters before going in to Robin Hoods Bay to meet Seebohm

---

[60] Margaret Rowntree (1893–1973), daughter of John Wilhelm Rowntree; m. 1918 George Spencer Crossley (1892–1968), Dir. of Rowntree & Co.

[61] George Prior (1846–1934), draper from Cumberland; active in Quaker mission work.

[62] John Cross, bro. of Richard Cross.

[63] Francis Sydney Marvin (1863–1943), Inspector Bd of Education 1890–1924. During the First World War he ran summer schools at Woodbrooke on 'the fundamental unities which underlie and are independent of national barriers and distinctions'.

[Rowntree] – I am wondering whether it would be right to ask
W.C.B.[raithwaite] to take Richard's place.[64] I'm sure it's a bigger
position than managing a Banbury bank and he perhaps more than
anyone else I know has the same kind of ability as Richard and
wonderful power of judgement. Peverett announces that his wife has
presented him with twins (a boy and a girl) – he finds it somewhat
overpowering!

2 October 1916
The Reform Club

I saw Tom Bryan, darling, this morning. He was better than I expected
but had a fairly continuous cough. I also saw E.G.[ilbert] and he has
agreed to undertake the work at Warwick[65] and begins tomorrow
expecting 50 COs on Thursday and shortly to make his family up to
250! [...].
I came up here and am now waiting for C.P. Scott.
Have just had a chat with Gulland who explains the L.G. outburst
last week[66] by the fact that he had to do something to get back his
standing with the military folk as he had got himself into considerable
difficulties in France by saying to General Foch,[67] one of the French
generals, that our generals were no use! General Foch took this
seriously, told Joffre[68] who told Douglas Haig[69] and then Joffre
would not see L.G. except with Haig! The story then got back
to England – the Morning Post had a severe general attack on
L.G.

[64] A.S.R. considered asking W.C. Braithwaite to succeed E.R. Cross as Chmn of Dirs
of the *Nation*. Braithwaite had become a Dir. of the JRSST, which owned the paper, in
December 1915. In fact, A.S.R. took this role himself.
[65] Since late July 1916 the Central Tribunal had been interviewing COs in prison and
offering many of them the chance of release to perform work of national importance
under the 'Home Office scheme'. One option was to send them to Warwick Work
Centre, in reality a disused prison. A.S.R. suggested Gilbert should be the Centre's first
director.
[66] Lloyd George's interview with the American journalist, Roy Howard, published in
The Times on 29 September 1916. It denounced any moves towards a negotiated peace
and called for a 'knock-out blow' against Germany. Lloyd George's indiscreet conversation
with Foch had been leaked to the *Morning Post* on 28 September 1916.
[67] Marshal Ferdinand Foch (1851–1929), Commander of French 9th Army 1914–1916,
Chief of Staff 1917–1918, Allied Generalissimo 1918–1919.
[68] Gen. Joseph Joffre (1852–1931), Commander-in-Chief of French Army 1914–1916.
[69] Field Marshal Sir Douglas Haig (1861–1928), Commander 1st Army 1914–1915,
Commander-in-Chief in France and Flanders 1915–1919, and Forces in Britain 1919–
1920; GCB 1915; cr. Earl Haig 1919.

C.P. Scott and Massingham are very indignant over the whole affair, rightly so.

[...]

6 November 1916
E.S. & A. Robinson Ltd, 1 Redcliffe St, Bristol[70]

I have had an interesting and encouraging time here, darling. The conference[71] on Saturday and Sunday with 15 hot Trade Union leaders was most informing and by the Sunday evening we had reached a fairly united decision and Wethered and I both felt able to say a few words about the need of mental and spiritual development. It was most interesting to see how easy it was to stimulate a really strong friendly atmosphere and I think many of the leaders really felt it was the most interesting weekend they had had in their lives – but more of this when we meet.

It was a soaking morning yesterday and only about 700 turned up to the meeting but I think it was felt to be a good time and it is a relief to have it behind me.

Today I have been with Tom King over his works and over Wills tobacco and having great talks about future relations between capital and labour with both King and Wills.[72] I am going to stay tonight with Wethered and go up to town by the breakfast train tomorrow.

7 November 1916
House of Commons

Thank thee, darling, for thy two notes. After writing thee last night I sat with Wethered for an hour at their Inner Advisory Labour Committee which reckons to be a model, afterwards had dinner and then went up to his house and talked till 1 AM and slept till 6.30 when I had to arise and catch the breakfast train to Paddington. I feel the gathering we have had at Penscott[73] opened up some rather serious issues as to one's work in the future but about these I must talk to thee when I return. This morning on reaching town I went straight to

[70] E.S. & A. Robinson, Liberal-owned firm of paper manufacturers in Bristol.
[71] A conference with a group of Bristol trade union leaders (including Ernest Bevin). A further conference with local employers and trade unionists in February 1917 led to the creation of the Bristol Association for Industrial Reconstruction.
[72] Presumably a member of the Wills family who owned Imperial Tobacco Co. Ltd.
[73] Penscott Guest House in Shipham, Somerset, venue of the conference with Bristol trade unionists.

Bensons and spent two hours there over advertizing matters. Then lunch with the Nation writers and this afternoon I have had a long talk with Whitley regarding the Penscott gathering. Whitley is the Chairman of the new Reconstruction Committee.[74] Ted [Harvey] has just gone off to France in good spirits. [...]

There is an awkward division tomorrow and if no pair is available I may have to stay, but I will wire thee tomorrow when I see the light.

14 November 1916
House of Commons

[...] George Masterman[75] came to breakfast as I wanted advice as to how to conduct Bonwick's[76] case before the Tribunal. Maclean the Chairman took a very strong line and he was given 6 mos. exemption with leave to appear again but then it was added he must join the volunteers. Then the fat was in the fire. Bonwick said he was a CO and at once the attitude of the Tribunal was different, but eventually his CO claim was postponed until Monday. I think Maclean means to do the right thing.

I spent the morning at the Nation office over various matters, lunched with the Staff, then appeared at the Tribunal and this afternoon have been to a very interesting gathering in the Harcourt Room addressed by Bryce and Gilbert Murray[77] on American relations. I sat next to Page,[78] the Ambassador, and had a talk with him. Now I am going to Buxtons to dinner which I regret as I should have liked to have heard the debate on the Cardiff Scandal.[79] The War Office have climbed down re the Birmingham inquisition.[80]

[74] J.H. Whitley had been chosen in October 1916 to head a cttee on employer–employee relations.
[75] George Masterman Gillett (1870–1939), A.S.R.'s first cousin; Dir. Gillett Bros. Discount Co.; LCC 1910–1922, Lab. (Nat.Lab. from 1931) MP Finsbury 1923–1935; PS Overseas Trade Dept 1929–1931, PS Ministry of Transport 1931; kt. 1931. In 1916–1918 served on HofC Appeal Tribunal for COs.
[76] Alfred James Bonwick (1883–1949), Sec. the *Nation*, later business manager of various newspapers owned by the JRSST; Lib. MP Chippenham 1922–1924.
[77] George Gilbert Aime Murray (1866–1957), Lib. academic; Regius Prof. of Greek at Oxford Univ. 1908–1936.
[78] Walter Hines Page (1855–1918), US Amb. to Court of St James' 1913–1918.
[79] *Hansard*, 5th series, 1916, LXXXVII, 711–750 for the debate on the breaking up of a meeting of the National Council for Civil Liberties in Cardiff.
[80] 'Birmingham inquisition'; Brigadier-Gen. Groves, the officer commanding in Warwickshire and the Midlands, had asked a number of local pacifists and Quakers, including George Cadbury, to produce details of their finances and the causes to which they subscribed. The matter was raised in the Commons by A.J. Sherwell; *Hansard*, 5th series, 1916, LXXXVII, 566–567.

28 November 1916
House of Commons

I have had a very busy day, darling, over chocolate negotiations first with Fry, then with Fry, Cadbury, Rowntree, Caley, then with the Confectionary Alliance, and here this evening with Gerald France, Runciman's secretary.[81] I hope we have come to a fairly amicable agreement.

I have been anxious all day about the Zepps – wondering whether York was attacked. Bertha wired to Bowes [Morrell] that all were well so I felt somehow that no harm had befallen you, and tonight I hear in the House that one was over York. Edward Cadbury heard during our sitting that the Lowestoft one was brought down by Bertie Cadbury![82] which has caused much amusement here. The other one thou willt have heard was brought down near Hartlepool. The seaplane that visited London was so high that no one saw it.

I am just going off to dine with Seebohm [Rowntree] and Bowes [Morrell] to talk Saccharine.[83]

Lloyd George resigned as Secretary of State for War on the morning of 5 December 1916. The crisis that lead to the reconstruction of the government was already well underway and Asquith resigned as Prime Minister later that evening. Lloyd George was appointed to that post on 6 December 1916 and set about forming a new government, without Asquith and his Liberal followers.

5 December 1916
Central Buildings

[...] I found Tom Bryan better I thought than last time I saw him. [...]
He wanted to tell me about his concern for Will [Harvey] – He says

[81] The Chanc. of the Exchequer had proposed in October 1916 that a quota set at one third of 1915 sugar usage should be imposed on the production of luxuries such as confectionary. In response, Rowntree & Co. decided to concentrate on its cheapest and most popular lines. Confectionary Alliance; Manufacturing Confectioners' Association, a group of leading confectionary makers formed in 1901 to lobby against increases in sugar duties.

[82] Egbert Cadbury (1893–1967), youngest s. of George Cadbury; joined Royal Navy 1914, transferring to Royal Naval Air Service 1915; ended war as a Major, with DSC and DFC; Dir. British Cocoa and Confectionary Ltd 1921, Managing Dir. Cadbury Bros. 1943–1963; kt. 1957.

[83] Wartime restrictions on imports produced an urgent search for substitute sweeteners and flavourings. In March 1915 Rowntrees set up Confectionary Ingredients Ltd to work on this subject and in November 1916 authorized it to investigate the production of saccharine.

that he more than anyone won the affection of the Fircroft boys and he feels that he is the *one* man to carry on the work – somewhere in the Yorkshire dales. I have told him to write Will expressing his concern. I left him a nice pot of white heather which pleased him and hope I may be able to see him again.

I didn't reach the Settlement at Warwick until after 10.30 PM. E.G.[ilbert]'s family has increased to 300 and on the whole things are going comfortably there but the men are getting *very* tired of mail bag making and amongst some of the stronger men there seems a spirit of revolt at the futility of it all.

I was at the Nation lunch for 45 minutes – the men in a state of almost despair at the way things are going and great uncertainty as to what to advise.

The news of L.G.'s resignation will probably clear the air. John Burns who I saw in the House thinks it much the best solution but if he fights and is supported by the whole of the Times and the Northcliffe press I should think it is doubtful if an Asquith coalition could live.

8 December 1916
Chalfonts

It is delightful to be back here, darling, after the whirl of London and to find the kiddies all well and in a very nice state of mind.

I had a comfortable journey last night – when I was having my supper in the train a lady offered me tea out of her thermos – and in going to Birmingham on Monday an officer pressed me to accept tea, toast and jam, so I am impressed with the breaking down of reserve which this war has brought.

[...]

The accident referred to by the Ministry of Munitions was at Garforth and several York people have been killed or injured. I heard that the wife of one of our men who had eight children was killed, also the sister of one of our girls.

I enclose an irreverent parody of the 23rd Psalm which I think either Frank[84] or Basil Neave[85] was responsible for. Oscar [Rowntree] is pleased with a story of Miss Milner[86] who went into one of the wards

---

[84] Francis Henry 'Frank' Rowntree (1868–1918), first cousin of A.S.R.; Dir. Rowntree & Co. 1897–1918.

[85] Basil Neave, commercial traveller for Rowntree & Co.; Quaker and CO.

[86] Edith Harriet Milner, member of family of local landowners who had occasionally represented York since the eighteenth century; leading figure in York Primrose League, wartime super-patriot and indefatigable writer of letters to local press, often denouncing the Rowntrees.

in the hospital and said to the soldiers, 'I have laid an egg on each one of your shelves!' (Loud laughter and cheers from the Tommies.)

J.R.[owntree] seemed to me very brisk, determined to see the best in this week's catastrophes and hopes now to see the nationalisation of the drink traffic.

I think if one tries to weigh the whole matter up one wants to remember the following points.

(a) It must be admitted that the old coalition were stale, tired and cross with one another.

(b) That this meant they were slow in making decisions and had lost their power of drive.

(c) That this lack of decision applied especially to the PM.

(d) That we were losing the war owing to innumerable blunders.

L.G. realising this felt that a change of government was essential in the national interest and owing to the extraordinary hold Asquith had over the people, extraordinary methods had to be employed. Hence the almost united suggestion that Asquith should be shunted from the War Council.

The great dangers ahead are I think the following:

(a) It is clear that L.G. seeing the impossibility of running the war with a large cabinet means to create a small war council probably of 4 who will have the power of deciding all large questions without reference to the cabinet. This means a virtual dictatorship and when you think of the composition of the council – L.G., Carson, Bonar Law and Henderson (probably) – you dread the dictatorship.

(b) L.G. believes some form of industrial conscription necessary. My own feeling is that unless great care is exercised here there will be serious industrial trouble.

(c) L.G. is a believer in the necessity of greatly strengthening our force in the *East* – this means the employment of large numbers of ships. I believe that without the employment of any more ships we shall be face to face with famine next summer owing to shortage of tonnage.

(d) With the pressure on the government to stiffen the Blockade I fear they will anger neutrals, especially America.

On the other hand it will be a real advantage having an informed opposition – a great upheaval like this forces an increasing number of people really to face the future. Thou knows I have come to the conclusion during the past four weeks that we cannot really improve our position even if we improve on the west. I fear our economic position in comparison to Germany's must steadily grow worse therefore I should be for making the best arrangement *now*.

It is however very difficult to say this in public and give reasons, because naturally if you do the Germans realise we are in a bad way and stiffen their demands.

I hope to breakfast on Tuesday with Battin who has just returned from Germany and I understand he feels now that the Germans realise they are on top and are hardening their hearts.

I think I shall try and have a private meeting of the Liberal Executive here next Friday and tell them my news.

[...]

CHAPTER 8

Letters 1917

28 February 1917
National Liberal Club

I have had a very full day, darling.

Breakfast with Seebohm [Rowntree] and Bowes [Morrell] to discuss new Cadbury Fry agreement.[1]

Meeting with Angell and Harold Wright regarding the future of 'War and Peace'.[2]

FAU Executive. Lunch with Little.

FAU Committee.

Friend Proprietors gathering including conference with J.E. Hodgkin and Marian Ellis.[3]

Dinner with G.N.[ewman] and W.C.B.[raithwaite] and then a long talk with W.C.B. about National Council matters. Now it's 11.30. I have promised to have a talk with Ernest Jones,[4] so in order to do this and catch the post, I must close. I will try to write thee hopefully tomorrow.

1 March 1917
House of Commons

I have just had tea with Gerty [Taylor], darling, who came to see me

---

[1] Cadbury Bros and Frys were already co-operating under the Cheltenham Agreement to dicuss price and sales strategy. In early 1917 the pressure of wartime shortages produced discussions about extending this co-operation to Rowntree & Co.

[2] *War and Peace*, monthly journal set up in 1913 by Norman Angell to propound his views; starting in May 1917, it was issued as a monthly supplement to the *Nation*.

[3] Marian Emily Ellis (1878–1952), daughter of John Edward Ellis; m. Ld Parmoor 1919; leading figure in FoR, and after the war Hon. Sec. Fight the Famine Council.

[4] Ernest Jones (1862–1941), Quaker businessman from Kendal and bro.-in-law of E.E. Taylor; served as unofficial chaplain to FAU 1917.

here. She is much exercised over the Criminal Law Amendment Act.[5] [...] I have had a very busy morning over conferences with various people about the 'Athenaeum'.[6] Hope very much I am getting the matter settled. I had lunch with Merrttens to talk over his trust matter and then visited the Home Office about COs. Mr Locke[7] is very hopeful that the Dartmoor scheme[8] will be liked by the COs as there is really good farming there; the reclamation work will certainly have no military flavour.

I am going to drive with Seebohm [Rowntree] – I fear the feud between him and G.N.[ewman] goes fairly deep – I should like to heal it if I could – I suppose as thou does not mention Frank [Rowntree] that he is going on well.

2 March 1917
National Liberal Club

I had dinner last night, darling, with Seebohm [Rowntree] and was glad to find that he had had a long talk with G.N.[ewman] and made it up as far as he was concerned. But the fact remains that Addison has made such alterations in the arrangements of the Welfare Department of the Ministry that Seebohm feels he cannot stay and unless they are modified he proposes to leave. As L.G. has asked him to join the reconstruction committee[9] this will provide him with ample scope for his energies.

I have been to the Meeting for Sufferings this morning. I thought on the whole there was a saner view and sweeter spirit amongst Friends than at some sittings which I have attended. The meeting, whilst declining to repudiate the document of the Friends Service Committee,

---

[5] Criminal Law Amendment Bill introduced by the govt 19 February 1917. Most controversially, it proposed to make the deliberate spreading of venereal disease and soliciting with such a disease criminal offences and authorized compulsory examinations of suspected carriers. The Bill provoked huge controversy and was shelved on 30 April 1917. Quakers were prominent in opposing the measure.

[6] *Athenaeum*, distinguished journal founded 1828; by 1917 it was a fortnightly review of society and politics, edited by Arthur Greenwood; its circulation was only 2,000 and it was losing money heavily. On 13 April 1917 the JRSST agreed to buy the journal for £1,000 and support it for two years. In 1921 the *Athenaeum* merged with the *Nation*.

[7] Arthur Locke (1872–1932), Asst Sec. Home Office.

[8] The Brace Cttee, which was in charge of the Home Office scheme offering work of 'national importance' to COs, obtained the use of Dartmoor Prison in early 1917. It was rechristened Princetown Work Centre.

[9] Reconstruction Cttee; cttee of fourteen 'experts' set up in March 1917 by Lloyd George to plan postwar social reform. Seebohm Rowntree devoted most of his time to housing.

refer the Public Prosecutor to the minute of the YM which blesses equally absolutists and those who are willing to undertake work of national importance.[10]

I had lunch with H.L.W.[ilson], and Harrison Barrow and was glad to resume one's interaction with two friends whom I don't often seem to see at present. On returning I heard the news that the Glenart Castle[11] had met with an accident last night (either mine or torpedo) and that the men had to take to the boats and that whilst they thought all were safe only one boat containing Alexander, Tony Wilson and Knowles[12] (and 4 others) had actually landed.

H.L.W.[ilson], Mrs Theodore Crosfield,[13] and Amy Sturge[14] all spoke to me about thy articles on Margaret [Ford][15] the last two thinking it almost the most beautiful thing they had ever read and *very* cheering and helpful to them spiritually. So thou wilt have to develop these great gifts! Thou wilt have noticed about Edward Backhouse – he is a brave man.[16]

Now I plunge into Adult School matters.

Arnold Rowntree became increasingly interested in industrial relations during the First World War. Largely due to the initiative of Henry Clay, who was teaching WEA classes in Tunstall, the pottery industry was selected as the field most suitable for an experimental joint industrial council of employees and employers. An employers' conference met on 21–22 April, following a trade unionists' conference on 24–25 February.

[10] The Dir. of Public Prosecutions had written to the Recording Clerk of YM on 12 February 1917, asking the YM to dissociate itself from two leaflets issued by the FSC which urged COs not to undertake alternative service.

[11] *Glenart Castle*, one of two hospital ships staffed by the FAU in 1916–1917. On the night of 1 March 1917 the ship was struck by a mine or torpedo off the Isle of Wight. Nobody was killed but the ship was severely damaged and the Unit was disbanded on 10 March 1917.

[12] Victor William Alexander (1887–1963), leader of FAU personnel on the *Glenart Castle*; later a teacher at Bootham. Tony Wilson and Knowles, FAU members on the ship.

[13] Mary Green Crosfield (1851–1940), m. George Theodore Crosfield (1849–1927), Croydon Quaker and tea merchant.

[14] Amy Elizabeth Sturge (1870–1943), Birmingham Quaker, sister of Winifred Sturge; Headmistress of the Mount School.

[15] An obituary of Margaret Ford appeared in the *Friend*, 23 February 1917, pp. 140–141.

[16] Backhouse stood as an Ind. 'Peace by Negotiation' cand. in the Stockton by-election on 20 March 1917. A.S.R. and T.E. Harvey spoke for him (against the Lib. candidate).

23 April 1917
en route London

I am sorry, darling, that circumstances have prevented my writing thee
a gathered letter – since Thursday. That day Fisher[17] spoke on education
and I had rather wanted to speak on the Education Estimate,[18] but I
found that so many members wanted to take part that both Ted and I
desisted. Ernest Jones came and had dinner with us after having seen Maxwell
and G.N.[ewman] about going out to help the unit as Quaker chaplain,
and I am glad both were pleased with him and gave him a most cordial
invitation. He will go after YM on Friday am. I travelled to Stoke (with
E.J.[ones] as far as Stafford) and was met there by Major Wedgwood[19]
and the Trades Unionist organizer – fixed up with the Major to go
and stay with him that night and then went off with Clowes[20] to see a
China factory. The Major is a very moderate man compared to his
brother, Josiah, in the House but he was most cordial and I enjoyed
the evening with him. He agreed to preside at the employer's conference
and from him I was able to learn a good deal about the manufacturer's
point of view.

On Saturday, I went over to two other factories and then after lunch
at the Wedgwood factory walked over to Lawton with the Major. On
arrival there we found several of the manufacturers in a mild state of
revolt because Miss Wilkinson, the manageress, without even saying
anything to us, had put five or six of them to sleep together in double
beds! However, we were soon able to make other arrangements and
treated it as a joke which I think really helped to break the ice.

I was told afterwards that soon after our last visit there someone was
visiting Lawton Hall and Miss W. told how 'she had been told that Mr
R. was bringing a party of his personal friends and so she had gone
out of her way to prepare a sumptuous repast and then he turned up
with 20 working potters! He was going to have another but next time
she was going to put two in a bed and give them plainer fare.' Hence
the new policy when the manufacturers turn up! Well it all turned out

[17] Herbert Albert Laurens Fisher (1865–1940), Lib. MP Sheffield, Hallam 1916–1918,
Combined English Univs 1918–1926; Pres. Bd of Education 1916–1922; an historian;
Fellow of New College, Oxford 1888–1912, Vice-Chanc. Sheffield University 1912–1916,
Warden of New College 1925–1940.
[18] *Hansard*, 5th series, 1917, XCII, 1887–1998 for the debate on the Education Estimates
on 19 April 1917.
[19] Francis Hamilton Wedgwood (1867–1930), eldest bro. of Josiah Wedgwood MP;
Chmn and Managing Dir. Josiah Wedgwood & Sons 1916–1930.
[20] Samuel Clowes (1864–1928), Sec. National Society of Pottery Workers 1916–1928;
Lab. MP Hanley 1924–1928.

right – they were somewhat stiff at first and didn't think it possible to come to an agreement in time to invite the men to meet them on Sunday so, alas, that hope had to be abandoned and we telephoned Clowes that we would arrange a conference later and by Sunday afternoon the manufacturers were quite keen for the joint conference and it is now arranged for Sunday week. (Don't be very angry!)

Wethered and Clay were there, also the Master of Balliol turned up and spoke excellently on Sunday afternoon. The feeding was again excellent and Lord Devonport's[21] regulation still unknown. Two colonels' wives waited on us as Miss Wilkinson was short of staff and so commandeered two of her permanent visitors! Wethered wanted his warmest regards given to thee and Christopher.

There was nothing very exciting at the board except the last Devonport threat[22] and, of course, a long discussion ensued as to how to combat it. I am meeting tomorrow Cadbury and Caley for lunch and then going to the meeting of the confectioners' alliance afterwards. Mamma and Essie [Sarah Elizabeth Rowntree] seemed nicely – Mamma had been to visit Frank [Rowntree] and also went to Meeting yesterday. Did thou see an account in the papers of Rendel [Harris] who it seems was four days in a boat[23] and saw some of his colleagues die! What an awful experience but I expect he was fine and certainly his prayers would be wonderful.

[...]

After ordering our hen house, it seems now that it is unpatriotic to keep hens which need feeding on grains!

I don't much like the Nation this week[24] – a little too personal I think and somewhat unbalanced. The letters are very impressive.

[21] Hudson Ewbanke Kearley (1856–1934), Lib. MP Devonport 1892–January 1910; PS Bd of Trade 1905–1909, Food Controller and Chmn Royal Commission on Sugar Supplies 1916–1917; Bt 1908, cr. Ld Devonport 1910, Vt 1917.

[22] Devonport threat; due to heavy shipping losses Vt Devonport was considering severely restricting the number and character of lines of confectionary in order to reduce sugar consumption.

[23] When Rendel Harris visited India in 1917 his ship was sunk by enemy action on both the outward and return voyages. He recorded his experiences in *Ulysses to his Friends* (Birmingham, 1917).

[24] On 29 March 1917 the War Office banned overseas circulation of the *Nation*, on the grounds that it could be used as enemy propaganda and Lloyd George defended the ban in the HofC on 17 April. The *Nation* of 21 April 1917 was particularly vitriolic in its denunciation of the PM and contained numerous letters from Lib. MPs and writers supporting their case. After Seebohm Rowntree had complained at the nature of the attacks on Lloyd George, the JRSST had resolved on 22 December 1916 that the paper should 'avoid all personalities as much as possible'.

25 April 1917
House of Commons

Thank thee, darling, for thy letters. Yesterday was given up to two trade meetings and later I was here for some time listening to the discussion on the Corn Production Bill,[25] dining with Ted [Harvey] at night. This morning we have had a long FAU meeting – the German attack on hospital ships has, of course, made great difficulties and if, as seems probable, the government give up running those ships under the Red Cross and make them into ordinary boats that can be convoyed, armoured and can carry transports, our men are, of course, put into a great difficulty and it looks as if we should have to withdraw.[26]

Tomorrow I have to stay here to see Devonport at 5 o'clock, so shall not get away until the 8 o'clock train and am, therefore, going to stay at the Station Hotel on arrival at York. I hope, of course, I shall be able to get off on Friday afternoon, but if Devonport is difficult I may be detained in conference at York [...].

4 May 1917
House of Commons

I had breakfast, darling, with Seebohm [Rowntree] this morning at the Automobile Club – then an interview with a very able man, Hayes, who has fallen on evil times whom we want to help if possible; since then have been at two trade meetings over Devonport's restrictions.

Now (4.30 pm) I am off to Stoke and trust that we may be of some help tomorrow in starting a new era in the pottery industry.[27] The weather is glorious but one's spirits are somewhat low in contemplation of all that is going on in France.

[...]

---

[25] Corn Production Bill; this Act empowered the govt to direct farmers to plough up grassland to grow cereals. In return they were guaranteed minimum prices for their crops and labourers received a minimum wage. A.S.R. was interested in the latter part of the Bill and secured an amendment ensuring that the minimum wage would be enough for 'physical efficiency', *Hansard*, 5th series, 1917, XCVI, 683–688, 706.

[26] The govt did take this course and the FAU relinquished responsibility for its one remaining hospital ship, the *Western Australia*, on 12 May 1917.

[27] The joint meeting of trade unionists and employers in the pottery industry was scheduled for 5–6 May 1917. It eventually resulted in the formation of the National Council of the Potteries Industry in January 1918 – the forerunner of the Whitley Councils.

21 June 1917
House of Commons

I had breakfast this morning, darling, with Norman Angell who has at last got a passport for the States and will be off shortly.[28] People here are getting anxious about America where opinion is somewhat faltering in expectation of a two years' war! and it will be very useful to have Angell there in touch with the President[29] who has I fear somewhat evil advice round him now. Afterwards, I worked at the office, bathed and went to see one of our wounded travellers at the University Hospital. Yesterday I visited another at St Thomas' Hospital.

This afternoon I have seen Fisher with Ken[30] and this evening am expecting him along with the Crosses and Margaret [Rowntree] to dinner. Afterwards I go to Jordans in order to lecture there first thing in the morning, I hope to get back tomorrow by 10.30 to catch the train to Birmingham. I fear I shall not get back to York until Saturday as the last train now leaves Birmingham at 4.40!

[28] Angell had initially been denied permission to return to the USA in 1916 because it was alleged he had written anti-war articles in the American press.

[29] Thomas Woodrow Wilson (1856–1924), Pres. of the USA, 1913–1921.

[30] K.E.T. Wilkinson helped A.S.R. in his work on Fisher's Education Bill in 1918.

CHAPTER 9

Letters 1918

9 January 1918
Friends' Ambulance Unit, 8 Weymouth St, Portland Place

I had a comfortable journey yesterday, darling, when once we got started! Arriving in London at 9 instead of 7.30, I went then to see Sally [Cross] and her family and found them all well and bright. Dorothy¹ was just off for a night at the Canteen – Margaret [Rowntree] is to be married on Tuesday at the Scarbro Meeting House at 11.20. Sally fears from the letters she is receiving that Con [Rowntree] feels the strain of all the arrangements. This morning I spent some time at the Nation office with Bonwick & Massingham.

L.G. has had talks with Buckmaster,² and Ramsay MacDonald evidently means to get peace if possible. He said that Alsace Lorraine is the main difficulty because we are under promise to France to restore it and cannot deliver the goods!

Then I had a talk with Pascall³ about the Trade Meeting tomorrow – lunch with R. Lambert⁴ at the NLC – he says the labour people are making difficulties over the new manpower bill⁵ and the shop stewards refuse to work the act unless accompanied with conscription of wealth!

This afternoon I have had a 'maintenance' committee⁶ here and am scribbling this now (5 pm) in order to catch the north post. It is very cold now and there was more snow this morning but the thaw has begun.

[...]

¹ Dorothy Cross, younger daughter of Richard Cross; engaged to Laurence Rowntree before his death in France in 1917.
² Stanley Owen Buckmaster (1861–1934), Lib. MP Cambridge 1906–January 1910, Keighley 1911–1915; Solicitor-Gen. 1913–1915, Ld Chanc. 1915–1916; kt. 1913, cr. Ld Buckmaster 1915, Vt 1933. Intermediary between Lloyd George and Asquith 1917–1918.
³ Charles Pascall (1853–1931), Chmn. and Managing Dir. of James Pascall Ltd, mint and sugar confectionary manufacturers.
⁴ Richard Cornthwaite Lambert (1868–1939), Lib. MP Cricklade December 1910–1918.
⁵ A new Military Service Bill was introduced on 14 January 1918, allowing the government to cancel exemptions from service based on occupation.
⁶ Members of the FAU were unpaid, but a few wealthy backers had set up a Special Allowance Fund in 1916 to provide allowances. This was converted in late 1917 into a Maintenance Fund, administered in England by a cttee chaired by A.S.R.

5 February 1918
House of Commons

Alternative vote carried by 1, darling.[7] So now thou will forgive my
running away. I fear however the Lords will refuse it again tomorrow
and in order to save the bill we shall have to give way. The Tories
however are short sighted with the rising tide of labour in a few years
they will rue that they hadn't the choice of getting the help of moderate
liberals.

I had a very comfortable journey with Oscar [Rowntree] and have
been able to entertain his two visitors that he had sent up here – one
the old postmaster at Brandsby who's almost off his head with joy at
having seen this place. The post is just off.

20 February 1918
House of Commons

I had a comfortable but uneventful journey, darling, last night and
happily found a room waiting for me at Peterboro and after a talk with
Middlebrook MP turned in. Currie Martin met me this morning at
King's Cross and I had an hour with him about his future. The question
of the provision of a pension arises as if we encourage him to refuse
the YMCA we naturally make ourselves responsible for his future
practically for life.

Then to the Nation office via St Pancras Hotel which I wanted to
see as one of the bombs on Sunday night fell just at the entrance to
the station and practically all the windows of the hotel are smashed
and several people were killed there.

I had lunch with Pringle[8] and Hogge at the House and then an
hour's talk with Ramsay MacDonald on his experiences in Paris last
week and the outlook generally.[9] I agree with him in thinking that the
meeting of the 'International' and the efforts to obtain agreement there

[7] Alternative Vote; the Representation of the People Bill 1917–1918 was shuttling
between the HofL and the HofC. The HofL wished to insert an experiment in
proportional representation, while the non-Con. majority in the HofC preferred the
Alternative Vote, if there was to be a change in the voting system. *Hansard*, 5th series,
1918, CI, 2191–2200 for the brief debate on 5 February, in which the alternative vote
was carried by 195–194.
[8] William Mather Rutherford Pringle (1874–1928), Lib. MP NW Lanarkshire January
1910–1918, Penistone 1922–1924.
[9] Ramsay MacDonald was part of a British Lab. delegation which left for Paris on 14
February to confer with the French Socialists. On 20 February 1918 the Inter-Allied
Socialist Conference on War Aims opened in London, comprising delegates from the
British, French, Italian, and Belgian Labour movements.

is on the practical road to peace. Folks generally are very gloomy about the outlook. I have been at the House for questions and am expecting an Athenaeum Board shortly.

27 February 1918
House of Commons

I travelled up, darling, with Dorothy [Cross], Ernest Taylor, Frank Pollard, Herbert Corder[10] – Dorothy leaving at Peterboro – stepping into the 9.12 train. Went straight to the FAU executive and then the Friend Trustees Meeting and met Mactavish[11] here afterwards and dined with him. Thou remembers that he is the WEA general secretary – I have been having a long talk with him regarding the relation of the Adult School to that body. I should like to see the two in much closer association. I wonder how Hettie [Rowntree] has got on at Haverford – do let me know how things develop. I think possibly I shall go out to Jordans tomorrow night. I have asked W.C.B.[raithwaite] if he will come a walk with me on Friday before the National Council. I am feeling to need a good tramp to freshen me up before those meetings.

28 February 1918
House of Commons, 3 pm

I will try and write later, darling, but I think probably I shall not have time as I have the meeting with Lord Parmoor[12] and others about a deputation to the PM regarding the treatment of COs and the whole question is to be raised in the House.[13]

I expect I must be there as much as I can, prepared to speak if necessary.

Unfortunately Whitehouse is raising the question and he is not exactly the man to carry the House!

[10] Herbert Corder (1864–1937), Quaker businessman from Sunderland; member of Meeting for Sufferings 1915–1936.

[11] J.M. Mactavish, Portsmouth shipwright; Gen. Sec. Workers Educational Association 1916–1928.

[12] Charles Alfred Cripps (1852–1941), Con. MP Stroud 1895–1900, Stretford 1901–1906, Wycombe January 1910–1914, when cr. Ld Parmoor; defended COs 1916–1918; m. 1919 Marian Emily Ellis, a Quaker, and joined postwar Lab. Party; Ld Pres. of Council 1924, 1929–1931.

[13] *Hansard*, 5th series, 1918, CIII, 1584–1591 for J.H. Whitehouse's speech on the treatment of COs, particularly H.W. Firth, who had just died at Dartmoor. A.S.R. had raised this case in the HofC on 26 February; *Hansard*, 5th series, 1918, CIII, 1224.

After leaving the House last night I had a long talk with W.S.R.[own-tree] and Frederick Andrews[14] and J.B. Clark[15] who were in the club and this morning have been busy at the office.

The outlook continues *very* black. I find it much harder to keep cheerful and equable here than at home. Tomorrow I hope to get a walk with W.C.B.[raithwaite] and late tonight I go to Gerrards Cross to the Morlands which seems more convenient than Jordans.

Lloyd George introduced the Military Service Amendment Bill on 9 April 1918, Hansard, 5th series, 1918, CIV, 1337–1365. It raised the age for conscription to 50 and gave the government power to dissolve all certificates of exemption. Most controversially, it allowed the government to extend conscription to Ireland. In return, the Irish were promised a measure of Home Rule and a Cabinet committee was appointed on 15 April 1918 to draw up a Bill. Though the new Military Service Act became law, conscription was not extended to Ireland and no Home Rule Bill appeared.

9 April 1918
House of Commons

Conditions here, darling, are very serious. The government have gone mad and George is proposing conscription to Ireland against the vehement opposition of the Nationalists without even consulting them and without even reading the unanimous report of the convention committee against the proposal! It is indeed an awful revelation of the way in which the country is governed at the present time.

One cannot tell yet what will happen but the government can't I think possibly get the Bill against the opposition of Ireland this week.
[...]

14 April 1918
Woodbrooke Settlement, Birmingham

The news from France last night and again this morning makes one hope that perhaps the British debacle is not coming but it is I fear too

[14] Frederick Andrews (1850–1922), Headmaster Ackworth School 1877–1920; Clerk of Meeting for Sufferings 1912–1915.
[15] John Bright Clark (1867–1933), eldest bro. of Roger Clark of Street, Somerset; Managing Dir. C. & J. Clark; Somerset County Councillor; Chmn E. Somerset Lib. Association.

early to speak as yet.[16] However it has helped me to be a little more cheerful, darling.

I think the gatherings here[17] have very distinctly grown in usefulness now there is a most excellent spirit running through the meetings. The Meeting for Worship this morning was most helpful and just the sort of feeling I thought that would help business men.

A collection for Woodbrooke is in progress that has already realised £200 so they will I hope have a kindly feeling towards us in future. After meeting this morning we had an interesting discussion on how to help Friends between 40 and 50 who may have to leave their businesses under the new act.

I think the FAU will probably form a new section and we shall try and get the government to let us undertake some definite work with regard to the training of discharged soldiers and sailors or work connected with food production.

I wonder if thou hast heard the York news. I fear there were awful casualties amongst the 'West Yorks' in which there were a large number of York men and I hear Dr Craig of York was killed and that Dr Hughes was taken prisoner.

Barrie Brown goes to prison tomorrow. I have just said goodbye to him – he is in excellent spirits.

PS George Hodgkin[18] goes off to the Caucasus on Tuesday. Many thanks for the letters. It is delightful to think of you all at Barmoor.

16 April 1918
House of Commons

Thank thee, darling, for thy letter – you all seem very happy and I wish I could be with you instead of at this centre of pessimism. I was sorry not to be able to get thee off a letter yesterday but just as I was going to write Arthur Greenwood[19] came in to ask advice about standing

---

[16] The second wave of the German Army's 'Ludendorff Offensive' had been launched on 10 April 1918.

[17] The first Quaker Employers' Conference met at Woodbrooke on 11–14 April 1918. A.S.R. served as Chairman.

[18] George Lloyd Hodgkin (1880–1918), Quaker banker, youngest s. of Thomas Hodgkin and son-in-law of H.L. Wilson; died on this journey to undertake relief work in Armenia.

[19] Arthur Greenwood (1880–1954), Asst. Sec. Ministry of Reconstruction and Joint Sec. to Whitley Cttee 1917–1919; Lab. MP Nelson and Colne 1922–1931, Wakefield 1932–1954; PS Ministry of Health 1924, Min. of Health 1929–1931, Min. without Portfolio 1940–1942 and 1947, Ld Privy Seal 1945–1947, Dep. Leader Lab. Party 1935–1945. Before 1914 Economics Lecturer Leeds Univ. and known to A.S.R. through his adult education work. Greenwood stood for Southport in 1918, while R.H. Tawney stood for Rochdale.

as Labour candidate for Rochdale and by the time he had gone the post had also! I advised him against as if he accepts it seems to me he will have to resign from the Ministry of Reconstruction and then it seems to me he would be called up! It was delightful seeing Ted [Harvey] yesterday. He and Irene crossed on Sunday night and told me of recent experiences. He says that he was told that already 700,000 people have left Paris as a result of the fear aroused by the big guns' activities[20] and that the municipality were discussing the advisability of moving all the children. He doesn't however think that this will be done.

He thinks the Paris people more excitable over this event than the Londoner over raids – on the other hand he says opinion there is steady and confident that the line can be held and the French have great faith in the capacity of Foch.

I had lunch yesterday with the Nation group but didn't find much inspiration there. Really folks don't know where they are and I have never felt it so difficult to forecast the future.

There is a serious conflict going on within the cabinet over the Irish position. Carson and several Unionist members have told the government they won't have Home Rule – and the Labour and some Liberal Ministers that they won't have conscription without it so that any time the government may fall over that question. On the other hand George told Asquith on Friday that if the Liberals generally voted against the inclusion of Ireland in the bill he would have to resign and Asquith with the terrible uncertainties of the position in France doesn't feel that immediately he can take office and so –

Runciman who has recovered from the measles told me yesterday that he was very anxious for his daughter to come to the Mount next term so I have written Winifred [Sturge] encouraging her to make room if possible and I think she told me a fortnight ago she had a vacancy.

Woodbrooke finished up very well – the employers are keen on some loose organisation for the dissemination of information and would like to arrange a summer school for foremen and forewomen. On the committee to plan future action we have got Philip Reckitt[21] and Hugh Fox and it is encouraging to feel we are getting such men with active association once more with Friends. Over £300 was raised for Woodbrooke so the committee in future may be very well disposed to such gatherings! Altogether we have much to be thankful for but the worst of all these efforts is they always mean *more* work! However we

---

[20] German 'Paris guns', able to shell the French capital from behind German lines.

[21] Philip Bealby Reckitt (1873–1944), Quaker manufacturer and Dir. Reckitt & Sons Ltd of Hull; succ. as 3rd and last Bt 1930.

are going to try to postpone the Pottery-Lawton Hall gathering on account of the crisis. I am going to lunch with Clay in a few moments and then this afternoon shall be taken up with trade meetings regarding Joint Councils in our own trade. I shall stay at the Station Hotel on Thursday night and shall try *very* hard to get off by the 3.30 on Friday.

17 April 1918
House of Commons

I spent a somewhat barren afternoon yesterday, darling, with Confectionary employees and Trades Union leaders and am doubtful whether we shall be able to get a Council formed. Afterwards I spent a good deal of time in the House[22] – heard Dillon, Barnes, Carson and George. Dillon too long – though his earlier comparison to England's attitude over American taxation and its consequences was very effective. Barnes poor man was very halting and feeble. Carson seemed as if he wanted to find an excuse for the great hostility of Ulster to conscription now that it has been enacted and he finds it in the promised Home Rule Bill which is to follow – and then L.G. a marvellously clever speech – the speech of an absolutely expert juggler but somehow it didn't ring true and the Irish don't believe he means to get them Home Rule but to make it the opportunity whereby he can resign!

I left the House again last night feeling that it was more like a madhouse than anything else and I was never clearer in my life about voting against an important measure than I have been during these days in the votes I have given against this measure.

Its just one of those acts of policy that might bring about the destruction of the Empire. To me its much more serious than the news from France – which I think is bad enough but military men seem still to think that Foch has the situation in hand and is doing nothing more than employing his usual retreating tactics of letting the opposing army spend itself before he makes the offensive – but our army can't retire much more without coming perilously near the sea! Of course all this news is depressing men terribly and I long to leave this home of pessimism and get to the moors.

[...]

---

[22] The Military Service Amendment Bill received its Third Reading on 16 April 1918; *Hansard,* 5th series, 1918, CV, 247–374. A.S.R. voted against the Third Reading and recorded three other votes against the Bill on the same day.

23 April 1918
The Cocoa Works, York

I enjoyed my journey to York last night, darling, as it was such a beautiful evening – Old Clark[23] amused me with his news about the influence of Wesleyan missioning on suicides in Farndale. He said he noticed that always after a Wesleyan preacher had had a three or four day mission in Farndale there was always a suicide! I took the daffodils round by 10 Grosvenor Terrace and hope that they have all been suitably distributed by this time, and then went on to T.[heodore Rowntree] and K.[atherine Rowntree]'s to supper and before going to bed tonight taught Theodore double demon. K. discouraged me this morning by taking a hopeless attitude over the appointment of Old Scholars representatives upon the school committee and I think for the sake of peace I shall recommend the QM to drop the proposal. I must draft a letter to the QM later this evening.

At the Board this AM the Directors agreed to my suggestion of giving £2,500 to the FAU to cover the expenses of the York hospital and also agreed to continue to meeting the expenses of £100 a month.

The budget is not quite as drastic as I expected.[24] I thought the Income Tax would have been 6/8 but I don't like the new postal arrangements and the sugar tax is irritating.

[...]

6 May 1918
The Grove,[25] Roundhay, Leeds, 10.45

I was sorry, darling, that there was no time to get any letter off to thee tonight but the Flounders Trust Meeting was unusually long – we didn't get away until 9.30 pm.

I hope thou managed to get back to Scalby comfortably. There was a good deal of rain on my homeward journey and I rather feared that thou might get drenched. All the trustees were present except J.E. Hodgkin – we passed the new scheme and probably it will come into effect in a year's time. Both Father and Ted [Harvey] were there – both seem very nicely. Father gives a good account of Will [Harvey] which is confirmed in a letter Father has from Mother this evening.

[23] 'Old Daddy Clark', resident of Kirbymoorside who met visitors at the station with a wagonette and drove them the three miles to the Harveys' house at Barmoor.
[24] Bonar Law's Budget of 22 April 1918 raised income tax from 5s to 6s, increased the charge for a letter to 1½d and introduced a new sugar tax at 11s 8d per cwt.
[25] The Grove, home of William and Anna Maria Harvey, parents of M.K.R.

There was a round robin signed by all the students asking that they might smoke in the House which request was granted. I wonder what old Bevan Braithwaite[26] would have said to such a decision! Ted [Harvey] seems very doubtful if he will come to the Committee next Tuesday – so I think probably we shall only have Fanny Thompson who I expect thou hast invited today and I found a letter from Florence Holmes[27] saying she wasn't coming so Winifred [Sturge] is asking Lucy Morland.[28] Father says that Lin and Carrie[29] have gone off to Italy, Rome, Naples and Florence – Lin is not very well suffering from a hardened knee. [...]

23 May 1918
House of Commons

The commemoration meeting in connection with the 250th meeting of YM was quite interesting, darling. I sat by G.R.T.[aylor] and Fred [Taylor]. W.C.B.[raithwaite] and Miss Godlee[30] were quite racy, A.N.B[rayshaw] and E.G.[rubb] less so. Afterwards I went and had supper with Fred and Gerty [Taylor] at the Maytree. We left in a tremendous thunderstorm. These are being repeated today with emphasis. Gerty said the morning session yesterday dealing with the presentation of the Service Committee was interesting and impressive, the meeting being practically unanimous with the decision to stand by the Committee in their trouble with the Censor.[31] The meeting during the trial today is to suspend its ordinary sitting and give itself to prayer.

This morning I have been to the Nation office about several matters and at lunch time the extension committee of the Woodbrooke Employers Gathering for a weighty sitting at the NLC so I am not attending the YM until the evening when I shall go to the session to be given up to the Victims, FAU and Emergency Committee.

---

[26] Joseph Bevan Braithwaite (1818–1905), lawyer and leading evangelical Quaker of the nineteenth century; father of W.C. Braithwaite.

[27] Florence Holmes, Quaker from Newcastle and member of York Schools Cttee.

[28] Lucy Fryer Morland (1864–1945), Quaker from Croydon; prominent on various Quaker education cttees and as a suffragist and pacifist.

[29] Dr Lionel Capper-Johnson (1874–1954), Quaker doctor from Leeds; his wife was Caroline (nee Menzies). 'Lin' was a cousin of M.K.R.

[30] Mary Jane Godlee (1851–1930), leading Quaker; in 1918 briefly served as acting Clerk of YM – the first woman to fill this role.

[31] Regulation 27C of the Defence of the Realm Act, published 25 December 1917, required a copy of all pamphlets concerning the war to be lodged with the censor three days before publication. The FSC refused to abide by this injunction.

24 May 1918
No. 1 – Central Buildings

I think we had a useful meeting of the Woodbrooke Employers' Committee yesterday, darling.

G.C.[adbury] Jr seems to me 'coming on' was helpful and constructive on the need of the provision of suitable opportunities for both practical and theoretical business education for both boys and girls leaving Friends schools who wish to go in for a business career and we talked over the possibility of getting Friends firms and others to let each year a few young people work in their factories with the idea of their getting practical knowledge of a well managed factory and afterwards, perhaps, have a year's course at a Woodbrooke hostel and Birmingham University combined. We also hope to arrange for the conference with foremen and forewomen belonging to Quaker firms. Then I went to the fag end of the afternoon YM sitting and heard the discussion on the revision of Part I of the Book of Discipline.[32] There wasn't unanimity at the meeting to go on with it so the QMs are to be burdened with the subject during the coming year. I believe it really would be best if E.G.[rubb] and W. Littleboy[33] and others who feel strongly about it would write a really good treatise on the Basis of Quakerism and then later probably the YM could accept it in whole or part. I believe really in that way a better treatise would be produced than having to continually compromise with good people like Howard Nicholson[34] and A.M. Hodgkin[35] and I am going to lay this upon E.G.[rubb].

I then had a good sardine on toast tea with Father, Mother and Nell [Helen Crosfield] at the GER Tea Shop and afterwards attended the sitting of the YM given up to Victims, Aliens and FAU. Herbert Wood spoke finely for the latter and the YM really seemed quite enthusiastic with the efforts of all three organizations, including the FAU! Afterwards I had supper with Barrow Cadbury and his wife and H.G.W.[ood] at the GE Hotel followed by a sombre talk with Ernest Jones there.

The YM is under the weight of the prosecution of the Service Committee and yesterday the Editor of the Venturer[36] and Headleys,

---

[32] Book of Discipline; document expressing Quaker views on their religion and its practice, first issued by YM in 1738. It was revised several times each century, but changes to Pt I on 'Christian doctrine' had been held up since 1911 by disagreements between liberals and evangelicals.

[33] William Littleboy (1853–1936), Quaker manufacturer of chandeliers from Birmingham; Warden of Woodbrooke 1904–1907.

[34] Howard Nicholson (1843–1933), leading evangelical Quaker and mission worker.

[35] Alice Mary Hodgkin (1860–1955), leading evangelical Quaker and mission worker.

[36] The *Venturer* was the monthly magazine of the FOR. On 23 May 1918 its editor, J.D.M. Rorke, was fined £50 and Headley Bros, its printers, were fined £100 for publishing 'A letter from the guard room' by G.M.L. Davies in the *Venturer* for 6 March

the publishers, were heavily fined for some article that had appeared. There seem some foolish men forcing these prosecutions with the inevitable result of increasing the interest in all the suppressed literature.

I have just been to the exhibition in the adjoining Hall showing what is to be done in different countries to help disabled soldiers. I met Hodge[37] the Pensions Minister there and startled him by saying I thought he would be prosecuted under DORA for allowing such an exhibition. It was really *most* gruesome but of course very wonderful.

I haven't been to YM this morning as I had work to do here and this afternoon I go to this YMCA University Education Committee which I have agreed to join and then on to Welders Wood[38] at 5.38 with Father and Mother [...].

On 23–24 May 1918 three leaders of the FSC were tried for refusing to submit the organization's pamphlet A Challenge to Militarism *to the official censor. The three were: Harrison Barrow, Chairman of the FSC; Edith Maud Ellis (1878–1963), Treasurer of the FSC and daughter of J.E. Ellis, MP; and Arthur Watts (1888–1958), Secretary of the FSC and veteran of the Australian campaign against compulsory military training. Barrow and Watts were sentenced to six months imprisonment and Ellis fined £150. Six members of Yearly Meeting (including T.E. Harvey) were deputed to attend the trial in order to show the solidarity of all Quakers with the defendants.*

25 May 1918
Welders Wood, nr Chalfont St Peter

[...] I didn't go to YM in the morning. I felt I must work at my address for Monday's YM sitting regarding the Woodbrooke Meeting of Quaker Employers, and in the afternoon I went to the first meeting of the YMCA Universities Committee regarding education in the army at home and abroad. Gilbert Murray was in the chair, and Princess Christian[39] amongst those present. I rebel at having to rise when she enters and departs!

The work the YMCA have been doing in connection with education is really very remarkable and I am glad that it is in the hands of a Committee of this kind, rather than run by officials in the war office

1918. The magistrate ruled the article contravened Regulation 27C of the Defence of the Realm Act.

[37] John Hodge (1855–1937), Lab. MP Gorton 1906–1923; Min. of Labour 1916–1917, Min. of Pensions 1917–1919.

[38] Welders Wood, nr Chalfont St Peter, Bucks., home of T.E. and Irene Harvey.

[39] Helena Augusta Victoria (1846–1923), third daughter of Queen Victoria; widow of Prince Christian of Schleswig-Holstein.

but I am doubtful whether I can help much or whether it will be worth my while giving time to it, however I suppose one must not decide hurriedly.

The chief interest in the YM yesterday I gather lay in the trial at the Guildhall. Father and Mother and Ted [Harvey] all attended and seemed much interested in the proceedings. They thought Harrison Barrow did well and after the Magistrate retired to consider his decision the 100 friends in court lapsed into prayer, one woman friend being vocal!

The three friends are appealing so little more will be heard of the case until the middle of July. It will be interesting to see whether the authorities will follow up their tussle with Friends by prosecuting the clerk of the YM after the YM Epistle has been published because naturally that can't be submitted to the Censor.

Friends' refusal to obey the law in this respect naturally brings fresh difficulties in its track. They cannot now call on the government to keep the law by doing the right thing with regard to COs so I gather they decided yesterday to issue an 'appeal to the nation'.

[...]

I am so glad, darling, that thy immediate anxiety about maids has been removed. I somehow felt all along that 'light would arise'. [...]

26 May 1918
Welders Wood

I don't know, darling, whether I shall find anyone at Meeting this morning to post this but I will write a few lines on chance. Frank [Sturge] will have told thee how well the Old Scholars gathering went off yesterday. I thought there was an excellent spirit and Ted [Harvey], Jean and Arthur [Rowntree] were admirable in their respective spheres.

I had some talk with G.N.[ewman] after most of the Old Scholars had left and found him troubled about the trial and the attitude Friends are taking. He feels strongly that Friends have made a mistake in allowing the issue to be raised in refusing to send material to the Censor – whereas he feels the really vital point would arise if and when the Censor had refused Friends to issue anything in the nature of a religious manifesto. I am dwelling carefully on the subject and shall hope to see William [Braithwaite] tomorrow. This seems the kind of questions that arise – if the YM Epistle is issued without submission to the Censor (as it will be) if the government want to take action they will prosecute Friends up and down for distributing a document not submitted to the Censor, whereas if it had been submitted and refused by him, then prosecutions would be for distributing a document stopped by the Censor and the whole emphasis would be put on the character of the document – a much stronger case and would give the document a publicity which no YM document had received before. Again it raises the question of obeying the law as far as ever you can etc.

[...]

26 May 1918
Welders Wood, Sunday evening

I think, darling, I better write now as tomorrow is very full and there may be no opportunity. The day here has been most restful. A good meeting at Jordans where we were ministered to by Shipley Brayshaw, Jonathan Lynn, Gilbert Stephens[40] & Ernest Warner[41] with prayers from Mrs Henry Cadbury[42] and Mrs Thompson.[43] Afterwards lunch at the Camp and quiet afternoon here and after tea a delightful walk through field and wood and lane. What wonderful lanes Buckinghamshire possesses. I do hope thou will't be able to come down before Cornwall and enjoy them.
[...]
Monday evening. No time to add. The Employer's debate went off fairly well and folks seemed interested. I had too much ground to cover in 30 minutes and felt hurried and fear did not do very well but people have been very kind in saying they felt the sitting helpful. I had lunch with Sally [Cross].

27 May 1918
National Liberal Club

I think I better write thee, darling, a few lines before going to bed because I see that I shall be full tomorrow and may not have a quiet opportunity.
   [...] Herbert Wood is probably coming to York to meet the Trustees and the FAU men for the previous weekend and if it suits thee I should

[40] John Gilbert Stephens (1862–1942), Quaker rope manufacturer from Falmouth; member of Meeting for Sufferings 1920–1943.
[41] Ernest Warner (1869–1934), Quaker metal broker; instrumental in buying Jordans Meeting House.
[42] Lucy Cadbury (nee Bellows) (1881–1956), m. 1912 Henry Tylor Cadbury.
[43] Jane Smeal Thompson (1857–1936), wife of Silvanus Thompson and member of Meeting for Sufferings.

like him to stay at Chalfonts as I want to get a good talk with him. I can't be quite sure about my return at present, probably Thursday morning – if I can manage Wednesday evening I will wire. After the meeting this afternoon 36 of the Quaker employers had supper together at Devonshire House, followed by a further meeting. Afterwards I had half an hour with W.C.B.[raithwaite] and E.E.T.[aylor] over the question I wrote thee about on Saturday. I expect it will have to remain where it is but I am not very happy about it.

17 June 1918
House of Commons

I had a comfortable journey, darling, though as my specks collapsed half way I had to doze the latter half of the journey because I find now I cannot read without glasses. I had lunch with the 'Nation' group – dictated letters to my new lady secretary in London – a Miss Jones and then was in the House for most of the discussion on the Trade Boards Bill and said a few words before it gets its second reading.[44]

I do hope thou art having a good time at Sutton – I was *very* sorry not to come with thee but I believe I was right to come here as this new bill is part of the new Industrial organisation which will have to be built up after the war. [...]

6 August 1918
House of Commons

I had dinner last night, darling, with Gulland[45] (the old Anti-Gambling man who is now in the Labour department of the Ministry of Munitions) and Ted [Harvey], as Gulland wanted to discuss Labour matters. Afterwards – after attending a little committee against the Lotteries Bill[46] which is coming on tonight which legalizes a grand lottery for the disposal of the 3000 pearls I retired early. This morning I had a

[44] *Hansard*, 5th series, 1918, CVII, 61–130 for the Second Reading of the Trade Boards Bill. It simplified the procedure for setting up trade boards and increased their powers. A.S.R. spoke briefly in its favour; *Hansard*, 5th series, 1918, CVII, 129–130.

[45] John Gulland, Scottish lawyer and Gen. Sec. National Anti-Gambling League 1906. His salary was paid by the Cadburys

[46] *Hansard*, 5th series, 1918, CIX, 1236–1282 for the Second Reading of the Lotteries (War Charities) Bill; this proposed to allow war charities to hold lotteries. One particular case it was aimed at was the Red Cross and St John's Ambulance who had organized a 'pearl contribution' from society ladies. The organizations hoped to raise more by holding a lottery for the pearls, rather than auctioning them. The Bill was defeated by 81–77 with A.S.R. voting in the majority.

good Turkish Bath – the place was closed yesterday, and then attended the deputation at the LGB. Poor Hayes Fisher[47] talked for 45 minutes but said nothing and so far our efforts have been in vain.

This afternoon I felt I must be in the House for a short time to listen to the India debate.[48] The House is always very small on such occasions but the speeches generally made by men who know their subject.

I tried to get at G.N.[ewman] today but failed so have not seen a Dr yet but I am feeling better.

I wish I were at Barmoor instead of here.

On 4 October 1918 the German Chancellor, Prince Max of Baden, sent President Wilson a note asking him to 'take in hand the restoration of peace' and accepting Wilson's '14 Points'. Wilson replied on 8 October, without consulting his allies as to whether they accepted the 14 Points, thus creating considerable inter-allied tension. On 12 October 1918 a further German note suggested Germany was prepared to evacuate occupied territories and rumours of an end to the war started to circulate. But it was not until 26 October that Lüdendorff was dismissed and the German government asked for armistice terms. The war finally ended on 11 November 1918.

15 October 1918
House of Commons

A comfortable journey, darling, with Edward [J.E. Hodgkin], with whom I was able to make arrangements regarding the next employers conference.

This afternoon we had a long meeting of the Confectionary Industrial Council[49] and so far I have not been able to talk much to members but I can see many Liberals are much impressed by the undercurrent of opposition to Wilson and his proposals amongst Conservatives and Militarists who don't like at bottom the idea of a League of Nations because they understand that that means the end of militarism and navalism and all that means in the way of position.

However the current view I think is that peace is not far off if only our statesmen will be reasonable.

[47] William Hayes Fisher (1853–1920), Con. MP Fulham 1885–1906, January 1910–1918 when cr. Ld Downham; junior whip 1895–1902, Fin. Sec. to Treasury 1902–1903, PS Local Govt Bd 1915–1917, Pres. Local Govt Bd 1917–1918, Chanc. Duchy of Lancaster 1918–1919.
[48] *Hansard*, 5th series, 1918, CIX, 1139–1236 for the Indian debate, mainly on constitutional reform.
[49] In 1918 the major confectionary companies and two of the bigger trade unions in the industry had set up an Interim Industrial Reconstruction Council to pave the way for a National Joint Industrial Council on the lines recommended by the Whitley Cttee.

16 October 1918
House of Commons

The post is very uncertain, darling, in these days. I haven't received
any letter so far from thee so I shall hope for two tomorrow! [...]
    I have had a fairly active day. Breakfast with Fleming, work at the
office afterwards with Crossland (advertising) and Philip Burtt (Headley
trouble) lunch at the Reform followed by several interviews here. Folks
are excited here over the news that Germany has capitulated accepting
Wilson's terms and that the Kaiser has abdicated but it may only be a
rumour – but opinion here evidently expects that this will soon come.
I was told last night that the Foreign Office had information that a
revolution might be expected there within 48 hours. If the news tonight
is true it will be immensely important to try to get the reconstruction
of Europe accomplished as rapidly as possible otherwise revolution will
spread quickly to other continents.
    It is thought that I hope will really prevent our militarists who are
out for blood becoming the predominant party. I still pin my faith to
Wilson.
    [...]

18 October 1918
Ministry of Reconstruction, 2 Queen Anne's Gate Buildings, Westminster, 10 am

Here I am, darling, waiting for the Housing Committee[50] (Seebohm's
ginger group) so I will fill up the vacant moment by writing to thee. I
forgot to mention yesterday that in the morning I took three of the
leading officials of the Civil Service Alliance[51] to the Treasury to have
a heart to heart talk with Mr Baldwin[52] (the Financial Secretary) about
conditions of employment within the service which I hope may prove
useful. In the evening I went with Noel Buxton and Joe King[53] to the
Trevelyans' reception where there was a goodly sprinkle of peace folk
and others all in very good spirits about the war – though many I
thought finding it difficult to explain their intellectual position, Wilson

[50] Housing Cttee; A.S.R. was Sec. of an all-party group of MPs and peers set up in
1916 to press for state action on housing.
[51] Civil Service Alliance, small civil service union, merged in the Civil Service
Confederation 1921.
[52] Stanley Baldwin (1867–1947), Con. MP Bewdley 1908–1937 when cr. Earl Baldwin
of Bewdley; Fin. Sec. to Treasury 1917–1921, Pres. Bd of Trade 1921–1922, Chanc. of
Exchequer 1922–1923, Prime Minister 1923–1924, 1924–1929, 1935–1937, Ld Pres. of
Council 1931–1935, Leader Con. Party 1923–1937.
[53] Joseph King (1860–1943), Lib. MP North Somerset January 1910–1918.

being the hero of the hour but his policy coming through force!

The House again was all agog with rumours yesterday and happy at the way in which news came of town after town delivered – what times these are!

Friday afternoon. Nothing further to report, darling, except that I am going to G.N.[ewman]'s for the night and hope to get a good walk tomorrow before going on to Bunhill.[54] I wonder if thou can somewhat rearrange thy Weybridge visit – I cannot get off my breakfast on the 31st but so far I have nothing else arranged that week.

29 October 1918
House of Commons

[...]

I have little to report. I think there is no doubt after last night's discussion that Fisher will get an amendment into the Superannuation Bill which will meet the York schools.[55] This morning I worked at the office and lunched here with Arthur Greenwood. He is always interesting with inside knowledge of government departments.

This afternoon I tried to get Sally [Cross] down to the House but failed – all kinds of rumours are floating about the lobby about armistice terms and peace and a general election are both expected quickly.

The House is very painful – awful accounts of bad treatment of prisoners[56] – the call for reprisals with now and then some realisation of the speakers of the difficulty of reconciling that with Xtianity!

[...]

13 November 1918
House of Commons

Thank thee, darling, for thine. I enclose a few letters that may interest thee. I think Sally [Cross] would come at once and help through the election and I have told her that thou will't write her saying how the

---

[54] Bunhill; Adult School in Finsbury, run by the Baker family.

[55] *Hansard*, 5th series, 1918, CX, 1211–1252 for the debate on the Teachers (Superannuation) Bill. Several MPs pressed for the bill to be extended to cover teachers in schools not receiving govt grants (a category which included Bootham and the Mount).

[56] *Hansard*, 5th series, 1918, CX, 1311–1390 for the debate on treatment of British prisoners of war.

land lies.[57] I expect it might be best to ask her to come Monday or Tuesday so as to be at the first meeting and help from the beginning in connection with the organisation but just as thou thinks best. I expected thou would feel her to be a help in the house. With regard to Mrs Smith I think she should certainly be asked to the meeting though I think probably it is best not to have her name put on the notice. After the meeting I think she will be prepared to stay in York for a time organising women voters and considering nothing has been done I think this is *very* important.

If thou spoke to E.E.T.[aylor] about Tuesday's meeting he would see that it was written up in the Gazette.[58]

Members here of *all* complexions have been extraordinarily kind in saying how glad they are that I am standing. I saw Butcher too, and he is in favour of a *short* speaking campaign.

There is much interest over George's tight rope performances and if only he was straight and people could trust him, what a power he would be.[59] Tonight I have dinner with Auckland Geddes[60] and later go to hear Asquith.

Farewell, darling, it was cheering at the FAU Executive spending most of the time on demobilisation.

[57] Lloyd George had seen George V on 5 November and informed him a dissolution was imminent. A.S.R. was re-adopted as Lib. cand. for York on 9 November 1918 and on 14 November Lloyd George decided to call a General Election for 14 December 1918.

[58] On 19 November 1918 A.S.R. addressed women voters at Peckitt St Adult School. The meeting was announced in the *Yorkshire Gazette*, 16 November 1918.

[59] Lloyd George had addressed a meeting of nearly 200 Liberals at 10 Downing St on 12 November 1918, in which he announced he would fight the election in alliance with the Conservatives, but reaffirmed his Liberalism. At an informal meeting of his supporters on 13 November Asquith was cautiously favourable to this speech, though hostilities soon broke out between the two wings of the party.

[60] Sir Auckland Campbell Geddes (1879–1954), Con. MP Basingstoke 1917–1920; Min. of National Service 1917–1919, Pres. Bd of Trade 1919–1920, Amb. to USA 1920–1923; KCB 1917, cr. Ld Geddes 1942. Originally Prof. of anatomy and archetypal Lloyd Georgian 'man of push and go'.

INDEX